SCOTTISH TRANSATLANTIC MERCHANTS, 1611–1785

by *David Dobson*

CLEARFIELD

Copyright © 2007 by David Dobson
All Rights Reserved.

Printed for
Clearfield Company by
Genealogical Publishing Co.
Baltimore, Maryland
2007

ISBN-13: 978-0-8063-5354-8
ISBN-10: 0-8063-5354-6

Made in the United States of America

Scottish Transatlantic Merchants, 1611 – 1785

INTRODUCTION

Scottish merchants were in the vanguard of Scottish emigration to Colonial America. Emigration from Scotland was, with exception, determined by trade routes. In the seventeenth century ships would leave Scotland bound for the Americas on trading voyages. The success of voyages led to the settlement of factors and their servants in a colony, and subsequently the merchant ships would carry passengers as well as goods. These passengers were, in part, indentured servants who had contracted for work in the colonies and were shipped there and sold there by the shipmasters or the supercargoes, who were the companies' representatives aboard ship. As transatlantic commerce expanded, the import/export firms in Glasgow and other Scots ports grew in size and scope of the operations. Probably the single most important commodity imported from America to Scotland in the colonial period was tobacco, and by the mid-eighteenth century Glasgow virtually controlled the trade. In Glasgow groups of merchants, known as 'Tobacco Lords' imported tobacco which they then distributed to markets all over western Europe. On the Chesapeake their operations were controlled by factors based throughout the region. These factors were often the sons of merchants or the gentry in the neighbourhood of Glasgow. While some of these factors eventually returned to Scotland, many chose to remain in the colonies and established branches of their families there. While this practice was at its most intense on the Chesapeake, it could be found to varying degrees in other colonies. By the late eighteenth centuries there were Scottish merchant families, generally connected by blood and business, forming a network all around the Atlantic rim.

This book identifies many of these merchants, and at a glance branches of the same family can be seen settled on both sides of the Atlantic. Research has been concentrated on primary sources in America and in Scotland and is fully referenced.

David Dobson
St Andrews, Scotland, 2007.

SCOTTISH TRANSATLANTIC MERCHANTS

REFERENCES:

Archives
ACA =	Aberdeen City Archives
AUL =	Aberdeen University Library
BA =	Barbados Archives
BM =	British Museum
CLRO=	Corporation of London Record Office
DA =	Dundee Archives
DSA =	Delaware State Archives
ECA =	Edinburgh City Archives
GA =	Glasgow Archives
GUL =	Glasgow University Library
MSA =	Maryland State Archives
NA =	National Archives, London
NAS =	National Archives of Scotland, Edinburgh
NEHGS	New England Historic Genealogical Society
NJSA=	New Jersey State Archives
NLS =	National Library of Scotland, Edinburgh
PCC =	Prerogative Court of Canterbury
SCS =	Scots Charitable Society of Boston
SCSA=	South Carolina State Archives
UNC =	University of North Carolina
VSA =	Virginia State Archives

Burgess Rolls
ABR =	Ayr Burgess Roll
EBR =	Edinburgh Burgess Roll
GBR =	Glasgow Burgess Roll
MBR =	Montrose Burgess Roll
STABR	St Andrews Burgess Roll

Publications
ActsPCCol	Acts of the Privy Council, Colonial
AJ =	Aberdeen Journal, series
ANY =	St Andrews Society of New York
AP =	St Andrews Society of Philadelphia
APS =	Acts of the Parliaments of Scotland
BS =	Bermuda Settlers
CMA =	Court Minutes of Albany
CTB =	Calendar of Treasury Books, series
DAB =	Dictionary of American Biography

SCOTTISH TRANSATLANTIC MERCHANTS

DCB =	Dictionary of Canadian Biography
DP =	Darien Papers
DPCA=	Dundee, Perth, and Cupar Advertiser, series
EA =	Edinburgh Advertiser, series
EEC =	Edinburgh Evening Courant, series
EMR =	Edinburgh Marriage Register
ERA =	Edinburgh Register of Apprentices
ESG =	Early Settlers of Georgia
ETR =	Edinburgh Tolbooth Records
F =	Fastii Ecclesiae Scoticanae
FD =	Family of Dallas
GaGaz	Georgia Gazette, series
GEU =	List of Graduates of the University of Edinburgh
HAF =	History of Ayrshire and its families
HM =	History of Maryland
Imm.NE	Immigrants to New England
Insh =	Scottish Colonial Schemes
IT =	Indian Traders of the Southeastern Borderlands
JHL =	Journal of the House of Lords, series
MAGU	Matriculation Albums of Glasgow University
MCA =	Records of Marischal College, Aberdeen
MdGaz	Maryland Gazette, series
MdMag	Maryland Magazine, series
Mowat =	East Florida as a British Province, 1763-1784
MR =	Muster Roll of Prince Charles Edward Stuart's
MWI =	Monument Inscriptions in the British West Indies
NCGSJ	North Carolina Genealogical Society Journal
NC =	Nisbets of Carfin
NGSQ	National Genealogical Society Quarterly
NWI =	New World Immigrants
NYCol.MS	New York Colonial Manuscripts
NYGBR	New York Genealogical & Biographical Register
PAB =	Passenger Arrivals at Boston
PaGaz=	Pennsylvania Gazette, series
PCCol	Calendar of the Privy Council, Colonial, series
P =	Prisoners of the '45
PTA =	Passengers to America
RGG =	Roll of Glasgow Graduates
RPCS=	Register of the Privy Council of Scotland, series
RSB =	Records of the Royal Burgh of Stirling
SA =	Scottish Americanus

SCOTTISH TRANSATLANTIC MERCHANTS

SAS =	St Andrew's Society of Charleston
SCHM	South Carolina Historical Magazine, series
SCGaz	South Carolina Gazette, series
SFV =	The Scottish Firm in Virginia, 1767-1777
SG =	The Scottish Genealogist, series
SHC =	Scottish House of Christie
SM =	Scots Magazine, series
SOF =	Some Old Families
SPAWI	State Papers, America and the West Indies, series
SSD =	Swedish Settlements on the Delaware
VaGaz	Virginia Gazette, series
VG =	Virginia Genealogies
VMHB	Virginia Magazine of History and Biography
VSP =	Calendar of Virginia State Papers, series
WMQ=	William and Mary Quarterly Journal

SCOTTISH TRANSATLANTIC MERCHANTS 1611-1785

ABERDEIN, ALEXANDER, a merchant in Aberdeen trading with Va. 1750. [NAS.E504.1.3]

ABERDEIN, WILLIAM, a merchant in Aberdeen trading with Va. 1750. [NAS.E504.1.3]

ABERNETHY, ALEXANDER, a merchant in Broadgate, Aberdeen, trading with Jamaica, 1780. [AJ#1684]

ABERNETHY, JOHN, from Haddington, a storekeeper in Va. before 1776. [NA.AO13.30.473]

ACHINCLOSS, JOHN, a merchant in Glasgow trading with Boston, 1766. [NAS.CS16.1.126]

ACHINCLOSS, THOMAS, a merchant in Portsmouth, New Hampshire, before 1775. [NA.AO13.96.1]

ADAIR, JOHN, a merchant in Antigua, 1771. [NAS.CS16.1.143]

ADAM, WILLIAM, a merchant from Culross, to the American colonies 1670. [RPCS.3.204]

ADAMS, JOHN, a merchant in Glasgow trading with Jamaica, 1756. [NAS.AC7.48.930]

ADDISON, CHARLES, a merchant in Bo'ness trading with Va., 1763, 1776. [NAS.CS16.1.115/168]

ADDISON, JAMES, a merchant in Bo'ness, trading with Va., 1772. [NAS.AC7.55]

ADDISON, JOHN, a merchant in Montrose trading with Africa and Antigua, 1754. [NAS.AC7.46.51]

AFFLECK, THOMAS, born 1730, a merchant in Prince William parish, S.C., probate 1758 S.C.

AGNEW, HUGH, a merchant in Barbados, 1699. [SPAWI.1699.68]

AGNEW, JAMES, born 1737, a merchant from Galloway who settled in Portsmouth, Va., before 1776. [NA.AO12.99.204]

AIKINE, JAMES, a merchant in St Kitts, 1722. [GBR]

AIKMAN, FRANCIS, a merchant from Edinburgh, settled in Va. by 1669. [EBR.3.63]

AIKMAN, JOSEPH, a merchant in Mobile, 1767. [NLS#ms119]

AINSLIE, JAMES, a merchant in Grenada, 1771. [MBR]

AINSLIE, THOMAS, a merchant in Quebec, 1780. [NAS.CS16.1.179]

AIRY and GILMOUR, merchants in Md., 1778. [NAS.CS16.1.173]

AITCHISON, JOHN, a merchant in Glasgow trading with Va., 1726. [NAS.AC9.1056; AC7.34.433-451]

AITCHISON, JOHN, trading between Port Glasgow and Va., 1749. [NAS.E504.28.4]

AITCHISON, JOHN, a merchant in Boston, pre 1776. [NA.AO12.81.36]

AITCHISON, JOHN, a merchant in Grenada, died in New London, Connecticut, on 25 August 1770. [SM.32.630]

AITCHISON, SAMUEL, a merchant in Northampton, Va., before 1773. [GA:T76.6.3]

AITCHISON, THOMAS, a merchant from Glasgow who settled in Norfolk, Va., before 1764. [VaGaz: 4.4.1766] [NAS.CS16.1.120; CS17.1.1/97] [NA.AO12.54.273][WMQ:2.22.532]

AITCHISON and RAE, merchants in Glasgow then in Va., 1764. [NAS.CS16.1.117]

AITKEN, CHARLES, a merchant in St Croix, 1771. [ANY.1.128]

AITKEN, ROBERT, born 1734, a merchant from Paisley who settled in Philadelphia during 1769, died there in 1802. [Hugh Simm pp. Princeton][AP#101]

AITKENSON, MURE, and BOGLE, merchants in Kingston, Jamaica, 1782. [NAS.RD3.295.734]

AITON, ANDREW, trading between Port Glasgow and Md., 1744; between Port Glasgow and Jamaica, 1745. [NAS.E504.28.1/2]

ALEXANDER, ALEXANDER JOHN, a planter and merchant in the Grenades, 1778. [NAS.CS16.1.171/173]

ALEXANDER, BOYD, a storekeeper in Baltimore before 1775. [GA:CFI]

ALEXANDER, CLAUD, trading between Greenock and Va., 1744, 1745; trading between Port Glasgow and Va. and Md., 1744, 1745, 1749; between Greenock and Boston, 1746. [NAS.E504.28.1/2/4; E504.15.2]

ALEXANDER, DAVID, trading between Port Glasgow and Maryland, 1747; between Port Glasgow and Va., 1749. [NAS.E504.28.3/4]

ALEXANDER, DAVID, born 1756, a merchant from Maybole, Ayrshire, emigrated from Greenock to Jamaica on the Isabella during July 1775. [NA.T47.12]

ALEXANDER, JOHN, a merchant from Glasgow who settled in Carolina by 1688, died 1699, probate S.C. 1700; testament Edinburgh 1707. [NAS.CC8.8.83; GD393.79; RD2.82.203; RPCS.13.xxxvii][Records of the Province of SC, 1692/1721]

ALEXANDER, JOHN, trading from Greenock to Jamaica, 1744; between Greenock and St Kitts, 1746. [NAS.E504.15.2]

ALEXANDER, JOHN, trading between Ayr and Antigua and Montserrat, 1764; between Ayr and Falmouth, N.E., 1770; between Ayr and Newfoundland, 1771. [NAS.E504.4.3/5]

ALEXANDER, ROBERT, a merchant who settled in Annapolis, Md., before 1732. [MSA.Md.Deeds.20.576]

ALEXANDER, ROBERT, settled in N.Y. 1762, a merchant in N.Y. City from 1770- 1776, partner of John Miller. [NA.AO12.22.288]

ALEXANDER, ROBERT, a merchant in Glasgow trading with America, 1782. [NAS.CS17.1.1]

ALEXANDER, THEODORE, a merchant in Grenada, 1772. [NAS.RS27.200.286]

ALEXANDER, THOMAS, a grocer/merchant in Boston 1763-1779. [NA.AO12.99.156]

ALEXANDER, WILLIAM, trading between Greenock and Jamaica, 1746; between Port Glasgow and Jamaica, 1748. [NAS.E504.15.2; E504.28.4]

ALEXANDER, WILLIAM, a merchant in Edinburgh, trading between Ayr and Va., 1749. [NAS.E504.4.1]

ALEXANDER, WILLIAM, a merchant from Galloway who settled in Cecil County, Md., died 17... [MSA.Md.Wills.24.75]

ALEXANDER, WILLIAM, a merchant in Antigua, 1778. [NAS.CS16.1.173]

ALEXANDER, WILLIAM, a purchasing agent in Richmond, Va., by 1784. [SA#155]

ALEXANDER and MITCHELL, merchants in Antigua, 1778. [NAS.CS16.1.174]

ALEXANDER, ..., from Leith to Va., 1667. [NAS.RD3.16.256]

ALISON, JOHN, a merchant from Glasgow who settled in Va. before 1748. [NAS.CS16.1.80]

ALISON, JOHN, a merchant in St Kitts, 1783. [NAS.CS17.1.2]

ALISON, ROBERT, trading between Port Glasgow and Va., 1746. [NAS.E504.28.3]

ALLAN, ANDREW, a merchant in Charleston, S.C., died 1735, probate S.C. 1735. [NA.CO5.509]

ALLAN, ANTHONY, a merchant in Edinburgh, trading with Md., 1783. [NAS.CS17.1.2]

ALLAN, HENRY, a merchant on Chapel Plantation, Barbados, 1763. [NAS.RS35.XX.197]

ALLAN, JAMES, a merchant in Kingston, Jamaica, 1781. [NAS.SC16.1.184]

ALLAN, JOHN, trading between Greenock and Va., 1743. [NAS.E504.1]

ALLAN, JOHN, a merchant from Hamilton who settled in Spotsylvania County, Va., probate Spotsylvania County 1750.

ALLAN, JOHN, a merchant in Kingston, Jamaica, 1781. [NAS.SC16.1.184]

ALLAN, ROBERT, a merchant from Alyth, Perthshire, settled on Chapel Plantation, Barbados, by 1759. [NAS.RS35.20.197; SH.15.2.1755]

ALLAN, ROBERT, trading between Port Glasgow and Md., 1745; between Ayr and Falmouth, Maine, 1768. [NAS.E504.28.2; 4.4]

ALLASON, DAVID, born 1736 in Glasgow, emigrated to America in 1760, a storekeeper in Rappahannock and Winchester, Va. [GA:CFI][VMHB/1931]

ALLASON, JOHN, son of Thomas Allason a Glasgow merchant, a merchant in St Kitts, 1782. [NAS.CS17.1.1/243]

ALLASON, ROBERT, born 1721 Glasgow, trading between Port Glasgow and Jamaica, 1749, emigrated to America in 1761, a merchant in Va. [GA:CFI][NAS.E504.28.4]

ALLASON, ROBERT, a merchant in Glasgow trading with the West Indies, 1778. [NAS.CS16.1.173]

ALLASON, WILLIAM, a merchant from Glasgow who emigrated in 1737, settled in Falmouth, Va.. [GA: CFI] [VMHB.85.45]

ALLEN, ROBERT, a merchant who emigrated to Barbados by 1755. [NAS.SH.15.2.1755]

ALRON, JOHN, a trader, from Glasgow to Boston in 1712. [PTA#129]

ALSTON, GEORGE, a merchant in N.C.., 1783. [NAS.CS17.1.1/22]

ALSTON, JOHN, jr., a merchant in Glasgow, trading between Port Glasgow and Va., 1748; trading with N.C., 1774; a landowner in Va., 1779. [NAS.E504.28/4; GD103/2/442; CS16.1.161/168; CS17.1.2; AC7.55] [NA.AO12.37.161]

ALSTON, CARMALT, and Company, merchants in Greenock, trading with America and the West Indies, 1782/1783. [NAS.CS17.1.1/2]

ALSTON, YOUNG, and Company, merchants of Glasgow and N.C. pre-1776. [NA.AO12.37.161]

ALVES, THOMAS, a merchant in Inverness trading with Va., 1729. [NAS.AC10.151]

ANDERSON, ANDREW, a merchant from Glasgow who settled in Va. before 1747. [NAS.CS16.1.79]

ANDERSON, ANDREW, a merchant in the Grenades and in Antigua, died pre 1784. [NAS.CC8.8.126/1]

ANDERSON, ANDREW, a merchant from Edinburgh who emigrated to Va. before 1755, settled in Jappahannock, died 1760. [NAS.RD4.198.558]

ANDERSON, DUNCAN, a merchant in Quebec and Chaleur Bay, 1769. [ActsPCCol.1769/601]

ANDERSON, GEORGE, trading between Leith and S.C., 1745, 1755. [NAS.E504.22]

ANDERSON, GEORGE, trading between Port Glasgow and Va., 1748; a merchant in Glasgow trading with Va., 1755, 1764, 1765. [NAS.E504.28/4; AC7.47.32; CS16.1.120/122]

ANDERSON, JAMES, a merchant in Barbados, 1703. [BA: RB6.43.67]

ANDERSON, JAMES, trading between Greenock and St Kitts, 1743, 1746; with Va., 1743, 1744, 1745, 1746; between Port Glasgow and Antigua, 1744; between Port Glasgow and Jamaica, 1744, 1745; between Port Glasgow and Va., 1747, 1748; between Port Glasgow and Md.,1747; between Port Glasgow and St Kitts, 1748. [NAS.E504.1/2; 28.1/2/3/4]

ANDERSON, JAMES, a merchant in Va., 1760. [NAS.RD4.198/2.558]

ANDERSON, JAMES, a merchant from Leith who emigrated to Va. before 1772, settled at Brokesbank,

Rappahannock, Essex County, died 1788, testament
Edinburgh 1788. [NAS.RD3.231.708; RD4.216.288;
CC8.8.127]

ANDERSON, JOHN, a merchant in Glasgow, trading between
Glasgow, Barbados, and the Caribee Islands, 1670.
[RPCS.3/3.259]

ANDERSON, JOHN, trading from Greenock to Antigua,
1742, to Va., 1745, 1746; between Port Glasgow and St
Kitts, 1746; between Port Glasgow and Va., 1749.
[NAS.E504.15.1/2: 28.2/4]

ANDERSON, JOHN, a merchant from Glasgow who settled
in Jamaica before 1748. [NAS.SC36.63.2]

ANDERSON, JONATHAN, a merchant in Glasgow trading
with the West Indies, 1782. [NAS.CS17.1.1]

ANDERSON, THOMAS, trading between Port Glasgow and
Jamaica, 1748. [NAS.E504.28.4]

ANDERSON, WILLIAM, a merchant trading between Port
Glasgow and Carolina in 1682.
[NAS.NRAS.0631.600][NAS.E72.19.6]

ANDERSON, WILLIAM, a merchant in Glasgow trading
with Guinea, Barbados, and Va., 1718, with Jamaica,
1730. [NAS.AC9.769; AC7.35.1065]

ANDERSON, WILLIAM, a merchant who settled in Va.
before 1750. [NAS.CS16.1.84]

ANDERSON and DALZIELL, merchants in Glasgow trading
with North America, 1772. [NAS.CS16.1.148]

ANDREW, WILLIAM, trading between Port Glasgow and
Va., 1745, 1749. [NAS.E504.28.2/4]

ANDREWS, ROBERT, a merchant in Edinburgh trading with
Jamaica, 1686. [RPCS.12.36]

ANGUS, JOSEPH, a merchant from Glasgow who settled in
St Kitts before 1763. [NAS.B10.12.2]

ANNAND, ALEXANDER, a merchant in Old Aberdeen
trading with Va., 1750. [AJ#133][NAS.E504.1.3]

ARBUCKLE, WILLIAM, a merchant, from Port Glasgow to
N.E. in 1683, a merchant in Glasgow trading with Va.,
1689. [NAS.E72.19.8][SCS] [RPCS.13.477]

ARBUTHNOTT, ALEXANDER, a merchant from
Inverbervie who settled in Philadelphia before 1720.
[NAS.B51.12.1]

ARMOR, JAMES, a merchant from Glasgow who emigrated
via Leith to East N.J. in 1685, settled in Perth Amboy

1687, in N.Y. 1690, then London 1724. [NAS.E72.15.32; RS.92.381][NJSA.EJD.B472/E89] [RPCS.10.206]

ARMOUR, HECTOR, trading between Ayr and Va., 1770. [NAS.E504.4.5]

ARMOUR, JOHN, a merchant in Glasgow trading with Va. in 1727. [NAS.AC7.36.328]

ARTHUR, JAMES, trading between Greenock and Va., 1745. [NAS.E504.15.2]

ARTHUR, JAMES, a merchant who settled on the James River, Va., before 1751. [NAS.CS16.1.85]

ARTHUR, ROBERT, and Company, trading between Greenock and Va., 1742, 1743, 1744, 1746; Greenock and N.C.., 1744; Greenock and S.C., 1746; Greenock and Jamaica, 1746; between Ayr and Antigua, 1760; between Port Glasgow and Va., 1745. [NAS.E504.15.1/2; 4.3/4; 28/2]

ARTHUR, ROBERT, merchant in Irvine, trading between Ayr and N.C.., 1757; trading between Ayr and Halifax, Nova Scotia, 1758; between Ayr and Barbados, 1758; between Ayr and Quebec, 1766, 1767; between Ayr and Antigua, 1768; between Ayr and S.C., 1768; between Ayr and Falmouth, Maine, 1769; between Ayr and Newfoundland, 1769; a merchant in Irvine trading with America, 1769. [NAS.E504.4.3/4/5; CS16.1.134]

ARTHUR, THOMAS, trading between Ayr and Charleston, 1769; between Ayr and St John's, Newfoundland, 1776. [NAS.E504.4.5/6]

ATCHISON, JOHN, trading between Port Glasgow and Va., 1747. [NAS.E504.28.3]

AUSTIN, ADAM, a merchant from Kilspindie, Perthshire, who settled in Charleston before 1782. [NAS.SH.3.7.1782]

BAILEY, ROBERT, a merchant in Edinburgh trading with Carolina pre 1757. [NAS.AC7.49.1293]

BAILLIE, ALEXANDER, a merchant in Glasgow trading with Va., 1726. [NAS.AC9.1056; AC7.34.433-451]

BAILLIE, ALEXANDER, a planter and merchant in St Andrew's parish, Ga., before 1776. [NA.AO13.90.9]

BAILLIE, EUAN, born 1747, a merchant who emigrated via Plymouth to St Vincent in 1775. [NA.T47.9/11]

BAILLIE, GEORGE, a merchant from Edinburgh who settled in Ga. in 1733. [NA.CO5.670.106]; a merchant in Savannah, 1763, [GaGaz#15]; a merchant in Ga. before

1776, moved to Edinburgh. [NA.AO12.74.101]
[NAS.RD3.279.116]

BAILLIE, HUGH, of Monkton, trading with Va., 1732. [NAS.AC9.1354]

BAILLIE, JAMES, son of Robert Baillie an Edinburgh merchant, a merchant in Jamaica, 1740. [NAS.GD1.1155.64]

BAILLIE, ROBERT, son of George Baillie of Haddington, a merchant in Jamaica, 1750s, later in Ga.. [NAS.GD1.1155.65]

BAILLIE, ROBERT, a merchant in Glasgow trading with Va., 1773. [NAS.CS16.1.154]

BAILLIE, THOMAS, son of Hugh Baillie in Orkney, a merchant in Charleston, S.C., 1743. [NAS.CS16.1.73/78]

BAIN, ALEXANDER, and Company, merchants in Greenock/Glasgow trading with N.Y., Charleston, and Newfoundland, 1772-1783. [NAS.CS96.71-180]

BAIN, ALEXANDER, a merchant in Va. before 1771. [NAS.RS.11.109; CS16.1.143]

BAIN, ROBERT, a merchant who settled in Richmond, Va., before 1775. [NAS.CS16.1.165]

BAIN, WILLIAM, born 1737, a shopkeeper from Wick who emigrated to Wilmington, N.C.., in 1774. [NA.T47.12]

BAINE, JOHN, a merchant trading between Greenock and Va., 1743. [NAS.E504.15.1]

BAIRD, DAVID, a merchant in Edinburgh trading with Md., 1748. [NAS.CS16.1.80]

BAIRD, GEORGE, a merchant in Kingston, Jamaica, 1760, 1778. [AUL.MS3175, 668, 3, bundle 4]

BAIRD, JAMES, and Company, merchants in Glasgow, trading between Greenock and Va., 1743, 1744; trading between Ayr and Cape Fear, N.C.., 1770; between Port Glasgow and Va., 1744, 1745, 1747, 1748. [NAS.E504.15.1/2/3; E504.4.5; 28.2/3][GA:T-MJ79]

BAIRD, JAMES, a merchant from Glasgow who settled in Va. by 1764. [NAS.CS16.1.120; CS17.1.1/197] [GA.T.MJ79]

BAIRD, JOHN, a merchant in Glasgow in Jamaica pre 1730. [NAS.AC7.35.485]

BAIRD, JOHN, trading between Port Glasgow and St Kitts, Va. 1742, 1744; with Md., 1744; between Greenock and Va., 1743, 1744, 1745; between Port Glasgow and Va.,

1736, 1745. [NAS.E504.28.1/2; E504.15.1/2; E512/1455]

BAIRD, PETER, a merchant from Glasgow who settled in Petersburg, Va., before 1740. [VSA.DB2.387]

BAIRD, ROBERT, a merchant who settled in Surinam before 1689. [NAS.RH1.2.772/3]

BAIRD, HAY, and Company, partners James Baird, John Hay, Ninian Menzies, and Peter Hay, merchants in Glasgow trading in Va., from 1772. [NAS.NRAS.0623.3]

BALFOUR, ANDREW, a merchant from Edinburgh and landowner in S.C., 1741. [SC Deeds, W#469]

BALFOUR, ARCHIBALD, a merchant in Edinburgh trading with Boston, 1736. [NAS.AC13.1; AC10.246]

BALFOUR, JAMES, a merchant trading with the West Indies before 1645. [APS.VI.i/457]

BALFOUR, JOHN, a merchant from Glasgow who settled on the Black River, Jamaica, died before 1750. [NAS.CC8.8.113]

BALFOUR, JOHN, a merchant on the Peedee River, S.C., died there 15 November 1781, testament, 1783, Edinburgh. [NAS.CC8.8.126][NA.AO12.48.238]

BALLANTINE, JAMES, trading between Ayr and Va., 1770. [NAS.E504.4.5]

BALLANTINE, JOHN, a merchant from Ayr who settled in Boston before 1684. [SCS]

BALLANTINE, JOHN, a merchant from Ayr who settled in Westmoreland County, Va., before 1763, later in partnership with Thomas Blane, Hugh Hamilton, and Patrick Ballantine, before 1776. [NA.AO13.90.122] [NAS.RD2.242.500; CS16.1.115]

BALLANTINE, PATRICK, trading between Ayr and Va. in 1746, 1749, 1750, 1759, 1765, 1766, 1769; between Ayr and Boston, 1769, 1770. [NAS.E504.4.1/2/3/4/5]

BALLANTINE, PATRICK, a tobacco merchant from Ayr who died in Va. 1770. [ACA.6.193]

BALLANTINE, PATRICK, a merchant in Westmoreland County, Va., in partnership with Thomas Blane, Hugh Hamilton, and John Ballantine, before 1776, later in Jamaica. [NA.AO13.90.122]

BALLANTINE, WILLIAM, a merchant trading between Ayr and Va., 1743, 1746, 1750, 1757, 1759, 1765, 1766, 1769; trading between Ayr and West Fla., 1768; trading between Greenock and Va., 1744, 1745, 1746, 1749; between Ayr and Boston, 1769, 1771. [NAS.E504.4.1/2/3/4/5; 15.1/2]

BAND, JOHN, trading between Greenock and Va., 1745. [NAS.E504.15.2]

BANKS, ALEXANDER, a factor who settled in Manchester, Va., before 1772. [University of Va.: John Smith pp]

BANKS, CHARLES, a merchant from Ross-shire who settled in Charleston around 1748, naturalised there in 1788. [S.C. Citizenship Book]

BANNATYNE, DUGALD, an assistant storekeeper who settled in Falmouth, Va., before 1776, returned to Glasgow. [SFV#229]

BANNATYNE, FRANCIS, a merchant from Glasgow who settled in New Providence, the Bahamas, probate 1760 the Bahamas.

BANNATYNE, JOHN, EBENEZER MCHARG, AND ANTHONY MCKITTERICK, merchants in Va., 1763. [NAS.CS16.1.115/120/122]

BANNERMAN, BENJAMIN, a merchant(?) in Portsmouth, Va., pre 1776. [NA.AO12.56.367]

BARBER, THOMAS, a merchant in Leith trading with Va. in 1667-1671. [NAS.E72.15.7][RPCS.3/3.331]

BARBOUR, JOHN, trading between Port Glasgow and St Kitts, 1745; between Greenock and St Kitts, 1746. [NAS.E504.28.2; 15.2]

BARBOUR, ROBERT, a merchant trading with the American Plantations, 1671. [RPCS.3/3.331]

BARCLAY, ANDREW, a merchant in N.Y. who died in 1775, probate 1775 N.Y.

BARCLAY, ANDREW, from Fife, a merchant and bookbinder in Boston before 1776, later settled in Shelburne, Nova Scotia, by 1783. [NA.AO13.24.23]

BARCLAY, DAVID, a merchant who emigrated from Leith to East N.J. in 1683. [NAS.E72.15.26]

BARCLAY, GEORGE, from Aberdeen, a merchant in Jamaica, 1741. [NAS.GD67.93]

BARCLAY, GILBERT, a merchant in Boston, 1763. [NAS.CS16.1.115/60]

BARCLAY, JAMES, a merchant who settled in Kingston, Jamaica, before 1748. [NAS.RD3.211/1.521; SH.15.11.1750]

BARCLAY, JOHN, trading between Greenock and Barbados, 1745. [NAS.E504.15.2]

BARCLAY, PATRICK, a merchant from Edinburgh who settled in Va. before 1745, probate Essex County, Va., 1749. [NAS.AC8.659; SH.24.8.1745]

BARKER, JOHN, a merchant in Kingston, Jamaica, 1778. [NAS.CS16.1.173/159]

BARLOW, THOMAS, trading between Scotland and Va., 1660s. [SPAWI.1666.1340]

BARNS, JOHN, a merchant in Glasgow, trading between Port Glasgow and Va., 1744. [NAS.E504.28.2; B10.15.7036]

BARRY, JAMES, trading between Greenock and Va., 1744; a merchant from Glasgow in Charleston, 1745. [GA.B10.15.7105][NAS.E504.15.2]

BARRY, ROBERT, a merchant in Glasgow trading with Va., 1744, Va. and Md., pre 1754. [NAS.AC7.46.185; E504.15.2]

BARTRAM, ALEXANDER, a merchant from Biggar who settled in Philadelphia before 1777. [NAS.RS42.20.426]

BEAN, SAMUEL, a merchant in Jamaica, 1781. [NAS.CS16.1.183]

BEATTIE, WILLIAM, a merchant from Dumfries who settled in Va. before 1749. [NAS.CS.1.81]

BEGG, JOHN, a merchant in Norfolk, Va., before 1776. [NA.AO12.100.1]

BELL, ALEXANDER, a merchant, from Glasgow to Boston in 1766. [PAB][SG#7.4.15]

BELL, ALEXANDER, a merchant from Glasgow who settled in West Fla. before 1777. [NA.CO5.613.414]

BELL, DAVID, a merchant from Glasgow who settled in Va. before 1745. [NAS.B10.15.5959]

BELLFOR, WILLIAM, trading between Leith and S.C., 1755. [NAS.E504.22]

BENNET, THOMAS, a merchant in Aberdeen trading with Va. 1750. [NAS.E504.1.3]

BERRIE, JAMES, merchant in Charleston, 1729. [SAS]

BERRIE, JAMES, trading between Port Glasgow and Va., 1744, 1745, 1746, 1747, 1748, 1749; between Greenock and Va., 1745; a merchant in Glasgow trading with America, before 1780. [NAS.E504.28.1/2/3/4; 15.2; CS16.1.179]

BERRIE, ROBERT, trading between Port Glasgow and Va., 1744, 1745, 1746, 1747, 1748, 1749; between Greenock and Va., 1746. [NAS.E504.28.1/2/3/4; 15.2]

BERTRAM, ALEXANDER, a merchant from Lanarkshire who settled in Philadelphia by 1772. [NAS.CS16.1.151/179]

BETHUNE, WILLIAM, a merchant from Portree, Skye, then in America, 1771. [NAS.CS16.1.148]

BINNIE, WILLIAM, a merchant in Edinburgh trading with the American Plantations, 1674. [RPCS.4.144/608]

BISSETT, DAVID, from Dunkeld, a storekeeper on the Bush River, Md., died 1758, probate Md. [MSA.Md.Wills.32.220/33.431]

BLACK, ALEXANDER, born 1750, a merchant from Lanarkshire who settled in Va. [BOA#28]

BLACK, ANDREW, a merchant from Glasgow who settled in Westmoreland County, Va., before 1782. [NAS.B10.15.8403]

BLACK, DAVID, merchant in Boston before 1775, 1783. [NA.AO12.10.362][NAS.CS17.1.2/233]

BLACKADDER, ADAM, born 16.., a merchant from Troqueer who settled in N.E. [F.2.302]

BLACKADDER, THOMAS, born in 1660s, later a merchant in N.E. [F.2.302]

BLACKBURN, ANDREW, trading between Greenock and Va., 1742, 1743, 1745, 1746; between Port Glasgow and Va., 1736, 1746, 1748, 1749 [NAS.E504.15.1/2; 28.2/3/4; E512/1455]; a merchant from Glasgow, land grant in Ga. 1751. [NA.CO5.668]; a merchant in Glasgow trading with Va., 1766. [NAS.CS16.1.126]

BLACKBURN, JOHN, a merchant from Glasgow who settled in Norfolk, Va., before 1752. [NAS.B10.15.6183]

BLACKWOOD, ROBERT, sr., a merchant from Edinburgh, possibly trading with East N.J., 1685. [NJSA.EJD.Liber A/227]

BLAIR, ALEXANDER, and Company, in St George's parish, Fredericksburg, Spottsylvania County, Va., before 1780. [NA.AO13.102.52]

BLAIR, DAVID, trading between Port Glasgow and Va., 1746, 1748. [NAS.E504.28.3]

BLAIR, DAVID, born 1732, a merchant who settled in Va. during 1762. [NA.AO12.99.268]

BLAIR, GEORGE, to Va. in 1762, a merchant in Smithyfield, Isle of Wight County, and later in Southampton County, and Norfolk, Va., partner of James Hunter. [NA.AO12.56.184]

BLAIR, JAMES, a merchant in Glasgow trading with Va. in 1727. [NAS.AC7.36.328]

BLAIR, JAMES, a merchant in Va. before 1774. [NAS.CS16.1.79]

BLAIR, JOHN, a merchant from Edinburgh who settled in Richmond, Va., before 1719. [NAS.SH.22.8.1719]

BLAIR, JOHN, a merchant from Edinburgh who settled in Williamsburg, Va., before 1746. [NAS.CS16.1.79]

BLAIR, JOHN, a merchant in Glasgow trading with Va., 1764. [NAS.CS16.1.120/122]

BLAIR, ROBERT, a merchant in Boston, 1778. [NAS.CS16.1.173]

BLAIR, THOMAS, a merchant from Dundee, probate 1767 N.Y.

BLAIR, WALTER, and Company, merchants in Glasgow trading with Virgina and Md., 1723. [NAS.AC7.28.715; AC7.33.44]

BLAIR, WILLIAM, a merchant, from Leith to Boston in 1765. [PAB]

BLANE, JAMES, a merchant in Grenada, 1778. [NAS.CS16.1.173]

BLANE, JOHN, a merchant in Glasgow in Jamaica pre 1730. [NAS.AC7.35.485]

BLANE, JOHN, from Ayrshire, a merchant in Antigua, 1751, died there in 1755. [NAS.RD2.211.1380; GJ#756]

BLANE, THOMAS, a merchant in Westmoreland County, Va., partner of John Ballantine, Hugh Hamilton, and Patrick Ballantine, before 1776. [NA.AO13.107.15]

BLANE, THOMAS, late a merchant in N.Y., 1784, then in London, 1787. [NAS.RD2.246/2.694; CS17.1.6/271]

BOG, ROBERT, a merchant in Greenock trading with N.Y., 1783. [NAS.AC7.61]

BOG, THOMAS, a merchant in N.C., 1774. [NAS.CS16.1.157]

BOGLE, GEORGE, trading between Greenock and Va., 1742, 1744, 1746; between Greenock and Md., 1744. [NAS.E504.1/2]

SCOTTISH TRANSATLANTIC MERCHANTS

BOGLE, JOHN, a merchant in Glasgow trading with Va., 1716; and with Guinea, Barbados, and Va., 1717. [NAS.AC13.1.160; AC9.769]

BOGLE, JOHN, a merchant trading between Greenock and Va., 1743; between Port Glasgow and Va., 1744, 1747. [NAS.E504.15.1; E504.28.1/3]

BOGLE, MATTHEW, a merchant from Glasgow who settled in Va. before 1729, returned to Glasgow in 1736. [SA#52]; a merchant trading between Greenock and Va., 1743, 1744, 1746; trading between Port Glasgow and Va., 1744, 1745, 1747, 1749. [NAS.AC9.1746; E504.15.1/2; E504.28.1/2/3/4]

BOGLE, PATRICK, a merchant trading between Greenock and Va., 1743, 1744, 1745, between Port Glasgow and Va., 1744, 1745, 1747, 1749. [NAS.E504.15.1/2; E504.28.1/2/3/4]

BOGLE, ROBERT, jr., a merchant in Glasgow trading with Guinea, Barbados, Nevis, and St Kitts, 1720. [NAS.AC7.33.433-583]

BOGLE, ROBERT, senior, a merchant in Grenada, died 1 June 1777. [SM.39.455]

BOGLE, ROBERT, a merchant from N.Y. who died in Wilmington, N.C.., in 1785. [GM#IX.427.80]

BOGLE, ROBERT, and WILLIAM SCOTT, merchants in Lovelane, Loudoun, trading with Tobago, 1771. [NAS.RD2.224/2.646]

BOGLE, THOMAS, trading with Va., 1745. [NAS.E504.28.2]

BOGLE, WALTER, trading between Greenock and Va., 1745. [NAS.E504.15.2]

BOGLE, WILLIAM, a merchant, from Port Glasgow to Va. in 1685. [NAS.E72.19.8]

BOGLE, WILLIAM, merchant in Glasgow, partner of Bogle, Somerville and Company, later Bogle, Jamieson and Company with stores in Va., at Falmouth kept by George Hamilton, at Culpepper kept by Gavin Lawson, at Northumberland kept by Robert Gilmour who also kept Lancaster. [NA.AO.12/100/31; 13/27/384; 90/100-121]

BOGLE, WILLIAM, trading between Port Glasgow and Va., 1747; a merchant of Glasgow trading with Va. before 1776. [NAS.E504.28.3][NA.AO.12.100.311]

BOGLE, SOMERVILLE, and Company, alias Bogle, Jamieson and Company, merchants in Glasgow with stores in Falmouth, Va., Culpepper, Va.,

Northumberland, Va., and Lancaster, Va., before 1776.
[NA.AO12.100.311][NAS.AC7.54]

BORELAND, JOHN, a storekeeper from Newmills, Ayrshire, died in Jamaica during September 1728.
[NAS.CC8.8.128]

BORLAND, FRANCIS, a merchant in N.E., 1743.
[NAS.CS16.1.72]

BORLAND, JOHN, a merchant in Boston by 1684.
[SCS][NAS.RS42.xi.67/xii.411; RH15.106.box 20]
[SPAWI.1690.806]

BORLAND, JOHN, trading between Ayr and N.Y., 1760, between Ayr and Antigua, 1764, 1765.
[NAS.E504.4.3/4]

BORRIE, JOHN, a merchant trading between Greenock and Boston, 1744. [NAS.E504.15.1]

BORRIE, ROBERT, and Company, trading between Greenock and Va., 1744. [NAS.E504.15.2]

BORTHWICK, JOHN, a merchant from Edinburgh in North America, 1772. [NAS.CS16.1.141/148]

BOWER, JAMES, a merchant from Dundee who emigrated to Darien in 1699, testament Edinburgh 1708.
[NAS.CC8.8.84]

BOWMAN, JOHN, a merchant in Glasgow trading with Va., 1726. [NAS.AC9.1056; AC7.34.433-451]

BOWMAN, JOHN, a merchant in Glasgow trading with Va., 1763; trading between Port Glasgow and Va., 1747, 1749; trading between Ayr and West Fla., 1768; in Charleston, 1769. [NAS.CS16.1.122; E504.4.5; 28/3/4] [Charleston County, Misc. Records#172]

BOYD, ALEXANDER, a merchant and planter from Ayrshire who settled in Mecklenburg, Va., in 1765. [VMHB#2]

BOYD, ANDREW, a merchant in Antigua and Va. before 1765. [NAS.CS16.1.122]

BOYD, JAMES, born 1742, a merchant from Galloway, emigrated from Stranraer to N.Y. in 1774, settled in Albany. [NA.T47.12][ANY.2.39]

BOYD, JOHN, a lawyer in Irvine then a merchant in N.Y., 1778. [NAS.CS16.1.174]

BOYD, JOSEPH, trading between Ayr and Falmouth, N.E., 1770; between Ayr and Newfoundland, 1770, 1771.
[NAS.E504.4.5]

BOYD, ROBERT, and Company, trading between Greenock and Va., 1743, 1745, 1746; between Port Glasgow and

Va., 1734, 1735, 1744, 1745, 1747. [NAS.E512/1455; E504.15.1/2; E504.28.1/2/3]

BOYD, ROBERT, a merchant in Charleston, S.C., 1767, 1773. [NAS.CS16.1.126/154; AC7.52]

BOYD, ROBERT, a merchant from Twynholm, Kirkcudbrightshire, died in Va. before 1783, testament Edinburgh 1783. [NAS.CC8.8.126/1][F.2.429]

BOYD, SPENCER, a physician and merchant who settled in West Point, King and Queen County, Va., before 1770, probate Williamsburg 1779. [NAS.RD2.233.108; GD1.26.60; CS16.1.168]

BOYD, WILLIAM, trading between Ayr and Antigua, 1768. [NAS.E504.4.4]

BOYLE, JAMES LAWRENCE, a merchant in St Croix, son of John Boyle, 1778, 1779, 1783. [NAS.CS16.1.173/175; CS17.1.1, 2]

BOYLE, STAIR, a merchant from Inverkip who settled in St Kitts before 1761. [NAS.B10.12.2]

BRABNER, JAMES, a merchant in Aberdeen trading with Va., 1711. [NAS.AC7.17.352]

BREADIE, ROBERT, a merchant from Perth in S.C., 1781. [NAS.CS16.1.183/184]

BREADY, WILLIAM, a merchant trading between Glasgow and Va., 1681. [NAS.E72.19.3]

BREBNER, ALEXANDER, a merchant from Peterhead who settled in Christianstad, St Croix, died there before 1775. [ACA: APB.4.65]

BREBNER, WILLIAM, and Company, trading between Aberdeen and Kingston, Jamaica, 1758, with N.Y. in 1765, and with Canada also N.Y. in 1777. [AJ#535/885/1516]

BRISBANE, EDWARD, partner in the Thistle Distillery, Norfolk, Va., dead by 1784. [NA.AO12/74/335]

BROCK, WALTER, trading between Port Glasgow and Va., 1744. [NAS.E504.28.2]

BROCK, WALTER, born 1746, a merchant in Glasgow who emigrated from Greenock to N.Y. in 1775. [NA.T47.12]

BRODIE, ALEXANDER, born 1738, a merchant from Morayshire who settled in St Mary's parish, Antigua, during 1760, died there in 1800. [Caribbeana.1.98]

BRODIE, ALEXANDER, a merchant who emigrated to N.C. in 1773 and settled in Wilmington. [NA.A012.100.204]

BROWN, ALEXANDER, a merchant in Md., 1708. [GBR]

BROWN, ALEXANDER, a merchant in St Kitts then in London pre 1765. [NAS.SH.10.4.1765]

BROWN, ARCHIBALD, a merchant and planter in Charleston, S.C., before 1776. [NA.AO12.92.5]

BROWN, GEORGE, a merchant who settled in Norfolk, Va., before 1766. [NAS.CS16.1.125]

BROWN, GEORGE, a merchant in Glasgow trading with Boston, 1768. [NAS.CS16.1.133]

BROWN, HUGH, trading between Port Glasgow and Va., 1749. [NAS.E504.28.4]

BROWN, JAMES, a merchant from Glasgow, and in Bladensburg, Md., before 1770. [NA.AO12.9.59]

BROWN, JOHN, a merchant trading between Scotland and Barbados, 1660s. [NLS.ms7003, fo.3/7033, fo.29/31] [NAS.GD103.214, 42]

BROWN, JOHN, trading between Port Glasgow and Md., 1745; between Port Glasgow and Barbados, 1746; between Ayr and Va., 1758; between Port Glasgow and Jamaica, 1748. [NAS.E504.28.2/3; 4.3]

BROWN, JOHN, a merchant in Va. 1783. [NAS.CS17.1.2/83]

BROWN, JOHN, a merchant in Norfolk, Va., before 1776, later in Nova Scotia by 1783. [NA.AO13.27.426]

BROWN, JOHN, a merchant and shipwright who settled in Va. during 1763, returned to Scotland after 1776. [NA.AO12.100.213]

BROWN, ROBERT, a merchant in Glasgow trading with Va., 1722. [NAS.AC7.27.2186; AC8.285]

BROWN, ROBERT, trading between Greenock and Va., 1745. [NAS.E504.15.2]

BROWN, SIMON, and Company, merchants in Glasgow, 1775. [NAS.CS16.1.165]

BROWN, THOMAS, a merchant from Glasgow who settled in King and Queen County, Va. during 1770. [NAS.RD2.233.108; CS17.1.2/145; CS17.1.1]

BROWN, WALTER, a merchant in Ga., 1780. [NAS.RD4.259.758]

BROWN, WILLIAM, a merchant trading between Scotland and Barbados, 1660s. [NLS.ms7003, fo.3/7033, fo.29/31]

BROWN, WILLIAM, a merchant from Ayr, in Boston 1684. [SCS]

BROWN, WILLIAM, jr., a merchant in Glasgow trading with N.Y., 1755. [NAS.CS16.1.95]

BROWN, WILLIAM, from Glasgow, a merchant in St Kitts before 1764, later in Tobago. [GA: B10.15.7493]

BROWN, WILLIAM, a merchant in Va., 1783. [NAS.CS17.1.2/83]

BROWN, GRIERSON and Company, merchants in Norfolk, Va., 1776. [NAS.CS16.1.168]

BRUCE, JOHN, trading between Port Glasgow and Philadelphia, 1747. [NAS.E504.28.3]

BRUCE, PETER, born 1758, a merchant from Inverurie who settled in N.Y. in 1770, died 1796. [ANY.I.228]

BRUCE, ROBERT, born 1758, a merchant from Inverurie who emigrated via Aberdeen to Va. in 1768, settled in Norfolk, died 1796. [ANY.I.160]

BRYCE, ARCHIBALD, a factor from Glasgow who settled in Richmond, Va., before 1776. [NAS.B10.12.4; AC7.58]

BRYCE, PATRICK, a merchant from Glasgow, in Boston 1684. [SCS]

BRYCE, WILLIAM, a merchant in Glasgow, trading with N.E., 1738. [NAS.AC7.43.4]

BUCHAN, GEORGE, trading between Greenock and Va., 1745. [NAS.E504.15.2]

BUCHANAN, ALEXANDER, trading between Greenock and Va., 1743, 1744, 1745; between Greenock and Boston, 1746; between Port Glasgow and Va., 1744, 1745, 1746; between Port Glasgow and Jamaica, 1745; between Port Glasgow and Md., 1747; between Port Glasgow and St Kitts, 1747; between Port Glasgow and Boston, 1748. [NAS.E504.1/2; E504.28.1/2/3]

BUCHANAN, ANDREW, a merchant in Glasgow trading with America and the West Indies, 1720, with Va., 1726. [NAS.AC7.24.710; AC9.6398]

BUCHANAN, ANDREW, trading between Greenock and Va., 1742, 1743, 1744, 1746, with St Kitts, 1746, pre 1761; between Ayr and Va., 1755; between Port Glasgow and Va., 1743, 1748. [NAS.E504.1/2; E504.4.2; 28.2/3; AC7.50]

BUCHANAN, ANDREW, born 1732, died in Baltimore 1786.

BUCHANAN, ANDREW, of Ravenscroft, Dinwiddie County, Va., before 1776. [NA.AO13.102.51][NAS.CS16.1.170]

BUCHANAN, ARCHIBALD, trading between Greenock and Va., 1743, 1744, 1746; between Port Glasgow and Va., 1736, 1744, 1745, 1748, 1749. [NAS.E512/1455; E504.15.1/2; 28.2/3/4]

BUCHANAN, ARCHIBALD, of Drumhead, a merchant in Williamsburg and Norfolk, Va., pre-1751. [NAS.RS10.8.250; CS16.1.85; CS16.1.84/85]

BUCHANAN, ARCHIBALD, a merchant from Glasgow, settled in Silverbank, Prince Edward County, Va., before 1757. [NAS.RS10.9.84]

BUCHANAN, ARCHIBALD, and ARCHIBALD COATS and Company, merchants in Glasgow trading with Va., 1748. [NAS.CS16.1.80]

BUCHANAN, GEORGE, trading between Greenock and Va., 1745, 1746; between Greenock and Boston, 1746; between Ayr and Va., 1755; between Port Glasgow and Va., 1745, 1748. [NAS.E504.15.2; 4.2; 28.2/3]

BUCHANAN, GEORGE, jr., a merchant in Glasgow trading with Va. and Barbados, 1755, with St Kitts pre 1761. [NAS.AC7.47.32]

BUCHANAN, GEORGE, a merchant from Glasgow who settled in Va. before 1773. [NAS.CS16.1.154]

BUCHANAN, GEORGE and ANDREW, merchants of Glasgow, and in Bladensburg, Md., pre 1776. [NA.AO12.9.1]

BUCHANAN, HASTIE, and Company, Charlotte County, Va., 1780. [NA.AO13.102.52]

BUCHANAN, JAMES, trading between Port Glasgow and New York, 1747; between Port Glasgow and St Kitts, 1748; between Port Glasgow and Virginia, 1749. [NAS.E504.28.3/4]

BUCHANAN, JAMES, a merchant from Dunbartonshire who settled in Falmouth, Va., 1758. [NAS.RS10.9.156; SH.16.3.1759; .RS10.9.40/160]

BUCHANAN, JAMES, of Middle Tillihaven, Dunbartonshire, a merchant in Jamaica, 1771. [NAS.RS10.361]

BUCHANAN, JAMES, and Company, merchants in St Inigo, Annapolis, and Chaptico, Md., before 1776. [NA.AO12.109.88]

BUCHANAN, JAMES, an assistant storekeeper who settled in Dumfries, Va., returned to Glasgow via N.Y. in 1777. [SFV#229/233]

BUCHANAN, JAMES, and DAVID COCHRANE, merchants in Glasgow trading with Va., 1753. [NAS.CS16.1.89]

BUCHANAN, JOHN, a merchant in Glasgow trading with S.C., 1728. [NAS.AC7.34.697]

BUCHANAN, JOHN, a merchant in Glasgow trading with Va., 1774. [NAS.CS16.1.157]

BUCHANAN, JOHN, merchant in Savannah, Ga., a partner of the firm Buchanan, Cochran and Company of Greenock and of Ga., dead by 1784. [NA.AO12.109.106]

BUCHANAN, JOHN, a merchant in Glasgow trading to Va., 1734. [NAS.AC7.40.137]

BUCHANAN, NEIL, trading with Va., 1726. [NAS.AC9.6398]

BUCHANAN, NEIL, trading between Greenock and N.C.., 1743. [NAS.E504.15.1]

BUCHANAN, NEIL, a merchant in Glasgow trading with Va., 1773. [NAS.CS16.1.154]

BUCHANAN, NEIL, merchant in Petersburg, Dinwiddie County, Va., dead by 1779, father of Mary, Anne, and Margaret. [ActsPCCol.1762/475] [NA.AO13.102.50][NAS.CS16.1.154/173/178]

BUCHANAN, ROBERT, a shopkeeper in Charleston, probate S.C. 1731.

BUCHANAN, ROBERT, trading between Greenock and Va., 1743, 1744; between Port Glasgow and Va., 1748. [NAS.E504.15.1/2; 28/3]

BUCHANAN, ROBERT, a merchant from Glasgow who settled in America in 1760, a merchant in Annapolis, and in Newport, Charles County, St Inigo, and Chaptico, Md., before 1776. [NA.AO12.6.239][ANY.I.262]

BUCHANAN, THOMAS, a merchant in N.Y., 1783. [NAS.RD4.235.686]

BUCHANAN and SIMPSON, merchants in Glasgow trading with Va., Md., Jamaica, Guadaloupe, St Kitts and Antigua, 1754-1773. [NAS.CS96.502-509]

BULL, ROBERT, a merchant in Edinburgh, trading with Jamaica and Boston, 1740s. [NAS.CS96.3823]

BUNTINE, NICOL, a merchant from Ayrshire who settled in Va., died 1740 in Ayrshire. [HAF.1.294]

BURNETT, JOHN, born 1611, a merchant from Aberdeen, emigrated via London to Va. in 1635. [SPC.1638.277][NA.E157.20][CSP.Col.1574/1660.277]

BURNETT, JOHN, a merchant in Aberdeen trading with Md., 1744/1749; with Dominica 1769. [NAS.AC9.1708/6464; GD23.3.51][AJ#1103]

BURNSIDE, ANDREW, a victualler in Port Royal, Jamaica, probate Jamaica 1676.

BURTON, ROBERT, born 1758, a factor from Haddington who settled in Richmond, Va., before 1776, died 1832. [NAS.SC70.1.58; RD3.309.682] [NA.AO13.33.153]

BURTON, WILLIAM, a merchant in Va., trading with Glasgow in 1756. [NAS.CS16.1.85]

BURTON, WILLIAM, a merchant, from Glasgow to Boston in 1763. [SG#4.4.14][PAB]

BUTCHER, ALEXANDER, trading between Port Glasgow and Va., 1745. [NAS.E504.28.2]

BUTCHER, JAMES, trading between Port Glasgow and Jamaica, 1748. [NAS.E504.28.3]

BYRES, JAMES, a merchant from Edinburgh who emigrated to Darien in 1699, possibly moved to Charleston, S.C., in 1700. [NAS.GD406]

CADENHEAD, JOHN, a trader among the Lower Creeks, 1735. [SPAWI.1735#157.vii]

CALDER, JAMES, trading between Port Glasgow and Va., 1749. [NAS.E504.28.4]

CALDER, THOMAS, a merchant trading with Va., pre 1733. [NAS.AC9.1248]

CALDERHEAD, THOMAS, a merchant from Glasgow who settled in Norfolk, Va. in 1775. [NA.AO12.54.147]

CALDERHEAD, WILLIAM, merchant from Glasgow who settled in Norfolk, Va., pre 1776, testament Edinburgh 1788. [NA.AO12/54/147; 74/293; 99/334; 109/100; AO13/2/355; 134/8; 137/33][NAS.CC8.8.127]

CALDWELL, WILLIAM, a merchant from Glasgow, probate Barbados, 1694. [BA: RB6.2.119]

CAMERON, JOHN, JOHN MCLAUCHLAN, and WILLIAM DRUMMOND of Balhadies, merchants in Fort William trading with America, 1736. [NAS.NRAS.1279/3]

CAMERON, RICHARD, a merchant from Glasgow in America, 1780. [NAS.CS16.1.179]

CAMPBELL, ALEXANDER, trading between Greenock and Md., 1745. [NAS.E504.15.2]

CAMPBELL, ALEXANDER, of Lossett, a merchant from Islay who settled in Kingston, Jamaica, later moved to Cumberland County, N.C., probate N.C.. 1779. [NAS.CS16.1.181]

CAMPBELL, ALEXANDER, a merchant in Glasgow trading with Jamaica, 1780. [NAS.CS16.1.181]

SCOTTISH TRANSATLANTIC MERCHANTS

CAMPBELL, ALEXANDER, a merchant in Tobago, 1776. [NA.T1.527.271/2]

CAMPBELL, ALEXANDER, a merchant in Va., died in Glasgow 178-. [NAS.CC9]

CAMPBELL, ALEXANDER, a merchant in Glasgow trading with Md., 1769, and Jamaica, 1780. [NAS.CS16.1.138/179]

CAMPBELL, ALEXANDER, and DANIEL, merchants in Glasgow trading with N.E., 1769. [NAS.CS16.1.134]

CAMPBELL, ANDREW, a merchant from Glasgow who settled in Jamaica before 1744. [NAS.RD2.169.74]

CAMPBELL, ARCHIBALD, a merchant trading between Greenock and Va., 1743; trading between Port Glasgow and Va./Md., 1745, 1749. [NAS.E504.28.2/4; 15.1]

CAMPBELL, ARCHIBALD, settled in Norfolk, Va., 1744 as a physician then as a merchant, partner in James Campbell and Company there. [NA.AO12/55/70, 70/10, 109/120; AO13/58/9, 134/27, 137/465]

CAMPBELL, ARCHIBALD, a factor who settled in Leonardstown in the Potomac, Md., 1775. [MSA.11.41][MdHistMag.44.247]

CAMPBELL, ARCHIBALD, a merchant in Bermuda, 1784. [NAS.CS17.1.3/375]

CAMPBELL, CHARLES, a merchant from Ayr who settled in Va. before 1752. [NAS.CS16.1.99]

CAMPBELL, CHARLES, trading between Ayr and Charleston, 1756; between Ayr and N.C.., 1757. [NAS.E504.4.3]

CAMPBELL, COLIN, a merchant from Greenock who settled in Jamaica before 1776. [NAS.CPD#73]

CAMPBELL, COLIN, a merchant from Glasgow then in America, 1783. [NAS.CS17.1.2]

CAMPBELL, COLIN, settled in Va. as a factor for Glasgow merchants, moved to Greenock before 1776 and traded with Dominica until 1778 [resident factor there was a Daniel Campbell], then moved to Penoscob, New Brunswick as a merchant. [NA.AO13.22.403]

CAMPBELL, COLIN, born 1751, a merchant from Perthshire, emigrated via Greenock to N.Y. in 1775. [NA.T47.12]

CAMPBELL, COLIN, jr., a merchant in Glasgow then in Jamaica, 1785. [NAS.CS17.1.4/344]

CAMPBELL, DANIEL, of Shawfield, a merchant in Glasgow trading with Boston and the West Indies, 1691-1714. [GA:Shawfield ms]

CAMPBELL, DANIEL, a merchant from Glasgow who settled in Falmouth, King George County, Va., before 1770. [Prince William County Deeds, R154]

CAMPBELL, DAVID, a bookseller in Boston by 1686. [SCS]

CAMPBELL, DOUGAL, of Laggan, a merchant in Campbeltown then in North America, 1777. [NAS.CS16.1.170]

CAMPBELL, DUNCAN, a merchant in Glasgow, then N.Y., later Kingston, Jamaica, afterwards London, and finally in Edinburgh, trading with S.C.. [NAS.RD2.28.1707; RH15.59][F.3.363]

CAMPBELL, DUNCAN, a merchant from Argyll, a partner in the merchant house of McDuffie and Campbell in Jamaica, 1771. [NAS.CS16.1.84/134/143/128; RS10.10.327; RD2.215.143]

CAMPBELL, GEORGE, a merchant who emigrated to N.Y. in 1742. [NYCol.ms#72/171]

CAMPBELL, HEW, a merchant trading between Port Glasgow and the West Indies, 1683. [NAS.E72.19.8]

CAMPBELL, HEW, a merchant from Glasgow who settled in Jamaica before 1744. [NAS.RD2.169.74]

CAMPBELL, HUGH, son of James Campbell a merchant in Edinburgh, a merchant in Bermuda from 1679, and by 1688 in Norfolk, Va.. [BS.28] *possibly in Boston before 1679 see Insh#191*

CAMPBELL, HUGH, trading between Port Glasgow and Va., 1745. [NAS.E504.28.2]

CAMPBELL, JAMES, an Indian trader in Augusta, Ga., 1756. [NA.CO5.646/C17]

CAMPBELL, JAMES, of Kames, Cowal, a merchant in Glasgow sometime in Jamaica, died in Rothesay, testament 1761 The Isles [NAS]

CAMPBELL, JAMES, settled in Norfolk, Va., in 1762 as a partner of James Campbell and Company (other partners being Robert Tucker, William Aitchison, Archibald Campbell, John Hunter, and James Parker). He moved to Grenada in 1769, Member of the Council there, [NA.AO12/90/3; AO13/97/151, 102/57, 134/30]

CAMPBELL, JAMES, a merchant in Kingston, Jamaica, then in Crieff, Perthshire, 1771. [NAS.CS16.1.143/128]

CAMPBELL, JAMES, a merchant who settled in Va. by 1769. [NAS.CC9.64]

CAMPBELL, JAMES and Company, merchants in Grenada, 1775, 1782. [NAS.RD2.242/2.338; AC7.58]

CAMPBELL, JOHN, a merchant from Glasgow who settled in Boston by 1684. [SCS]

CAMPBELL, JOHN, a merchant in N.C.., 1748. [British Library, add.ms#32/71/140]

CAMPBELL, JOHN, of Whitehaugh, a merchant in Ayr, trading with Va. in 1750. [NAS.CS16.1.84]

CAMPBELL, JOHN, emigrated to America as an indentured servant of Young, Miller and Company in 1764, later a merchant in Guildford County, N.C. [NCGSJ.xi.26]

CAMPBELL, JOHN, a merchant from Glasgow who settled in Occoquan and Bladensburg, Va., in 1760. [GA:CFI]

CAMPBELL, JOHN, merchant in Ayr, trading between Ayr and Montserrat and Antigua, 1764, 1765, 1766, 1768, 1769, 1770, 1771, 1773 ; between Ayr and Grenada, 1769; between Ayr and N.Y., 1769, 1771; between Ayr and Bath, N.C.., 1769; between Ayr and Antigua, 1774. [NAS.E504.4.3/4/5/6]

CAMPBELL, JOHN, a merchant, from Glasgow to Boston in 1769. [PAB]

CAMPBELL, JOHN, a merchant in St Croix, later in Greenock, testament Glasgow 1769. [NAS.CS16.1.170; CC9.9]

CAMPBELL, JOHN, a merchant in Glasgow trading with Md., 1771. [NAS.CS16.1.143]

CAMPBELL, JOHN, a merchant in Tobago, 1776. [NA.T1.527.271/2]

CAMPBELL, JOHN, a merchant from Glasgow then in America, 1783. [NAS.CS17.1.2/236]

CAMPBELL, LACHLAN, a merchant from Glasgow, who settled in Fredericksburg, Va., in 1764 as a factor for John Glassell. [NA.AO12/106/23; AO13/28/81, 97/160, 137/35]

CAMPBELL, MARTIN, an Indian trader in Augusta, Ga., 1756. [NA.CO5.646/C15]

CAMPBELL, PATRICK, trading between Port Glasgow and Va., 1748. [NAS.E504.28.4]

CAMPBELL, PETER, emigrated from Glasgow to Va. in 1775, a tobacco factor in Prince George County, Va.. [GA.CFI]

CAMPBELL, PETER, born 1755, a merchant from Glasgow who emigrated via Greenock to Jamaica in 1775. [NA.T47.12]

CAMPBELL, ROBERT, a merchant from Glasgow who settled in Jamaica before 1744. [NAS.RD2.169.74]

CAMPBELL, SAMUEL, a merchant in Wilmington, N.C.., partner of Robert Hogg, before 1775, moved to Shelburne, Nova Scotia, by 1785. [NA.AO12.35.4]

CAMPBELL, WILLIAM, a merchant who settled in Accomack County, Va., probate Accomack 1716.

CAMPBELL, WILLIAM, a merchant from Glasgow who died in Va. during 1718, probate PCC 1718.

CAMPBELL, WILLIAM, a storekeeper in Westmoreland County, Va., before 1731. [NAS.GD1.455]

CAMPBELL, WILLIAM, a merchant from Montrose, emigrated from Gravesend to Ga. in 1737. [SPAWI.1737.107]

CAMPBELL, WILLIAM, trading between Ayr and the Va. and Md., 1747, 1749, 1750, 1752, 1753, 1754, 1757, 1760, 1761, 1763, 1765, 1769; between Ayr and St Kitts, 1759; between Ayr and Philadelphia, 1760; between Ayr and Boston, 1769. [NAS.E504.4.2/3]

CAMPBELL, WILLIAM, born in Cowal, Argyll, settled in Worcester, Massachusetts, 1768, a merchant in partnership with Andrew Duncan pre 1775. [NA.AO13.24.72]

CAMPBELL, WILLIAM, a merchant in Cross Creek, N.C.., before 1776. [NA.AO13.97.154]

CAMPBELL, ZACHARIAH, born 1740, a merchant from Glasgow who emigrated to America by 1763, and settled in Vienna, Md., and in Fredericksburg, Va.. [NAS.B10.15.6863]

CAMPBELL, BLANE and Company, merchants in Grenada, 1776, 1782, 1783. [NAS.CS16.1.170; CS16.1.185; CS17.1.1]

CAMPBELL, MCNEILL, and CAMPBELL, merchants in Campbeltown trading with St Kitts, 1775. [NAS.CS1116.1.165]

CANT, JAMES, a merchant in Va. around 1656 to 1671. [NAS.RD2.27.30; RD2.26.638; RD2.27.501; RD2.30.483]

CARGILL, JOHN, born 1744, a merchant in Jamaica, died there in 1780. [Kingston Cathedral gravestone]

SCOTTISH TRANSATLANTIC MERCHANTS

CARLYLE, ALEXANDER, a merchant from Dumfries-shire who settled in Hopewell, Somerset County, Md., before 1712, died 1726. [MSA.MdProv.Ct#12.297][WMQ.1.18.208]

CARLYLE, ALEXANDER, a merchant planter in Va., before 1739. [NAS.S/H. 1767; RS23.13.197]

CARLYLE, JOHN, born 1720, a merchant from Dumfries who emigrated via Glasgow and settled in Alexandria, Va. before 1748, died 1780. [NAS.SC36.63.1; RS10.16.31][RAV#19]

CARLYLE, JOHN, and Company, merchants in Glasgow trading with Va., 1775. [NAS.CS16.1.161]

CARMICHAEL, GEORGE, and Company, merchants in Glasgow trading with S.C. and Va., 1757, 1769. [NAS.CS16.1.99/100/134]

CARMICHAEL, JAMES, a merchant from Glasgow who settled in Jamaica by 1750. [NAS.B10.15.7166]

CARMICHAEL, JOHN, a merchant in Edinburgh trading with S.C., 1734, 1756, with Boston, 1744. [NAS.AC9.1960; AC7.49.14; E504.15.2]

CARMICHAEL, ROBERT, a merchant in Va., 1770. [NAS.RS10.10.295][GA.CFI]

CARMICHAEL, WALTER, a merchant from Edinburgh who settled in Queen Anne County, Md., before 1767. [EMR.21.6.1767][NAS.RD4.239.714/6] [MSA.MdWills.37.130]

CARMICHAEL, WILLIAM, a merchant who settled in Barbados before 1695. [NAS.RD2.80.10; RD4.78.1253]

CARMICHAEL, WILLIAM, a merchant from Glasgow who settled in Jamaica by 1750. [NAS.B10.15.7166]

CARMONT, JOHN, a shopkeeper who settled in Norfolk, Va., before 1770. [NA.AO12.102.152]

CARNEGIE, JOHN, a merchant trading between Greenock and St Kitts, 1743; between Port Glasgow and Jamaica, 1745. [NAS.E504.15.1; 28.2]

CARRICK, JAMES, a merchant from Fife, who settled in Boston before 1747. [SCS][NAS.SH.5.4.1754]

CARRICK, ..., a merchant who emigrated via Portsmouth to Tobago in 1775. [NA.T47.9/11]

CARSE, EDWARD, a merchant trading between Ayr and Barbados, 1642. [NAS.RD1.544.6]

CARSON, JAMES, a merchant in Charleston, S.C., 1786. [NAS.CS17.1.5/162]

CATHCART, ANDREW, a merchant, trading from Ayr to the Caribbee Islands in 1680s. [NAS.E72.3.12][RPCS.14.584]

CATHCART, ANDREW, a merchant in Glasgow trading with N.E. and Md., 1739-1741, dead by 1741. [NAS.AC9.1476]

CATHCART, ELIAS, trading between Ayr and Va., 1742, 1745, 1749, 1753, 1754, 1755, 1756, 1759; between Ayr and Antigua, 1750; between Port Glasgow and Va., 1744. [NAS.E504.4.1/2/3; 28.1]

CATHCART, FERGUS, a merchant in Greenock trading with Barbados, pre 1715. [NAS.AC8.196]

CATHCART, WILLIAM, born 1732, a merchant from Glasgow who settled in Kingston, Jamaica, before 1768. [NAS.SC36.63.12.51]

CHALMERS, DONALD, a merchant from Glasgow who settled in Va. before 1765. [NAS.CS16.1.125]

CHALMERS, JAMES, a merchant in St Kitts, a burgess of Ayr, 1665. [ABR]

CHALMERS, JAMES, a merchant in Jamaica, 1765, brother of John Chalmers a merchant in Glasgow and Donald Chalmers a merchant in Va.. [NAS.CS16.1.125/13]

CHALMERS, JAMES, trading between Ayr and Antigua, 1768; between Ayr and Grenada, 1769. [NAS.E504.4.4/5]

CHALMERS, JOHN, and Company, merchants in Glasgow trading with Va., 1772. [NAS.CS16.1.148]

CHAMBERS, ANDREW, a merchant trading between Glasgow and Va., 1681. [NAS.E72.19.3]

CHAPLIN, GEORGE, a merchant from Arbroath who settled in Kingston, Jamaica, died 1723. [NAS.CC8.8.89]

CHAPMAN, DANIEL, a merchant in Edinburgh then in America, 1773. [NAS.CS16.1.154]

CHARITY, JAMES, a merchant who settled in Boston before 1762. [SCS][NAS.SC36.63.8.168]

CHARTERS, CHARLES, a merchant in Edinburgh trading with N.E., 1674. [NAS.AC7.4]

CHEAP, HUGH, trading between Leith and S.C., 1775. [NAS.E504.22]

CHEAP, JAMES, trading between Leith and S.C., 1775. [NAS.E504.22]

CHEAP, PATRICK, a trader, from Glasgow to Boston in 1712. [SCS][PTA#129]

CHIESLEY, SAMUEL, a merchant in Glasgow trading with Va., 1722. [NAS.AC7.27.2186; AC8.285]

CHISHOLM, ADAM, trading between Port Glasgow and St Kitts, 1744; between Port Glasgow and Jamaica, 1744, 1745. [NAS.E504.28.1/2]

CHISHOLM, ALEXANDER, a merchant at Ticonderoga, N.Y., pre 1776, later in Quebec and Montreal. [NA.AO12.27.141]

CHISHOLM, JOHN, from Ross-shire, settled in Camden District, S.C., as a merchant around 1764, moved to the West Indies after 1778. [NA.AO12.49.417]

CHISHOLM, WILLIAM, a farmer and merchant who settled in Pittenweem, Norfolk, Va., in 1754, moved to the Bahamas in 1779. [NA.AO13.2.259]

CHRISTALL, WILLIAM, a merchant from Kippen who settled in Va., died 1751, probate Accomack 1751.

CHRISTIAN, JOHN, trading between Ayr and Halifax, Nova Scotia, 1776; between Ayr and Dominica, 1776. [NAS.E504.4.6]

CHRISTIE, ADAM, jr., a merchant in Pensacola, West Fla., 1778. [NAS.CS16.1.173/159]

CHRISTIE, CHARLES, a merchant who settled in Joppa, Baltimore County, Md., died 1763. [MSA.Prov.Ct.Deeds.DD3.165]

CHRISTIE, JAMES, born 1695, a merchant from Stirling who settled in Baltimore, Md., died 1745. [SHC#20]

CHRISTIE, JAMES, possibly from Fife, a merchant in Md. before 1776. [NA.AO12.6.419]

CHRISTIE, PATRICK, a merchant who emigrated via Aberdeen to West N.J. in 1682. [NAS.E72.1.7]

CHRISTIE, ROBERT, a merchant from Culross, in Fla. and Mexico in 1667. [RPCS.4.297]

CHRISTIE, ROBERT, trading between Greenock and Va., 1744, 1745; with Md., 1746; between Port Glasgow and Va., 1745, 1747, 1748, 1749; between Port Glasgow and Md., 1746, 1747. [NAS.E504.15.1/2; 28.2/3/4]

CHRISTIE, THOMAS, a merchant in Montrose trading with Africa and Antigua, 1754. [NAS.AC7.46.51]

CHRISTIE, ROBERT, settled as a merchant in Baltimore from 1764 to 1776. [NA.AO12.8.73]

CLARK, ARCHIBALD, trading between Port Glasgow and Jamaica, 1747. [NAS,E504.28.3]

CLARK, COLIN, born 1750, a merchant in Wilmington, N.C.., before 1776, moved to London by 1784. [NA.AO12.34.203][NAS.CS17.1.8/130]

CLARK, DANIEL, trading between Port Glasgow and Va./Md., 1745. [NAS.E504.28.2]

CLARK, DANIEL, an Indian trader in Augusta, Ga., later in Charleston, S.C., probate S.C. 1757. [NAS.CS16.1.107]

CLARK, JAMES, a merchant from Glasgow who settled in Va. before 1754. [NAS.B10.15.6653]

CLARK, JAMES, a merchant in Kilmarnock trading with Va., 1767. [NAS.CS16.1.130]

CLARK, JOHN, trading between Port Glasgow and Boston, 1748. [NAS.E504.28.3]

CLARK, JOHN, born 1739, a merchant in Halifax, Nova Scotia, died in Roxburgh, Boston, 1761. [AJ#710]

CLARK, ROBERT, a trader, from Glasgow to Boston in 1712. [SCS][PTA#129]

CLARK, THOMAS, a merchant in N.E., 1695. [NAS.GD3.4.469]

CLARKSON, JAMES, a merchant from Linlithgow who emigrated via Leith to S.C. in 1684, settled in Woodbridge, East N.J., by 1697, died there 1729. [NAS.RD4.83.421; RD4.38.1501][RPCS.8.527] [NJSA.EJD.Liber A]

CLARKSON, THOMAS, a merchant from Lanarkshire who settled in Barbados before 1765. [NAS.RS32.18.33; RD3.246.893; CS16.1.122]

CLAYTON, FRANCIS, a merchant from Edinburgh who settled in Wilmington, New Hanover County, N.C.., died 1790, probate N.C. 1790. [NAS.CC8.8.128/2]

CLAYTON, ROBERT, a merchant in St Kitts, 1720. [GBR]

CLELAND, JAMES, a merchant from Edinburgh who emigrated via the Clyde to Darien in 1699, testament Edinburgh 1707. [NAS.CC8.8.83]

CLELAND, JAMES, a merchant in Philadelphia, Pa., probate Barbados 1720.

CLELAND, WILLIAM, a merchant from Edinburgh who settled in Barbados before 1705, died there 1719. probate Barbados 1719 [RB6/4.519][SPAWI.1705.409]

CLERK, HUGH, trading from Greenock to Va., 1744. [NAS.E504.15.1]

CLERK, HUGH, a merchant in Edinburgh trading with S.C., 1745, 1748, 1751. [NAS.E504.22;AC8.723; GD18.5321]

CLERK, JAMES, a merchant from Penicuik who settled in Boston before 1716. [NAS.GD18.5288/2573/5296]

CLERK, JONATHAN, a merchant in Boston, trading with Leith, 1739. [NAS.AC7.44.185]

CLERK, THOMAS, a merchant in Charleston, S.C., then in London, 1789. [NAS.CS17.1.8/130]

CLYDESDALE, ROBERT, a merchant trading between Port Glasgow and the West Indies, 1683. [NAS.E72.19.8]

COATS, ARCHIBALD, and JOHN, trading from Greenock with S.C., 1745, Va., 1745, 1746; between Port Glasgow and Va., 1745, 1747, 1748; between Port Glasgow and Jamaica, 1748, 1749. [NAS.E504.15.2; 28.2/3/4]

COATS, ARCHIBALD and WILLIAM, merchants in Glasgow trading with America, 1769. [NAS.CS16.1.134]

COATS, CHARLES, trading between Port Glasgow and Maryland, 1747. [NAS.E504.28.3]

COATS, JOHN, a merchant in Glasgow, trading between Port Glasgow and Maryland, 1747; between Port Glasgow and Va., 1749; trading with Philadelphia, 1751. [NAS.E504.28.3/4; CS16.1.85]

COCHRAN, ANDREW, trading between Greenock and Va., 1742, 1743, 1744, 1746; between Port Glasgow and Jamaica, 1745; between Port Glasgow and Va., 1745, 1747. [NAS.E504.15.1/2; 28.2/3]

COCHRAN, ANDREW, a merchant in Glasgow trading with Va., 1764. [NAS.CS16.1.117/120/122]

COCHRAN, DAVID, trading between Port Glasgow and Va., 1747. [NAS.E504.28.3]

COCHRAN, DAVID, a merchant in Va., 1777. [NAS.AC7.56]

COCHRAN, DAVID, and JAMES BUCHANAN, merchants in Glasgow trading with Md., 1749. [NAS.CS16.1.80]

COCHRAN, MUNGO, a merchant from Glasgow who emigrated from Leith to the West Indies in 1678. [RPCS.6.76]

COCHRAN, CUNNINGHAM and Company, in Henrico County, Va., pre 1776. [NA.AO13.102.56]

COCHRANE, DAVID, born 1739, a merchant from Glasgow who settled in Richmond, Va., before 1766. [NAS.RD3.242.127; CS.GMB#56; CS17.1.3/314; AC7.56; CS16.1.125]

COCHRANE, DAVID, trading between Port Glasgow and Va., 1749. [NAS.E504.28.4]

COCHRANE, DAVID, trading between Ayr and Va., 1773. [NAS.E504.4.6]

COCHRANE, WILLIAM, trading between Port Glasgow and Virginia, 1748. [NAS.E504.28.3/4]

COCHRANE, WILLIAM, a merchant from Glasgow then in Jamaica, 1780. [NAS.CS16.1.125/13/179]

COCKBURN, ARCHIBALD, a merchant in Edinburgh trading with Boston, pre 1739. [NAS.AC7.44.185]

COGLE, RICHARD, a merchant in Md., 1778. [NAS.CS16.1.173]

COLHOUN, JAMES, and Company, merchants in Glasgow trading with Boston, 1728. [NAS.CS96.3814]

COLHOUN, JAMES, trading between Greenock and Va., 1745. [NAS.E504.15.2]

COLQUHOUN, HUGH, a merchant in Glasgow trading in Bermuda, 1784. [NAS.RD4.243]

COLQUHOUN, ROBERT, a merchant in St Kitts, 1729. [NAS.B10.15.6183; GD237.12.47/4]

COLQUHOUN, WALTER, a merchant in Va. then in Jamaica, 1783. [NAS.CS17.1.2/188]

COMYN, THOMAS, born 1756, a merchant in Michael Street, Pensacola, West Fla., 1786. [PC.Col.V.593] [Spanish Census of Pensacola, 1784-1820]

CONNELL, JAMES, a merchant in Port Royal, Jamaica, a burgess of Ayr, 1710. [ABR]

CONNOR, EDWARD, a storekeeper from Greenock who settled in Loudoun County on the Potomac River, Va., died 1766. [Loudoun County Deed Book. F48]

COOK, ARCHIBALD, trading between Greenock and Va., 1743. [NAS.E504.1]

COOK, JOHN, a merchant in Tobago, 1782. [NAS.CS17.1.1]

COPLAND, CHARLES, jr., a merchant in Aberdeen trading with Va., 1751. [AJ#200]

COPLAND, WILLIAM, and Company, merchants in Aberdeen, trading with Md., pre 1750. [NAS.AC9.1748; E504.1.3]

CORBETT, EDWARD, born 1754, a merchant from Edinburgh, emigrated via Greenock to Charleston, S.C., in 1774. [NA.T47.12]

CORBETT, EDWARD, trading between Leith and S.C., 1775. [NAS.E504.22]

CORBETT, JAMES, a merchant in Dumfries, trading with Va. and Barbados, 1745-1762. [NAS.CS96.2147-2162]

CORBETT, JAMES, trading between Port Glasgow and Va., 1743, 1745, 1747; between Greenock and N.C.., 1744, with Va., 1746. [NAS.E504.28.1/2/3; 15.2]

CORBETT, JOHN, a merchant trading between Greenock and Va., 1743, 1745; trading between Port Glasgow and Va. and Md., 1744, 1748. [NAS.E504.15.1/2; 28.1/3]

CORBETT, JOSEPH, a merchant in Va., 1782. [NAS.CS17.1.1/97]

CORBETT, THOMAS, merchant in Dumfries trading with Va., 1745-1753. [NAS.CS96.2156/62]

CORBETT, WILLIAM, son of James Corbett a merchant in Glasgow, a merchant who settled in Boston before 1756, died 1767. [GA.B10.15.7137/7234][SCS]

CORDINER, JAMES, a merchant from Paisley who settled on the Rappahannock, Va., dead by 1724, testament Edinburgh 1724. [NAS.CC8.8.89]

CORDINER, JOHN, a merchant from Glasgow who settled in Boston before 1686, dead by 1712. [NAS.SH.17.10.1712][SCS]

CORRIE, ARCHIBALD, a merchant from Dumfries who settled in Bath and Edenton, N.C.., before 1770. [NAS.CS16.1.143]

CORRIE, JOHN, a factor in Providence, Rhode Island, 1740. [NAS.CS16.1.69]

CORRIE, JOSEPH, a merchant who settled in Dominica before 1782, then in St Thomas. [NAS. CS17.1.1; SH.12.2.1783]

COULTER, HUGH, born 1717, a merchant from Glasgow who settled in Md., died in 1763, testament Edinburgh 1766. [NAS.CC8.8.120/1]

COULTER, JAMES, a merchant in Glasgow, trading between Port Glasgow and Md., 1745; trading with Va. and Barbados, 1755; with America, 1776; with the Va. and Md., 1779. [NAS.E504.28.2;AC7.47.32; CS16.1.170/175]

COULTER, JOHN, a merchant in Edinburgh trading with Va., 1727. [NAS.AC9.976]

COULTER, JOHN, trading between Port Glasgow and Md. 1745. [NAS.E504.28.2]

COULTER, MICHAEL, a merchant in Edinburgh trading with Va., 1727. [NAS.AC9.976]

COUTTS, HERCULES, a merchant from Montrose, died in Newcastle, Pa.. pro.1709 PCC

COUTTS, HERCULES, born 1714, a merchant from Montrose who settled in Md. before 1751. [NAS.RD4.177.298]

COUTTS, JAMES, a merchant, possibly from Montrose, who settled in Philadelphia by 1699. [SPAWI.1699.138/1]

COUTTS, PATRICK, a merchant from Aberdeen who emigrated to Va. in 1747, settled at Port Royal, and at Richmond Falls, died in 1777. [NAS.RD4.212.846][ACA: APB.4.106]

COWAN, JOHN, trading between Greenock and Va., 1745. [NAS.E504.15.2]

CRAIG, GEORGE, a merchant in Glasgow trading with America and the West Indies, 1717. [NAS.AC7.24.710]

CRAIG, GEORGE, a merchant, from Orkney to Boston in 1765. [PAB]

CRAIG, JOHN, a storekeeper from Ayrshire who settled in Va. in 1769. [NAS.CS.C4.13]

CRAIG, ROBERT, trading between Port Glasgow and Boston, 1748. [NAS.E504.28.3]

CRAIG, WILLIAM, a merchant in Glasgow trading with Jamaica, 1730. [NAS.AC7.35.1065]

CRAMOND, JOHN, a merchant from Glasgow who settled in Norfolk, Va., 1759, moved to Jamaica by 1777. [NAS.CS16.1.170/173/159][NA.AO13.28.120] [VaGaz: 4.4.1766]

CRAWFORD, ANDREW, a merchant in Va., 1760. [NAS.RD4.198/2.558]

CRAWFORD, ARCHIBALD, trading between Ayr and Antigua, 1768. [NAS.E504.4.4]

CRAWFORD, DANIEL, a merchant in S.C., 1756. [MAGU#54]

CRAWFORD, DAVID, a merchant in S.C. around 1737. [SC Deed of Sale book T#381]

CRAWFORD, DAVID, a merchant in St Eustatia, 1773. [NAS.RD4.213.1232]

CRAWFORD, GEORGE, a merchant who settled in Va. before 1769. [NAS.CS16.1.134]

CRAWFORD, GEORGE, a merchant in Glasgow then in Jamaica, 1777. [NAS.CS16.1.171]

CRAWFORD, GEORGE, and **WILLIAM FRENCH,** Richmond, Henrico County, Va., 1779. [NA.AO13.102.54]

CRAWFORD, HUGH, born 1680, a merchant in Kingston, Jamaica, died 1719. [Kingston gravestone]
CRAWFORD, JAMES, a merchant, from Port Glasgow to Va. in 1684. [NAS.E72.19.9]
CRAWFORD, JAMES, a merchant in Boston, died 1777. [NA.AO12.10.253]
CRAWFORD, JAMES, a merchant who emigrated via Greenock to Jamaica in 1773. [NAS.CE60.1.7]
CRAWFORD, JAMES, a merchant in Greenock trading with Va., pre 1781. [NAS.AC7.58]
CRAWFORD, JOHN, a merchant trading from Port Glasgow to the West Indies in 1684. [NAS.E72.19.9]
CRAWFORD, JOHN, a merchant from Ayr in Boston by 1684. [SCS]
CRAWFORD, JOHN, jr., a merchant from Ayr, to S.C. in 1682. [NAS.NRAS.0631.600; E72.19.6]
CRAWFORD, JOHN, a merchant trading between Ayr and the Caribbee Islands, 1691. [NAS.E72.3.23]
CRAWFORD, JOHN, trading between Ayr and Antigua, 1773. [NAS.E504.4.6]
CRAWFORD, MATTHEW, a merchant in Glasgow in Jamaica pre 1730. [NAS.AC7.35.485]
CRAWFORD, MUNGO, a merchant in Boston, 1684. [SCS]
CRAWFORD, PATRICK, a merchant who emigrated via London to N.Y. by 1699. [DP#153]
CRAWFORD, ROBERT, a merchant in St Kitts, a partner in Crawford, Johnston and Company there, 1783. [NAS.CS18.714.25; AC7.51; RD3.243.146; SH.2.4.1784]
CRAWFORD, ROBERT, and Company, merchants in Glasgow trading with Boston, 1781. [NAS.CS16.1.183]
CRAWFORD, SAMUEL, and Company, merchants in Glasgow trading with Antigua, 1773, with Va., 1781. [NAS.CS16.1.154; AC7.58]
CRAWFORD, THOMAS, a merchant in Glasgow trading with the Plantations, 1671. [RPCS.3.298]
CRAWFORD, THOMAS, a merchant who emigrated via Port Glasgow to S.C. in 1684. [NAS.E72.19.9]
CRAWFORD, WILLIAM, a merchant in Funchal, Madeira, 1620. [Tombo, Funchal Archives, Codex 1503]
CRAWFORD, WILLIAM, a merchant who emigrated via Port Glasgow to N.E. in 1685. [NAS.E72.19.9][SCS]

CRAWFORD, WILLIAM, a merchant in Glasgow, trading between Greenock and Va., 1743, 1758; trading between Port Glasgow and Va., 1745, 1748. [NAS.E504.1: 28.2/3; CS16.1.100]

CREIGHTON, ALEXANDER, born 1753, a merchant from Glasgow who emigrated via Greenock to Nevis in 1774. [NAS.CE60.1.7]

CREIGHTON, WILLIAM, born 1757, a merchant from Edinburgh, who emigrated via Greenock to Jamaica in 1775. [NA.T47.12]

CROCKETT, CHARLES, a merchant in Edinburgh trading with Charleston, 1738. [NAS.AC7.43.213; CS16.1.69]

CROCKETT, JAMES, a merchant in Charleston by 1730. [NAS.RD4.178.252; RS27.144.179; CS16.1.69; AC7.43.213][NA.CO5.401.249][SAS]

CROCKETT, JOHN, a merchant who emigrated to Charleston in 1737, probate 1740 PCC; probate 1759 S.C.. [NA.CO5.667][NAS.CS16.1.69/78; AC7.43.213][SAS]

CROCKETT AND SEAMAN, merchants in Charleston, S.C., from 1737. [NA.CO5.667.46; CO5.640.229; CO5.667.102D][SPAWI.XLIV.86]

CROSBIE, JAMES, a merchant from Cambuslang who settled in Williamsburg, Va., probate Chesterfield County, Va., 1753.

CROSS, DAVID, trading between Port Glasgow and Va., 1749. [NAS.E504.28.4]

CROSS, DAVID, of Glenduffhill, a merchant in Glasgow, then in Jamaica 1780. [NAS.CS16.1.177]

CROSS, JAMES, a merchant in Glasgow trading with Va. and Barbados, 1755. [NAS.AC7.47.32]

CROSS, JAMES, a merchant from Glasgow who settled in Manchester, Prince Edward County, Va., before 1776, died in Norfolk in 1787. [GA: TD131.13] [NAS.SH.7.5.1788][VaGaz.25.1.1787]

CROSS, JOHN, a merchant from Glasgow, a factor in the Canary Islands, 1695-1703. [NAS.PC2.28.271]

CRUDEN, JAMES, a merchant in N.C.., partner in John Cruden and Company, before 1776, moved to Jamaica in 1776. [NA.AO12.37.9]

CRUICKSHANK, ALEXANDER, a merchant in Antigua, died there in 1713. [ACA.APB.2.111]

CRUICKSHANK, ALEXANDER, a merchant in Albany, N.Y., pre 1776. [NA.AO12.26.270]

CRUICKSHANK, CHARLES, born 1746, a merchant from Glasgow who settled in Md. before 1775. [GA:CFI]

CULBERT, SAMUEL, trading between Port Glasgow and Jamaica, 1745. [NAS.E504.28.2]

CULLEN, WALTER, born 1755, a merchant from Edinburgh who emigrated via Greenock to Jamaica in 1775. [NA.T47.12]

CUMMING, ROBERT, from Aberdeenshire, a merchant in Concord, N.E., 1720s. [NAS.GD105.339] [St Paul's Episcopal church register, Aberdeen, 1728]

CUMMING, ROBERT, a merchant from Kilmarnock who settled in Va. before 1763. [NAS.CS16.1.115]

CUMMING, THOMAS, a merchant from Ayr trading with Antigua, 1768; between Ayr and Falmouth, N.E., 1771; between Ayr and Va., 1771; then in America, 1775. [NAS.E540.4.4/5; CS16.1.165]

CUNNING, GEORGE, trading between Greenock and St Kitts, 1746. [NAS.E504.15.2]

CUNNINGHAM, ARCHIBALD, merchant from Haddington who settled in Boston by 1765, settled in Shelburne, Nova Scotia, after 1776. [NA.AO.13.24.96]

CUNNINGHAM, GEORGE, an assistant storekeeper who settled in Falmouth, Va., before 1776. [SFV#229]

CUNNINGHAM, JACK, a merchant who settled in Va. before 1776. [AHR.5.294]

CUNNINGHAM, JOHN, a storekeeper and clerk to George Logan in Va. from 1768. [NA.AO32.124]

CUNNINGHAM, WILLIAM, a merchant in St Kitts, 1720. [GBR]

CUNNINGHAM, WILLIAM, a merchant in Glasgow trading with the West Indies, 1726, with Jamaica pre 1730. [NAS.AC9.1098; AC7.35.485]

CUNNINGHAM, WILLIAM, a merchant in Glasgow and in Westmoreland County, Jamaica, 1744. [NAS.RD2.169.70]

CUNNINGHAM, WILLIAM, born 1727, merchant in Glasgow and Ayr, trading between Ayr and Va., 1746, 1753, 1754, 1756, 1757, 1761, 1765, 1769; between Ayr and Boston, 1769, 1771; between Ayr and Falmouth, N.E., 1771; partner in Va. and Md. in Cunninghame Findlay and Company, Cunningham, Browne and

Company, from 1748 to 1768, returned to Ayrshire in 1776; a merchant in Glasgow trading with Va., 1779. [NAS.E504.4.1/2/4/5; GD247.140; CS16.1.133/174] [NA.AO12.56.289] [SFV.xi.232]

CURRIE, ALEXANDER, a merchant from Linlithgow who settled in Curacao, died there in 1728, testament 1741 Edinburgh. [NAS.CC8.8.104]

CURRIE, GEORGE, and GEORGE THOMSON, merchants in Glasgow trading with Va., 1729. [NAS.AC9.1085]

CURRIE, JAMES, a merchant in Edinburgh trading with Va. and Barbados, 1660s. [RPCS.3/2.358/446]

CURRIE, JOHN, a merchant from Haddington who settled in Jamaica, died there in 1747, testament 1785 Edinburgh. [NAS.CC8.8.126/2]

CURRIE, WALTER, a merchant in New Providence then in Linlithgow, 1741. [NAS.CC8.8.104]

CURRIE, WILLIAM, settled in western S.C., a merchant there from 1772 to 1778, moved to Edinburgh by 1784. [NA.AO12.51.65]

CURRY, GEORGE, settled in Ga. 1736, an Indian trader in Augusta. [ESG#70]

CUTHBERT, LEWIS, a merchant in Kingston, Jamaica, 1782. [NAS.CS17.1.1]

CUTHBERT, SAMUEL, trading between Ayr and Antigua, 1750; between Ayr and Va., 1755. [NAS.E504.4.2]

CUTHBERTSON and SYME, merchants in Glasgow trading with Quebec, 1783. [NAS.CS17.1.2]

DALE, DAVID, a merchant in Glasgow trading with the Va. and Md., 1777. [NAS.CS16.1.170]

DALGLEISH, ANDREW, a merchant, from Greenock to Boston in 1764. [SG#7/14][PAB]

DALGLEISH, JAMES, a merchant in Bo'ness trading with the West Indies, 1778. [NAS.CS16.1.173]

DALLAS, ALEXANDER, born 1757, a merchant from Aberdeen who emigrated via Greenock to Jamaica in 1775. [NA.T47.12]

DALLAS, WALTER, a merchant in Charleston, 1729. [SAS]

DALLAS, WALTER, born in 1690s, a merchant from Edinburgh who settled in Annapolis, Md., and died there before 1772. [NAS.CS.GMB.282; CS16.1.95/99] [FD#344]

DALLING, WILLIAM, a merchant in Jamaica, 1744. [NAS.RS.Edinburgh.130.123]

DALRYMPLE, CATHCART, trading between Port Glasgow and Virginia, 1747. [NAS.E504.28.3]

DALRYMPLE, DAVID, and Company, merchants in Glasgow, trading with Va., 1764. [NAS.CS16.1.120]

DALYELL, ANDREW, a merchant, from Greenock to Boston in 1764. [SG#7/14][PAB]

DALYELL, DAVID, trading between Greenock and Va., 1744, 1745, 1746; between Port Glasgow and Va., 1745, 1746, 1748, 1749. [NAS.E504.15.2; 28.2/3/4]

DALYALL, DAVID, and GEORGE OSWALD, and Company, in Fairfax County, Va.. before 1776. [NA.AO13.102.59]

DALYELL, GEORGE, a merchant from Lanark who emigrated to Antigua before 1765. [NAS.RS42.17.79]

DANSKINE, JAMES, a merchant from Stirling who settled in Fla. by 1780. [NAS.CS16.1.181]

DARLING, ANDREW, a merchant in St John's parish, Sunbury, Ga., 1770, [Ga. Land Grant book #H41], probate Ga. 1772.

DAVIDSON, ANDREW, a merchant from Paisley who settled in Va. before 1764. [NAS.CS16.1.120]

DAVIDSON, WILLIAM, alias John Godsman, a merchant in Miramachi, from 1765, died 1790. [DCB.IV.195]

DAVIDSON, ..., a merchant from Kincardineshire who settled in Md., died 1779. [Garten gravestone]

DEAN, HUGH, a merchant who emigrated from Scotland to America, and settled in Somerset County, Md., during 1770, moved to the Bahamas by 1783, later in N.Y.. [ANY.I.275][MdHistMag.2.33.134]

DEAN, JOHN, a merchant probably from Glasgow, settled in Tappahannock, Va., before 1757. [NAS.B10.15.7036]

DEANS, JAMES, a merchant who settled in Chesterfield County, Va., probate Chesterfield 1764.

DEAS, DAVID, born 1722, a merchant from Leith who settled in Charleston in 1738, died there in 1775. [SAS] [NAS.RD3.224.627-630; CS16.1.165/170][SM#37.637]

DEAS, DAVID, trading between Leith and S.C., 1745. [E504.22]

DEAS, JOHN, born 1735, emigrated to S.C. in 1749, a merchant in Charleston, died there 1790, probate S.C.

1790. [NA.AO12.73.129][SM.52.517]
[NAS.CS16.1.165/170][SAS]

DEAS, ROBERT, from Leith, a merchant in Charleston, 1755. [NAS.CS16.1.95]

DENHAM, THOMAS, a merchant who settled in Charleston, S.C., in 1774, later in Shelburne, Nova Scotia. [NA.AO13.25.138]

DENHOLM, ROBERT, a merchant in Savannah, Ga., testament. Edinburgh 1786. [NAS.CC8.8.127/1]

DENNISTOUN, JAMES, a merchant in Glasgow trading with the Va. and Md., pre 1754. [NAS.AC7.46.185]; trading from Port Glasgow to Va. 1742, 1744, 1746, 1747, 1749; between Port Glasgow and Barbados, 1746; trading between Port Glasgow and Jamaica, 1747, [NAS.E504.28.1/2/3/4]

DENNISTOUN, RICHARD, a merchant from Glasgow who settled in Hanover County, Va., before 1776, returned to Glasgow. [NA.AO13.33.124]

DENNISTOUN, BROWN, and Company, merchants in Glasgow trading with Grenada, 1782. [NAS.AC7.58]

DEWAR, ROBERT, a merchant from Edinburgh who settled in Antigua and in St Eustatia before 1768. [NAS.SH.14.1.1772; SH.15.1.1768; RS27.180.276; RGS.110.95; CS16.1.173]

DICK, JAMES, born 1706, a merchant from Edinburgh who emigrated to Md. in 1734, settled in London Town on the South River, died during 1782 in Lewistown, Md.. [NYGaz: 11.11.1782][MSA.All Hallows church register#56]

DICK, THOMAS, a merchant from Edinburgh who settled in Annapolis, Md., before 1758. [NAS.SH.21.3.1758]

DICKIE, ROBERT, a merchant in Montrose trading with Africa and Antigua, 1754. [NAS.AC7.46.51]

DICKSON, JOHN, a merchant in Glasgow trading with Va., 1722. [NAS.AC7.27.2186; AC8.285]

DICKSON, ROBERT, a merchant in Glasgow trading with N.J., 1770. [NAS.CS16.1.138]

DINWIDDIE, JOHN, born 1698, a merchant from Glasgow who settled in Hanover, King George County, Va., died in Glasgow during 1726, testament Glasgow 1726. [NAS.CC9.7.52][King George County Wills#1A.45]

DINWIDDIE, LAWRENCE, a merchant trading between Greenock and Va., 1743; between Port Glasgow and Md., 1744, 1745. [NAS.E504.15.1; 28.1/2]

DINWIDDIE, CRAWFORD and Company, in Mecklenburg County, Va., pre 1776. [NA.AO13.102/59]

DOBBIE, GEORGE, an assistant storekeeper who settled in Halifax County, Va., from 1770 to 1776. [SFV#34]

DOBSON, PETER, a merchant in Glasgow trading with Antigua, 1782. [NAS.CS17.1.1]

DOCHERTY, DANIEL, a merchant, from Greenock to Boston in 1764. [SG#7/14][PAB]

DONALD, ALEXANDER, partner in the Thistle Distillery, Norfolk, [NA.AO12.74.335]; a merchant from Glasgow, then in Richmond, Va., 1787. [NAS.CS17.1.6/96]

DONALD, JAMES, a merchant trading between Greenock and Va., 1743, 1744, 1745, 1746; between Port Glasgow and Va., 1745, 1747, 1749. [NAS.E504.15.1/2; 28/2/3/4]

DONALD, JAMES, Chesterfield County, Va.. 1779. [NA.AO13.102.59]

DONALD, JAMES, a merchant in St Augustine, Fla., 1776. [NAS.NRAS.0159.C4]

DONALD, JAMES & ROBERT, Henry County, Va.pre 1776. [NA.AO13.102.61]

DONALD, ROBERT, and Company, trading from Greenock to Antigua, 1742, to St Kitts, and Va., 1743, 1745, Barbados, 1744, with Boston, 1744, 1745, 1746; with Md. and Va., 1744, 1745, with S.C., and Boston, 1745; with Jamaica, 1745, 1746; trading between Port Glasgow and Md. 1745; between Port Glasgow and Boston, 1748; between Port Glasgow and Va., 1748, 1749. [NAS.E504.15.1/2; 28.2/3/4]

DONALD, ROBERT, a merchant from Dunbartonshire who settled in Va., 1757. [NAS.RS10.9.97]

DONALD, ROBERT, a merchant from Ayr who settled in Warwick, Va., before 1778; then in Pensacola, W.Fla., died in Ayr, test Glasgow 1791. [NAS.CS16.1.173; SH.11.4.1788]

DONALD, ROBERT, a merchant in Glasgow trading in Bermuda, 1784. [NAS.RD4.243]

DONALD, THOMAS, trading between Port Glasgow and Jamaica, 1746. [NAS.E504.28.2]

DONALD, THOMAS, a merchant in Glasgow trading in Bermuda, 1784. [NAS.RD4.243]

DONALD, WILLIAM, a merchant in Ayr trading with Va., 1756, 1759; between Ayr and Falmouth, N.E., 1769, 1770. [NAS.E504.4.2/5; CS16.1.103]

DONALD, WILLIAM, and Company, trading between Greenock and Boston, 1743. [NAS.E504.15.1]

DONALDSON, JAMES, a merchant from Dunbartonshire who settled in Annapolis, Md., probate Md. 1737. [NAS.CS16.1.69/80/81][MSA.Wills.21.891]

DONALDSON, JAMES, a merchant in Glasgow trading with the Va. and Md., 1777. [NAS.CS16.1.171]

DONALDSON, JOHN, a merchant, probate Newcastle, Delaware, 1702

DONALDSON, WILLIAM, a merchant in Glasgow trading with Va., 1748. [NAS.AC11.231]

DONALDSON, WILLIAM, a merchant in N.Y. by 1758, later in London. [NAS.CS96/1834/41]

DONALDSON, WILLIAM, merchant in Norfolk, Va., pre 1776, possibly settled in Shelburne, Nova Scotia, by 1783. [NA.AO12.55.112, etc]

DOUGAL, ADAM, trading between Greenock and Va., 1744. [NAS.E504.15.1]

DOUGLAS, ANDREW, a merchant in Surinam, inv.1706 NY. [N.Y. wills, liber 3-4, fo.453-455]

DOUGLAS, ARCHIBALD, a merchant in Va., 1775. [NAS.CS16.1.165]

DOUGLAS, GEORGE, a merchant trading between Greenock and Va., 1743, 1745. [NAS.E504.15.1/2]

DOUGLAS, GEORGE, a merchant in N.Y., 1782. [NAS.GD185.29.5]

DOUGLAS, JAMES, born 1722, a merchant in Glasgow who emigrated to Va. before 1754, settled in Dumfries, Prince William County, died 1766. [NAS.CS16.1.165] [SM.29.55][VMHB.19.94; 22.273][MAGU#19] [Frederick Deeds#25.357]

DOUGLAS, JAMES, a merchant in Kingston, Jamaica, 1781. [NAS.RD4.231.242]

DOUGLAS, JAMES, a merchant in N.Y., 1782. [NAS.GD185.29.5]

DOUGLAS, JAMES, a merchant in Va., 1785. [NAS.CS17.1.4/264]

DOUGLAS, SAMUEL, a merchant in Jamaica, burgess of Ayr, 1751. [ABR]

DOUGLAS, SAMUEL, a merchant in Savannah, Ga., 1776, then in Jamaica. [NA.AO12.71.1]

DOUGLAS, SAMUEL, a merchant in N.Y., 1782. [NAS.GD185.29.5]

DOUGLAS, THOMAS, a merchant in Montrose, trading with the Potomac River, Va., 1751; trading between Montrose, Africa and Antigua, 1754. [NAS.RD211.2.107; AC7.46.51]

DOUGLAS, WILLIAM, a merchant in Philadelphia, 1698. [N.Y. wills, Liber 3/4, fo.280]

DOVE, JAMES, a merchant in Jamaica, 1761. [Edinburgh Marriage Register, 1.3.1761]

DOW, JOHN, born 1723, a merchant in Philadelphia c1763-1773. [NA.AO12.42.319]

DOW, STEWART, born 1748, a merchant in Bermuda, died 1786. [F.3.79]

DREGHORN, ALLAN, trading between Greenock and Va., 1742, 1743, 1744, 1746; trading between Port Glasgow and Va., 1745. [NAS.E504.15.1/2; 28.2]

DREGHORN, ROBERT, trading between Greenock and Va., 1742, 1743, 1744, 1746, between Greenock and Boston, 1744; between Port Glasgow and Virginia, 1748, 1749. [NAS.E504.15.1/2; 28/3/4]

DRUMMOND, GAVIN, a merchant from Edinburgh who emigrated via Leith to East N.J. in 1684. [NJSA.EJD.Liber B/148/132]

DRUMMOND, JAMES, trading between Greenock and Md., 1744, 1745. [NAS.E504.15.1/2]

DRUMMOND, JOHN, merchant in Blandford, Prince George County, Va., and in Md. from 1749 to 1776, then in Glasgow. [NA.AO13.4.195][NAS.CS16.1.80/84/89/115]

DUCAT, GEORGE, a merchant in Charleston, 1729. [SAS]

DUFF, WILLIAM, of Dipple, a merchant in Inverness trading with the American Plantations, 1690. [NAS.E72.11.16]

DUFF, WILLIAM, a merchant on the island of Rattan, America, 1751. [NAS.CS16.1.85]

DUN, JAMES, a merchant, possibly from Edinburgh, who settled in Md. before 1760. [NAS.CS16.1.107; CS17.1.2]

DUNBAR, GEORGE, a merchant from Edinburgh who settled in N.Y. before 1782. [NAS.RD2.235.17]

DUNBAR, JAMES, a merchant bound for Barbados, 1666. [RPCS.2.128]

DUNBAR, JOHN, a merchant who emigrated via Liverpool to Va. in 1716, later settled in Newport, Rhode Island. [NAS.GD298; GD103][SPAWI.1716.310][CTB.31.208] [VSP.1.185]

DUNBAR, JOHN, a merchant in Sunbury, Ga., died 1768. [NAS.CS16.1.138][SM.30.503]

DUNBAR, ROBERT, a merchant in Montrose trading with Africa and Antigua, 1754. [NAS.AC7.46.51]

DUNBAR, WILLIAM, a merchant in Edinburgh trading with the American Plantations, 1674. [RPCS.4.608]

DUNBAR, WILLIAM, born 1749, emigrated to Philadelphia in 1771, an Indian trader at Fort Pitt, later a planter and merchant in Natchez, Adams County, Mississippi, died there 1810. [UNC.William Dunbar pp, ms#231] [NAS.GD188.12.5]

DUNCAN, ALEXANDER, a merchant in Jamaica, burgess of Edinburgh, 1758. [EBR]

DUNCAN, ALEXANDER, a merchant from Edinburgh who emigrated before 1758, a member of the firm of Duncan, Schaw and Sutherland in Wilmington, N.C.., died there 1767. [REB.1758.60][St James church register] [NAS.CS16.1.117]

DUNCAN, ANDREW, from Glasgow, a merchant in Worcester, Massachusetts, in partnership with William Campbell. [NA.AO13.24.72][NAS.CS16.1.161]

DUNCAN, GEORGE, a wine merchant who settled in Charleston from 1763 to 1778, moved to London during 1779. [NA.AO13.127.42]

DUNCAN, JAMES, a storekeeper from Midlothian who emigrated via Leith to Philadelphia in 1775. [NA.T47.12]

DUNCAN, JAMES, born 1760, a storekeeper from Falkirk who emigrated via Greenock to N.Y. in 1775. [NA.T47.12]

DUNCAN, JOHN, a brush-manufacturer and merchant from Glasgow who settled in Md. before 1778. [NAS.CS16.1.170/171/173]

DUNCAN, THOMAS, a merchant in Philadelphia, 1767. [NAS.CS16.1.130]

DUNCAN, THOMAS, a bookseller from Glasgow then in North America, 1783. [NAS.CS17.1.2/289]

DUNCAN, WALTER, a merchant in Glasgow trading with Va., 1726. [NAS.AC9.1056; AC7.34.433-451]

DUNCAN, WILLIAM, a merchant from Glasgow in N.E. by 1778, and in Va. by 1781. [NAS.CS16.1.173/88/184]

DUNCAN, ANCRUM AND SCHAW, merchants in Wilmington, N.C.., in 1760s. [SCHM]

DUNCANSON, ROBERT, a merchant from Forres who settled in Fredericksburg, Va., died 1764. [Spotsylvania Deeds, #G266][ActsPCCol.1762/475]

DUNDAS, ALEXANDER, a factor who settled in Barbados by 1716. [NAS.CS.GMB#25.946; GD220.5/704; AC9.769; AC7.25.946]

DUNDAS, CHARLES, a merchant who settled in Barbados before 1718. [BA: RB.6.6.139][NAS.AC9.769; AC7.25.946]

DUNDAS, JAMES, a merchant who emigrated via Leith to East N.J. in 1685. [NAS.E72.15.32]

DUNLOP, ALEXANDER, a merchant who settled in Va. before 1751. [NAS.RD4.177.480]

DUNLOP, ARCHIBALD, a merchant from Glasgow who emigrated to Va. in 1762, settled at Cabin Point on the James River. [NAS.CS.GMB.51; AC7.51; CS16.1.134][GA.CFI]

DUNLOP, COLIN, trading between Greenock and Md., 1743, with Va., 1744, 1745; with Md., 1746, with Va., 1746, with St Kitts, pre 1761; trading between Port Glasgow and Va., 1745, 1746, 1747, 1749; between Port Glasgow and Md., 1747. [NAS.E504.15.1/2; AC7.50; E504.28.2/3/4]

DUNLOP, COLIN, merchant in Glasgow, partner with James Wilson and Company of Kilmarnock, in business in Va. and Md. before 1776. [NA.AO13.28.275] [NAS.CS16.1.134]

DUNLOP, COLIN, and Son and Company, merchants in Prince William County, Va., pre 1776. Partners were Colin Dunlop, his son James, James Wilson, his son James, and Cumberland Wilson in America. Properties in Dumfries, Dettingen County, and in Alexandria, Fairfax County, 1779. [NA.AO13.102.58] [NAS.GD1.572.33.1-31]

DUNLOP, JAMES, born 1754, a merchant from Lanarkshire who settled as a storekeeper in Va. and N.C.. before 1776, then in Georgetown, Md.. [GA.Dunlop pp/LC1.1][NAS.CS16.1.168; RD3.282.551]

DUNLOP, JAMES, trading between Ayr and Philadelphia, 1760. [NAS.E504.4.3]

DUNLOP, JAMES, a merchant in Glasgow trading with Va., 1746, 1765. [NAS.E504.28.2; AC7.51]

DUNLOP, JAMES, a merchant from Glasgow, in North America, 1769, [NAS.NRAS.0631.4; CS16.1.134/141]; in Va., 1771, [NAS.NRAS.0623.T-MJ, 327-5]; in Canada 1773, [NAS.GD1.151.1]; in Montreal 1784, [NAS.NRAS.0620.wc, bundle 4]; in Port Royal, Va., 1785. [NAS.GD1.850.43]

DUNLOP, JAMES, born 1757, a merchant from Glasgow who emigrated to America in 1773, settled on the James River, Va., moved to Quebec in 1779, died in Montreal during 1815. [DCB.4.284][NAS.SH.9.5.1799]

DUNLOP, JOHN, a merchant from Garnkirk who emigrated via Gravesend to N.Y. in 1683, a merchant in N.Y. who died in Curacao 1683, probate PCC 1684, probate Jamaica 1684. [Dunlop of Garnkirk ms, Mitchell Library, Glasgow][NGSQ.71.3.171]

DUNLOP, JOHN, a merchant from Glasgow who settled in Va., died before 1751. [NAS.RD4.177.480]

DUNLOP, JOHN, a merchant and planter possibly from Kilmarnock, settled at Aranlise Creek, Pasquotank County, N.C.., before 1776, later captain of a privateer and died at sea. [NA.AO12.36.321]

DUNLOP, JOHN, of Garnkirk, a merchant in Glasgow then in Va., 1776. [NAS.CS16.1.168]

DUNLOP, ROBERT, trading between Greenock and Va., 1742, 1744, 1745, with Boston, 1744; between Port Glasgow and Va., 1736, 1746, 1747, 1748, 1749. [NAS.E512/1455; E504.1/2; 28.2/3/4]

DUNLOP, ROBERT, trading between Ayr and Antigua and Montserrat, 1764. [NAS.E504.4.3]

DUNLOP, THOMAS, trading between Greenock and Va., 1742, 1743, 1744, 1745, between Greenock and Boston, 1744; between Port Glasgow and Va., 1747, 1748, 1749. [NAS.E504.1/2; 28/3/4]

DUNLOP, THOMAS, a merchant in Glasgow trading with Va., 1769. [NAS.CS16.1.134]

DUNLOP, WILLIAM, a merchant who emigrated via Port Glasgow to S.C. in 1684. [NAS.E72.19.9]

SCOTTISH TRANSATLANTIC MERCHANTS

DUNLOP, WILLIAM, born 1708, a merchant from Glasgow who settled in Dumfries, Prince William County, Va., died there in 1739. [WMQ.19.294]

DUNLOP, WILLIAM, trading between Port Glasgow and Va., 1744, 1747, 1748, 1749; between Greenock and Va., 1746; between Port Glasgow and Va., 1746; between Port Glasgow and Boston, 1748 [NAS.E504.28.1/2/3/4; 15.2]

DUNLOP, WILLIAM, a merchant in Va., 1752. [MAGU#47]

DUNLOP and MONTGOMERIE, merchants in Glasgow trading with Va., 1781. [NAS.CS16.1.185]

DUNLOP and RALSTON, merchants in Va., 1767. [NAS.CS16.1.130]

DUNLOP and WILSON, merchants in Glasgow trading with N.Y. and Grenada, 1781. [NAS.CS16.1.183]

DUNMORE, ROBERT, and Company, merchants in Glasgow trading with Jamaica, 1780. [NAS.AC7.57]

DUNMORE, ROBERT, merchant in Norfolk, Va., partner in Logan, Gilmour and Company before 1776, returned to Glasgow after 1783. [NA.AO13.3.243]

DUNMORE, BLACKBURN, and Company, (Robert Dunmore and Andrew Blackburn), merchants in Glasgow trading with Va., 1783. [NAS.CS17.1.2]

DUNN, JOHN, trading between Ayr and Newfoundland, 1773. [NAS.E504.4.6]

DUNSMURE, THOMAS, trading between Greenock and Va., 1745; between Port Glasgow and Va., 1745, 1746, 1748. [NAS.E504.15.2; 28.2/3]

DURIE, WILLIAM, a merchant in Barbados, 1655. [NAS.RD#6/15]

DURWARD, WILLIAM, a merchant in Aberdeen trading with St John's and Quebec, 1774. [AJ#1365]

DYCE, ALEXANDER, jr., merchant in Aberdeen, trading with Jamaica, 1763. [AJ#826]

EASDALE, JAMES, a merchant in St Kitts, 1765. [NAS.CS16.1.122]

EASON, ROBERT, a merchant in Stirling trading with Grenada, 1782. [NAS.AC7.58]

EATON, THOMAS, born 1746, a chapman from Edinburgh who emigrated via Greenock to Philadelphia in 1774. [NA.T47.12]

ECCLES, GILBERT, a merchant in Cross Creek, N.C.., 1783. [NAS.RD2.237.825]

ELLIOT, GEORGE, born 1747, emigrated to America around 1747, a timber merchant in Elderslie, Little Lower River, Cumberland County, N.C.., died 1807. [SFV][SAS]

ELPHINSTONE, JOHN, a merchant in Aberdeen trading with Antigua, 1748, with Va., 1749. [AJ#42/54/70] [NAS.E504.1.3]

ELRICK, ANDREW, a merchant in Jamaica, burgess of Aberdeen, 1751. [ABR]

ERSKINE, ARCHIBALD, a merchant in Boston by 1684. [SCS]

ESDAIL, JAMES, a merchant in Basseterre, St Kitts, 1778. [NAS.CS16.1.173/322]

EWING, DAVID, a merchant in Ayr, trading between Ayr and Va., 1770; between Ayr and Antigua, 1774, 1776. [NAS.E504.4.5/6]

EWING, PATRICK, trading between Greenock and Barbados, 1746; trading between Ayr and Barbados, 1747, 1756. [NAS.E504.15.2; 4.2]

EWING, ROBERT, trading between Ayr and Antigua, 1765, 1775. [NAS.E504.4.4/6]

FAIRBAIRN, JOHN, trading between Leith and S.C., 1775. [NAS.E504.22]

FAIRHOLM, GEORGE, trading between Port Glasgow and Virginia, 1747, 1748. [NAS.E504.28.3]

FAIRHOLM, THOMAS, a merchant from Edinburgh, in Tobago, 1776. [NAS.CS16.1.170/175]

FAIRHOLM, THOMAS, and ADAM FAIRHOLM, merchants in Edinburgh trading with Pa., 1744. [NAS.CS16.1.75]

FAIRIE, JOHN, trading between Port Glasgow and Jamaica, 1748. [NAS.E504.28.4]

FAIRLIE, JAMES, merchant in N.Y. and in Warwick, Va., pre 1776, partner in the Thistle Distillery in Norfolk, Va.; moved to Pensacola, West Fla., in 1781, then in Kingston, Jamaica, 1783-1796, returned to Kilmarnock. [NAS.NRAS.00396/337,TD248.2; NRAS. 0905/1; CS16.1.181; CS17.1.3/375]

FAIRLIE, RALPH, and Company, trading between Greenock and Va., 1743, 1744, 1745. [NAS.E504.15.1]

FALCONER, DAVID, a merchant from Edinburgh with lands in East N.J., 1683-1690. [NJSA.EJD.Liber A/106, 230; Liber B/324]

FALCONER, PETER, a merchant in Woodbridge, East N.J., 1688. [NJSA.EJD.Liber B174/420]

FALL, WILLIAM, and Brothers, merchants in Dunbar, trading with Va., 1727, 1729. [NAS.AC9.1016; AC10.152]

FALLS, CHARLES, and ROBERT FALLS, merchants in Dunbar, trading with Charleston, 1767. [NAS.CS16.1.133]

FALLS, JAMES, a merchant, arrived in Boston during 1768. [PAB]

FARQUHAR, DAVID, a merchant in Kingston, Jamaica, died there in 1758, testament Edinburgh 1763. [NAS.CC8.8.119]

FARQUHAR, JOHN, trading between Leith and S.C., 1765. [NAS.E504.22]

FARQUHAR, JOHN, a merchant and writer from Edinburgh who settled in Spanish Town, Jamaica, died there before 1767. testament Edinburgh 1767. [NAS.CC8.8.120]

FARQUHAR, ROBERT, a merchant from Aberdeen who settled in Charleston, S.C., by 1783, probate S.C. 1784.

FARQUHAR, THOMAS, a merchant from Edinburgh then in Va., 1782. [NAS.CS17.1.1/97]

FARQUHARSON, HARRY, a merchant from Aberdeenshire who died in Jamaica during 1755. [ACA:APB.3.183]

FERGUSON, ALEXANDER, a merchant, from Scotland to Boston in 1766. [SG#7.4.15][PAB]

FERGUSON, ARCHIBALD, from Ayr, a merchant in Marblehead, N.E., by 1684; 1692. [SCS][AyrBR]

FERGUSON, DAVID, a merchant trading from Ayr to the Caribee Islands in 1683, 1693. [NAS.E72.3.12] [EBR:29.11.1693]

FERGUSON, JAMES, trading between Ayr and Barbados, 1742, between Ayr and Va. 1746, 1752. [NAS.E504.4.1/2]

FERGUSON, ROBERT, merchant in Ayr, trading between Ayr and Antigua, 1770; between Ayr and the York River, Va., 1771, 1773. [NAS.E504.4.5/6]

FERGUSON, ROBERT, a merchant who settled in Jappahannock, on the Rappahannock River, Va., before 1755; in Ayr 1772. [NAS.RD4.198.558; CS16.1.148]

FERGUSON, ROBERT, a storekeeper from Dumfries-shire who settled in Md. before 1774. [NAS.CS16.1.161]

FERGUSON, ROBERT, born 1719, a slave-trader in Newport, Rhode Island, pre-1776, then in Perth. [NA.AO12.84.2]

FIDDES, ROBERT, a merchant, from Scotland to Boston in 1766. [SG#7.4.15]

FIFE, JAMES, born 1739, a merchant from Renfrewshire who emigrated via Greenock to Charleston, S.C., in 1774. [NA.T47.12]

FINDLAY, ROBERT, a merchant trading between Greenock and Md., 1743, Boston 1744, Va., 1745; trading between Ayr and Quebec, 1766; trading between Port Glasgow and Jamaica, 1745, 1748 [NAS.E504.15.1/2; E504.4.4; E504.28.2/3]

FINDLAY, ROBERT, and company, merchants in Glasgow trading with Pensacola, West Fla., 1777. [JCTP]

FINLAYSON, JAMES, a merchant on the James River, Va., 1770. [NAS.CS17.1.9/233]

FISHER, ADAM, from Inveraray, a merchant and mariner in N.Y. in 1755. [NAS.CS16.1.95/125/148; RD4.178.596]

FISHER, JOHN, emigrated to America in 1760, a merchant in Orangeburg, S.C., before 1775, later in Jamaica. [NA.AO12.50.1]

FISHER, JOHN, a merchant who settled in Va. before 1778. [NAS.CS16.1.173/178]

FISHER, THOMAS, emigrated to N.Y. in 1756, a merchant there pre 1776. [NA.AO12.24.298]

FLEMING, DAVID, a merchant from Edinburgh who settled in S.C. by 1773. [NAS.CS16.1.154/103]

FLEMING, GARDNER, a merchant who settled in Suffolk, Va., before 1764. [NAS.CS16.1.120; AC7.51]

FLEMING, JOHN, a merchant from Leith who settled in Barbados by 1689, probate Barbados 1695. [BA: RB6.11.111]

FLEMING, JOHN, a merchant, from Scotland to Boston in 1764. [PAB]

FLEMING, THOMAS, a merchant from Edinburgh bound for Barbados in 1659. [ECA.EBR.9.2.1659]

FLEMING, WILLIAM, a merchant in Cumnock trading with Va., 1774. [NAS.AC7.62]

FLETCHER, DANIEL, traded from Barbados to Scotland in 1659. [NAS.RD1.553.406]

FOGGO, DAVID, a merchant who settled in Antigua before 1749. [NAS.SH.20.1.1749]

FOGGO, HENRY, and Company, merchants in Glasgow, trading between Greenock and Va., 1743, 1744, 1745; between Port Glasgow and the Va. and Md., 1744, 1745. [NAS.AC9.1658; E504.15.1/2; 28.1/2]

FOGGO, JAMES, a merchant from Glasgow who settled in Clarendon, Jamaica, before 1771. [NAS.B10.15.7475]

FOGGO, WILLIAM, a merchant trading between Greenock and Va., 1744, 1745; between Port Glasgow and Va. and Md., 1744, 1749. [NAS.E504.15.1/2; 28.1/4]

FORBES, ALEXANDER, a merchant from Aberdeenshire who settled in Philadelphia by 1748. [NAS.CS16.1.80/85]

FORBES, ARTHUR, a merchant who emigrated via Aberdeen to East N.J. in 1683. [NAS.E72.1.10]

FORBES, GEORGE, a merchant from Aberdeen who settled at Good's Bridge, Va., probate Chesterfield, Va., 1754.

FORBES, GEORGE, a merchant from Aberdeen who settled in St Thomas, Jamaica, in 1753, died before 1766. [ACA: APB.2.5]

FORBES, GILBERT, a merchant in N.Y., probate 1769 N.Y.

FORBES, HUGH, a merchant in Philadelphia, 1764. [MBR]

FORBES, JOHN, a merchant formerly in Charleston, died in Savannah, 1775. [GaGaz#2/2]

FORBES, JOHN, born 1767, settled in St Augustine, East Fla., in 1784, a partner in the firm of Panton, Leslie and Company, Indian traders, probate Mobile 1820.

FORBES, THOMAS, an Indian trader and partner in firm of Panton, Forbes and Company of St Augustine, 1775, moved to Nassau, the Bahamas, by 1783, died there in 1808. [GM.78.364][IT#21]

FORBES, WILLIAM, a merchant from Aberdeenshire who settled in Jamaica and died there before 1783. [NAS.SH.19.7.1783]

FORDYCE, GEORGE, a merchant in Aberdeen trading with Va., 1711. [NAS.AC7.17.352]

FORRESTER, JOHN, a merchant trading with N.Y., 1669. [RPCS.3/3.46]

FORSYTH, WILLIAM, a merchant in Va. by 1778. [NAS.CS16.1.173]

FOTHERINGHAM, JAMES, a merchant in Dundee, trading between Dundee and S.C., 177.. [NAS.E504.11

FOULIS, JAMES, a Scots merchant in London, trading with America, 1670s/1690s. [SPAWI.1699.763] [NA.HCA.13.vol.82]

FOULIS, WILLIAM, a merchant in Edinburgh trading with Va., 1668. [NAS.GD217.586]

FOWLER, JAMES, a merchant in Va. 1703, possibly from Inverness. [NAS.CS96.3309]

FRANCIS, THOMAS, trading between Port Glasgow and Va., 1747. [NAS.E504.28.2]

FRASER, ALEXANDER, a merchant in Charleston, 1740s. [SAS]

FRASER, ALEXANDER, a merchant who died in Jamaica 1773. [SM.36.166]

FRASER, DAVID, a merchant in Jamaica, 1771. [NAS.RS27.192.342]

FRASER, JAMES, a merchant from Aberdeenshire who settled in Va. before 1703. [NAS.CS96.3309]

FRASER, JAMES, in Augusta, Ga., 1749 as storekeeper for William Yeoman of Charleston, S.C.. [NA.CO5.668.305]

FRASER, JAMES, a merchant in Barbados, 1786. [NAS.RD2.248.627]

FRASER, JOHN, emigrated to S.C. around 1700, an Indian trader in Coosawhatchie, died in Charleston in 1754. [SCHM.5.56]

FRASER, JOHN, a merchant and shipmaster from Aberdeen who settled in St Kitts and died there before 1747. [ACA: APB.3.137]

FRASER, JOHN, trading between Ayr and Port Hampton, Va., 1763; between Ayr and Falmouth, N.E., 1770; between Ayr and Newfoundland, 1771; between Ayr and Antigua, 1774. [NAS.E504.4.3/5/6]

FRASER, JOHN, a merchant in N.Y., 1782. [NAS.RS38.34]

FRASER, SIMON, jr., a merchant from Inverness who emigrated via Glasgow to North America in 1761. [NAS.SC29.55.10.266]

FRASER, SIMON, a merchant in Va., 1784. [NAS.CS17.1.3/375]

FRASER, THOMAS, trading between Ayr and Antigua, 1773. [NAS.E504.4.6]

FRASER, WILLIAM, a Scots merchant in London trading with Va., Boston, and Antigua, 1699-1711. [NAS.CS96.524]

FRASER, WILLIAM, a merchant in Inverness trading with Va., 1729. [NAS.AC10.151]

FRASER, ..., an Indian trader, killed en route for Mobile, 1768. [GaGaz#3/1]

FREEBAIRN, DAVID, a merchant in Kingston, Jamaica, 1767. [NAS.AC7.52]

FREEMAN, JAMES, born 1741, a merchant and planter from Aberdeen who emigrated via London to Md. in 1729. [NAS.NRAS.0809][CLRO/AIA]

FRENCH, ROBERT, a merchant from Annandale in Boston by 1685. [SCS]

FULLARTON, GEORGE, a merchant from Ayrshire who settled in Charleston, S.C., died there before 1709, probate PCC 1709, probate S.C. 1709; [Admin. Act Book #1691/91].

FULLARTON, ROBERT, a merchant trading from Ayr to the West Indies in 1681. [NAS.E72.3.6/7]

FULLERTON, ROBERT, trading from Montrose to East N.J., 1684. [NAS.E72.16.3]

FULTON, WILLIAM, a merchant who settled in Bristol, N.E., before 1687. [SCS][SPAWI.1699.501]

FYFFE, ALEXANDER, a storekeeper and Indian trader in Savannah, Ga., by 1761; died in Charleston, S.C., during 1766, probate Ga. 1766. [SCGaz#1406][GaGaz#1/1; 13/271]

FYFFE, PATRICK, a merchant trading from Edinburgh to Va. and Barbados in 1667/1669/1670. [RPCS.3.21/358/446][EBR]

GALBRAITH, PETER, a storekeeper in N.C.. before 1776, moved to Glasgow by 1778. [NAS.CS16.1.173/281]

GALBRAITH, THOMAS, a merchant from Glasgow or Ayrshire who emigrated to N.Y. before 1776, later in London. [NAS.B10.12.4; CS17.1.3/114; RD2.242/2.4; CS16.1.170]

GALE, ROGER, a merchant who settled on the Bay of Honduras before 1775. [NAS.RD4.228.1092; CS16.1.173/181/184; AC7.55/58]

GALLOWAY, DAVID, trading between Ayr and Va., 1750, 1754, 1755, 1756, 1759, 1761; between Ayr and Barbados 1755, 1756, 1757, 1758. [NAS.E504.4.2/3]

GALLOWAY, HUGH, a merchant, from Glasgow to Boston in 1769. [PAB]

GALT, JOHN, a merchant in Edinburgh trading with S.C., 1775. [NAS.CS16.1.165]

GAMMELL, JAMES, merchant in Greenock, trading with Md., 1744, with Va. and N.C.. before 1776, with St Kitts, pre 1781; with N.Y. in 1783. [NA.AO12.36.194][NAS.AC7.58; CS17.1.2; E504.15.1]

GAMMELL, WILLIAM, trading between Port Glasgow and Md., 1743, 1745; between Port Glasgow and Va., 1749. [NAS.E504.28.1/2/4]

GARDEN, ALEXANDER, a merchant in Boston, 1754. [NAS.AC7.46.101]

GARIOCH, ANDREW, a merchant in Aberdeen trading with Antigua, 1748. [AJ#42/54][NAS.E504.1.3]

GARVINE, EDWARD, a merchant in St Kitts, burgess of Ayr 1737. [Ayr Burgess Roll, 3.10.1737]

GATT, WILLIAM, a merchant who emigrated to America in 1775, died in Richmond, Va., during 1825. [DPCA#1189]

GAY, WILLIAM, a merchant who settled in Va. before 1772. [NAS.SH.8.10.1772]

GED, WILLIAM, a merchant from Edinburgh who died in St James, Jamaica, before 1767. [SM.29.389]

GEILLS, ANDREW, a tobacco merchant in Glasgow who emigrated to Va. before 1744. [NAS.B10.15.5959]

GEILLS, ANDREW, trading between Greenock and Va., 1744, 1745, 1746; between Port Glasgow and Va., 1749. [NAS.E504.15.2; 28.4]

GELLATLY, JOHN, a merchant trading with Barbados and Newfoundland, 1698. [NAS.RH15.1013]

GEMMELL, DAVID, a merchant in N.Y., died 1763. [N.Y. Postboy: 15.9.1763; N.Y. Mercury: 29.8.1763]

GEMMILL, ROBERT, trading between Ayr and Charleston, 1769. [NAS.E504.4.5]

GIBB, ROBERT, a merchant trading between Glasgow and Va. in 1681; from Leith to N.Y. in 1681. [NAS.E72.19.3; 15.32]

GIBBONS, ..., a merchant in Charleston, S.C., 1724. [GBR]

GIBSON, JAMES, a merchant from Glasgow who settled on Pungataigue Creek, Accomack County, Va., before 1731. [NAS.CS.GMB.36/328; AC7.36.328]

GIBSON, JAMES, a merchant from Dumfries-shire who settled in Suffolk, Va., by 1769, dead by 1788. [NAS.RD4.204.2; RS23.XX.372; CS17.1.7/111]

SCOTTISH TRANSATLANTIC MERCHANTS

GIBSON, JOHN, a factor from Glasgow who settled in Colchester, Va., before 1770. [GA#779.21]

GIBSON, JOHN, a merchant in Glasgow trading with America before 1781. [NAS.CS16.1.184]

GIBSON, WALTER, a merchant in Ayr trading with Montserrat and the West Indies in 1673. [NAS.E72.3.4]

GIBSON, WALTER, a merchant in Glasgow trading with America, 1684. [RPCS.8.379/709][NAS.AC7.8]

GIBSON, DONALDSON, HAMILTON, & Co, Nansemond Co., Va. 1782. [NA.AO13.102.64]

GIELS, ANDREW, trading between Port Glasgow and Virginia, 1747. [NAS.E504.28.3]

GILCHRIST, ANDREW, a merchant from Glasgow who settled in Accomack County, Va., before 1733, testament Glasgow 17.. [NAS.CC9.7.62]

GILCHRIST, JAMES, a merchant in Barbados, probate Barbados 1677. [BA: RB6.13]

GILCHRIST, JOHN, a merchant from Premnay, Aberdeenshire, who settled in Norfolk, Va., died there in 1762. [NAS.GD180.629/2][ACA: APB.3.221]

GILCHRIST, JOHN, a merchant from Galloway who settled in Norfolk, Va., probate Norfolk 1773.

GILCHRIST, ROBERT, a merchant from Duns, Berwickshire, who settled in Barbados and died there in 1649. testament, Edinburgh 1653. [NAS.CC8.8.67]

GILCHRIST, ROBERT, a merchant in Glasgow then in Va. by 1750. [NAS.AC9.1746]

GILCHRIST, ROBERT, a merchant from Kilmarnock who settled in Md. before 1774. [NAS.RD3.246.375]

GILCHRIST, THOMAS, a merchant from Dumfries who settled in Suffolk, Va., and Halifax, N.C.., before 1783. [NAS.RD4.235.686]

GILCHRIST, WILLIAM, trading between Greenock and Boston, 1744; trading between Port Glasgow and Boston, 1748. [NAS.E504.15.2; 28.3]

GILLAN, JOHN, a merchant and planter in Dominica, 1776. [NAS.NRAS.0631/GDB3]

GILLESPIE, GEORGE, a merchant from Tynwald, Dumfries-shire, who settled in St Mary's, Md., and died there before 1724, probate PCC 1724.

GILLIES, ROBERT MCLAURIN, born 1750, a merchant from Glasgow who settled in Jamaica and died there in 1778. [MAGU#80][F.3.399]

GILLIES, ROBERT, a merchant, from Scotland to Boston in 1766. [SG#7.4.15][PAB]
GILLIES, ROBERT, a factor for James Gammell of Greenock in Wilmington and in Cross Creek, N.C.., before 1776. [NA.AO12.36.194]
GILLIES, WILLIAM, an assistant storekeeper who settled on the James River, Va., returned to Glasgow in 1777. [SFV#233]
GILLON, JOHN, merchant in Dominica, 1776. [NAS.NRAS.0631.76]
GILMOUR, GAVIN, and Son, merchants in Md. before 1778. [NAS.CS16.1.173]
GILMOUR, ROBERT, trading from Greenock and Port Glasgow with St Kitts, 1742; with Va., 1743, 1744, 1746; between Greenock and S.C., 1746. with Md., 1746; with Boston, 1746; with Jamaica, 1746; between Port Glasgow and Va., 1746, 1747, 1749. [NAS.E504.15.1/2; E504.28.1/2/3/4]
GILMOUR, ROBERT, a storekeeper in Lancaster, Va., before 1776. [NA.AO12.100.311]
GILMOUR, ROBERT, born 1748, a merchant from Kilmarnock who settled in Oxford, Md., 1767, moved to Baltimore, later in Va., probate Williamsburg, Va., 1782. [NAS.RD3.246.375; RS42.21.92; SH.6.10.1794; SH.25.3.1795; CS16.1.151/173]
GILMOUR, ROBERT, partner in the merchant houses of Logan Gilmour and Company in Norfolk, Va., and in Logan and Gilmore and Company pre 1776; in Glasgow 1782. [NAS.GD1.850.30][NA.AO12.74.335]
GIRDWOOD, ALEXANDER, a merchant in Glasgow trading with Va., 1771. [NAS.CS16.1.143]
GLASFORD, JOHN, and **ARCHIBALD HENDERSON,** Prince William Co., Va., pre 1776. [NA.AO13.102.63]
GLASS, HUGH, trading between Greenock and Va., 1744, 1745. [NAS.E504.15.2]
GLASSELL, JOHN, born 1734, a merchant from Dumfriesshire who emigrated via Glasgow to Va., settled in Fredericksburg, Spottsylvania County, in 1775, brother of Andrew Glassell. [NA.AO13.102.63]; in Longniddry, Scotland, 1779, died 1806. [NAS.RGS.119/271; RS27.247.237] [AGB.1.10]
GLASSFORD, JAMES, a merchant from Glasgow; trading with St Kitts, 1756; emigrated to Quebec in 1770, later

settled in Boston, and in Norfolk, Va., by 1776.
[GA.CFI][NAS.CS16.1.98/168]

GLASSFORD, JOHN, and Company, merchants of Glasgow trading between Port Glasgow and Va., 1749; trading with N.Y., Md. and Va., 1753-1764, [NAS.E504.28.4; NRAS.0396.192/244/281]; trading in Va. and Md. as Glassford, Gordon, Monteath and Company before 1776. [NA.AO12.9.35][NAS.CS16.1.168]

GLASSFORD, ROBERT, a merchant from Glasgow who emigrated to St Kitts and Grenada before 1764. [GA.T-MJ]

GLEN, WILLIAM, a merchant who emigrated via Ayr to America in 1766, settled in Newhaven, Connecticut, until 1776. [NA.AO12.92.5]

GLEN, WILLIAM, a merchant in Glasgow trading with North America, 1776, and Jamaica, 1779.
[NAS.CS16.1.170/175]

GLEN and PETER, merchants in Glasgow trading with Va., 1778. [NAS.CS16.1.174]

GLENCROSS, WILLIAM, a merchant in N.Y., probate N.Y. 1713.

GLOAG, JOHN, and Company, merchants in Edinburgh trading with Antigua, 1779. [NAS.CS16.1.175]

GLOVER, JAMES, a merchant, from Port Glasgow to Va. in 1682. [NAS.E72.19.8]

GORDON, ALEXANDER, a merchant who emigrated to Boston in 1754. [NAS.AC7.46/101; CS16.1.107]

GORDON, ALEXANDER, a merchant in Madeira, 1765. [NAS.RS35/21/566]

GORDON, CHARLES, born 1719, a merchant from Aberdeen, who settled in Jamaica. [SAA#203]

GORDON, CHARLES, a merchant who died in Jamaica during 1755. [SM.17.514]

GORDON, CHARLES, a merchant in Jamaica, dead by 1773. [NAS.GD67.105]

GORDON, FRANCIS, a merchant from Kirkcudbrightshire who settled in Yeocomico, Va., by 1759, and died there before 1770, testament Edinburgh 1770.
[NAS.CC8.8.121/2; CS16.1.103]

GORDON, GEORGE, a merchant, via Aberdeen to East N.J. in 1685. [NAS.E72.15.32][NJSA.EJD.Liber A, 247-269]

GORDON, GEORGE, a merchant and planter from Roxburghshire who died in Md. before 1748. [ACA: APB.3.139]

GORDON, GEORGE, a merchant who emigrated to Va. before 1747. [Rathven gravestone]

GORDON, JAMES, a merchant in St Kitts, 1767, died there in 1770. [NAS.RGS.109.165][Clatt gravestone]

GORDON, JAMES, settled in Georgetown, S.C., from 1763 to 1776, also in Augusta, Ga., later in the West Indies. [NA.AO12.5.38; AO12.3.104]

GORDON, JAMES, of Corestoun, a merchant from Stromness then in Savannah, Ga., by 1778. [NAS.CS16.1.171/173; CS16.2.282]

GORDON, JAMES, a merchant in Newfoundland then in Aberdeen, 1779. [NAS.CS16.1.177]

GORDON, JAMES, a merchant from Aberdeen then in Jamaica, 1782. [NAS.CS17.1.1]

GORDON, JOHN, settled in Beaufort, S.C., in the 1740s, a merchant in East Fla., 1764, a partner in firm of McQueen, Gordon and Company, in Charleston, S.C., 1760, partner of Gray Elliot in Beaufort and in Sunbury, Ga., 1762 to 1767, then partner of Gordon and Netherclift in Charleston and Savannah, died in Bordeaux, France, 1778, probate PCC 1778. [NAS.NRAS.771, bundles 403/489; GD172.2548] [NA.T1.522.44/5; AO12.100.11][AJ#1578]

GORDON, JOHN, a merchant from Aberdeen who settled in Va. before 1766. [NAS.CS16.1.125]

GORDON, JOHN, a merchant who emigrated before 1771, settled in Va. and N.C. [NAS.B10.15.8270]

GORDON, RICHARD, a merchant in N.Y., 1782. [NAS.CS17.1.1]

GORDON, ROBERT, a merchant in New Providence, the Bahamas, probate the Bahamas 1723

GORDON, SAMUEL, a merchant in Charleston, S.C., before 1776. [NA.AO12.100.58]

GORDON, THOMAS, a merchant in St Michael's, Barbados, 1714. [BA: RB6.37.406]

GORDON, THOMAS, factor in Lunenberg County, Va., for William Cunningham and Company during the 1770s [NA.AO13.102.55]

GORDON, THOMAS, a merchant from Aberdeen trading in Md. from 1763 to 1778. [NA.AO13.40.61]

GORDON, THOMAS, a factor who settled in Halifax County, Va., before 1770. [SFV#34]

GORDON, WILLIAM, a merchant in Glasgow trading with Barbados and Antigua, 1734; trading between Port Glasgow and Va., 1744, 1747, 1748; with Md., 1744, 1745; trading between Greenock and Md., 1745; between Port Glasgow and Va., 1744, 1746, 1748, 1749; between Port Glasgow and Jamaica, 1745, 1748; between Port Glasgow and Antigua, 1745, 1747; between Port Glasgow and St Kitts, 1746, 1747, 1748; between Port Glasgow and Boston, 1748. [NAS.AC40.166; E504.28.1/2/3/4; 15.2]

GORDON, WILLIAM, born 1750, a merchant from Aberdeen who emigrated via Greenock to Ga. in 1775. [NA.T47.12]

GOURLAY, JOHN, a merchant in Dundee then in Carolina, 1740. [NAS.CS16.1.69]

GOURLAY, WILLIAM, a merchant in Boston, 1769. [NAS.CS16.1.134]

GOVAN, ARCHIBALD, trading between Port Glasgow and Va., 1735, [NAS.E512/1455]

GOVAN, ARCHIBALD, settled in Va. as a factor in 1758, in partnership with two trading companies in Glasgow; also of Aylett's Warehouse, Hanover Town, King William County; agent for Murdoch Donald and Company of Glasgow in 1774, returned to Glasgow. [NA.AO13.30.378]

GOVAN, DONALD, a merchant from Glasgow in Boston, 1684. [SCS]

GOVAN, JAMES, trading between Greenock and Va., 1744. [NAS.E504.15.2]

GRAHAM, ANDREW, a factor who settled at New Severn, Hudson Bay, before 1770. [NAS.RD2.216.766]

GRAHAM, DAVID, trading between Leith and S.C., 1755. [NAS.E504.22]

GRAHAM, DUNCAN, a merchant from Perthshire who settled in Ledard, Caroline County, Va., before 1764. [NAS.RD2.197.470]

GRAHAM, JAMES, a merchant in N.Y. trading with Barbados, 1679, probate N.Y. 1700. [CMA#498]

GRAHAM, JAMES, a merchant in Edinburgh trading with NE & N.Y., 1682, 1683. [RPCS.6.534; 8.193]

GRAHAM, JAMES, a merchant and Indian trader who settled in Savannah, Ga., by 1760.
[NA.CO5.648.E46][SM.29.557]

GRAHAM, JOHN, born 1711, a merchant from Perthshire who emigrated to America before 1742 and settled in Md., Stafford County, Va., and Prince William County, Va., died 1787. [VG#162][NER.21.189]

GRAHAM, JOHN, trading between Leith and S.C., 1745; between Port Glasgow and Va., 1749. [NAS.E504.28.4]

GRAHAM, JOHN, a merchant from Dunbar who settled in Savannah, Ga., before 1754. [NAS.GD105; GD110.999.2/1046]

GRAHAM, JOHN, Lunenburg County, Va., agent for Glasgow merchants, later in Kilsyth, Scotland, by 1783. [NA.AO13.96.347]

GRAHAM, RICHARD, a merchant in Glasgow trading with Guinea and Va., pre 1720. [NAS.AC9.718]

GRAHAM, RICHARD, a merchant from Dumfries who settled in Prince William County, Va., by 1757.
[VMHB.19.4]

GRAHAM, RICHARD, a merchant in N.Y., 1782.
[NAS.CS17.1.1]

GRAHAM, WILLIAM, a vintner in Quebec, probate 1780, PCC

GRANT, ALEXANDER, a merchant who settled in Portsmouth, Va., moved to Nova Scotia, by 1781.
[NA.AO13.25.190]

GRANT, ANDREW, a merchant from Edinburgh who settled in Ogychee, Ga., in 1734. [NA.CO5.670.108] [NAS.RD2.171.33][SAS]

GRANT, ANDREW, a merchant from Berwickshire who settled in Jamaica then in London, 1774.
[NAS.RS19.16.317]

GRANT, ANDREW, a merchant in Edinburgh then in Grenada, 1781. [NAS.CS16.1.183]

GRANT, CHARLES, a merchant planter in Grenada, 1778.
[NAS.CS16.1.174]

GRANT, DUNCAN, a merchant in Antigua, 1760. [EBR]

GRANT, Captain JAMES, a merchant in Boston, 1703.
[GBR]

GRANT, GEORGE, son of John Grant a Leith merchant, a merchant in Jamaica, burgess of Stirling 1768.
[NAS.GD29.2167]

GRANT, JAMES, a fur trader in Quebec from 1770s.
[DCB.IV.311]

GRANT, JOHN, a merchant and planter from Aberdeen who settled in Grenada, died there in 1768. [ACA:APB.4.31]

GRANT, LUDOVICK, settled in S.C. in 1716, an Indian trader. [Charleston Probate Court Book, 1754-1758, fo.301]

GRANT, ROBERT, trading between Leith and S.C., 1745. [NAS.E504.22]

GRANT, WILLIAM, of Glenbeg, a merchant-planter in Jamaica, 1778. [NAS.CS16.1.174]

GRAY, ANDREW, a merchant in Glasgow trading with Jamaica pre 1730. [NAS.AC7.35.354]

GRAY, ARCHIBALD, a merchant in Glasgow trading with Va., 1724-1725, 1734, Jamaica pre 1730. [NAS.AC9.1116; AC7.40.137; AC7.35.354]

GRAY, DAVID, a merchant, from Glasgow to Boston in 1768. [PAB]

GRAY, GEORGE, a merchant in Glasgow trading with Antigua, 1715. [NAS.AC7.22.440]

GRAY, GEORGE, a tobacco factor from Glasgow who settled in Portobacco, Md., and after 1784 in Dumfries, Va.. [GA:CFI]

GRAY, JAMES, a storekeeper in Albany, N.Y., from 1771 to 1776. [NAS.AO12.14.180]

GRAY, JOHN, a merchant in Glasgow trading with Guinea, Barbados, Nevis, and St Kitts, 1720; with Va., 1727, with S.C., 1728. [NAS.AC7.33.433-583; AC7.34.697; AC7.36.328]

GRAY, JOHN, a merchant from Glasgow who settled in Port Royal, Caroline County, Va., from 1748 to 1777, moved to Glasgow, died 1787. [NA.AO13.30.398/424] [SM.50.362][NAS.CC8.8.128]

GRAY, JOHN, trading between Port Glasgow and Va., 1745, 1747. [NAS.E504.28.2/3]

GRAY, JOHN, a merchant in Glasgow trading with Va., 1774, 1775. [NAS.AC7.55]

GRAY, JOHN, a merchant in Quebec, 1781. [NAS.CS16.1.183]

GRAY, THOMAS, a merchant from Glasgow who settled in Boston before 1766. [NAS.B10.15.7234]

GRAY, WILLIAM, trading between Port Glasgow and Va., 1744, 1749; between Greenock and Va., 1746. [NAS.E504.28.1/4; 15.2]

GRAYSON, BENJAMIN, a merchant who settled in Dumfries, Va., before 1750. [VG#303]

GREEN, ANDREW, trading between Ayr and Va., 1757. [NAS.E504.4.3]

GREENLEES, JOHN, trading between Leith and S.C., 1745. [NAS.E504.22]

GREENLEES, JOHN, a merchant in Va. before 1753, 1766. [NAS.GD90.2.236; AC7.51]; 1782. [NAS.CS17.1.1]

GREENLEES, JOHN, and THOMAS HARDIE, merchants in Norfolk, Va., 1766. [NAS.CS16.1.125; AC7.51]

GREENLEES, ROBERT, trading between Leith and S.C., 1745. [NAS.E504.22]

GREENSHIELDS and WARDROPE, merchant in Glasgow trading with Va. and the West Indies, 1766. [NAS.CS16.1.125]

GREGG, ROBERT, a storekeeper from Ochiltree who settled in Hampton, Va., before 1762. [Library of Congress, Neil Jamieson pp]

GREGORIE, JAMES, born 1740, a merchant in Charleston, S.C., died there 1807. [Old Scots gravestone]

GREGORY, JAMES, merchant in Urbanna, Va., from 1758-1776, moved to the West Indies, [NA.AO13.29.723]

GREGORY, WILLIAM, born 1742, a merchant from Kilmarnock who settled in Fredericksburg, Va., before 1765. [WMQ.13.222]

GRINDLAY, ALEXANDER, a merchant in Glasgow, landowner in Virginia, 1779. [NAS.GD103/2/442]

HADDOW, GAVIN, a merchant in Jamaica before 1763. [EMR:18.12.1763]

HAGGINS, JONATHAN, a merchant, trading from Port Glasgow to S.C. in 1684. [NAS.E72.19.9]

HAIG, JAMES, a merchant in Edinburgh trading with Jamaica, 1780. [NAS.CS16.1.179; CS17.1.2]

HAIG, WILLIAM, born in Berwickshire 1670, a merchant in Antigua. [Haigs of Bemersyde, p.443, Edinburgh, 1881]

HALDANE, JAMES, a merchant from Jedburgh who emigrated via Glasgow to N.E. in 1722. [NAS.JC.12.3]

HAMILTON, ALEXANDER, a merchant from Bo'ness who emigrated to Darien in 1699, testament Edinburgh 1707. [NAS.GD406, bundle 163; CC8.8.83]

HAMILTON, ALEXANDER, a factor from Glasgow who settled in Piscataway, Md., and Va., before 1766, died in Portobacco, 1799. [GA: CFI] [MHS.ms#1301][GC1263][NAS.NRAS.0396.251]

HAMILTON, ARCHIBALD, a merchant in Glasgow trading with Va., 1742. [NAS.CS16.1.70]

HAMILTON, ARCHIBALD, of Overton, a merchant in Va. 1778. [NAS.CS16.1.173/162]

HAMILTON, ARCHIBALD, a merchant from Glasgow who settled in Suffolk, Nansemond County, N.C.., before 1776. [GA: CFI][NA.AO13.95] [NAS.CS16.1.170]

HAMILTON, ARCHIBALD, & Company, merchants in Va. and N.C.., Glasgow partners, sons of John Hamilton in Glasgow, (from 1760) John and Archibald H. (to America 1755) [Archibald died in 1777 leaving Jane his widow and 4 sons/4 daughters in Glasgow].

HAMILTON, ARCHIBALD or ARTHUR, a merchant, from Greenock to Boston in 1766. [SG#7.4.15][PAB]

HAMILTON, GAVIN, a merchant, trading between Glasgow and Va., 1681; from Port Glasgow to N.E. in 1684. [NAS.E72.19.3/9]

HAMILTON, GAVIN, a merchant from Glasgow who settled in Norfolk, Va., before 1750. [NAS.B10.15.6087; CS16.1.170/171]

HAMILTON, GEORGE, a storekeeper in Falmouth, Va., before 1776. [NA.AO12.100.311]

HAMILTON, GILBERT, a merchant in Glasgow, trading with N.C.before 1784. [NA.AO13.96.362]

HAMILTON, GUSTAVUS, in Boston 1690, [SCS]; factor in Pa., 1690s. [SPAWI.1696.213/558]

HAMILTON, HUGH, a merchant trading with the West Indies, 1689. [RPCS.14.584]

HAMILTON, HUGH, a merchant in Edinburgh trading with Jamaica, 1772. [NAS.CS16.1.151]

HAMILTON, HUGH, a merchant in Westmoreland County, Va., in partnership with Thomas Blane, John Ballantine, and Patrick Ballantine, before 1776. [NA.AO13.90.122]

HAMILTON, JAMES, a merchant trading from Edinburgh with Va. and Barbados in 1669. [RPCS.3/3.21/301/446][EBR]

HAMILTON, JAMES, a merchant in Boston, 1753. [NAS.CS16.1.89/92]

HAMILTON, JOHN, of Boighall, a trader in the West Indies by 1644. [APS.V.i/227]

HAMILTON, JOHN, a merchant from Ayr who settled in Barbados by 1723. [NAS.GD1.521.91]

HAMILTON, JOHN, a merchant in Kingston, Jamaica, 1735. [ABR]

HAMILTON, JOHN, a merchant from Glasgow who settled in Norfolk, Va., in N.C.., and in 96 District, S.C., before 1770, later in New Brunswick. [GA: T79.18] [NA.AO12.47.92]

HAMILTON, JOHN, a merchant in Va. by 1778. [NAS.CS16.1.170/173/162]

HAMILTON, PAUL, a merchant in S.C., 1724. [GBR]

HAMILTON, ROBERT, trading between Greenock and Va., 1745; between Port Glasgow and Va., 1748. [NAS.E504.15.2; 28.4]

HAMILTON, THOMAS, a merchant in Edinburgh trading with N.Y., 1682, 1683. [RPCS.6.534; RPCS.8.193]

HAMILTON, WILLIAM, a merchant in N.Y., 1676. [NY Hist. NS Dutch.xx/xxi.102]

HAMILTON, WILLIAM, a merchant in St Kitts, probate PCC 1698.

HAMILTON, WILLIAM, son of John Hamilton of Dowar, went to Va. and N.C.. as a storekeeper for Hamilton and Company in 1771, returned to Scotland by 1785. [NA.AO12.101]

HAMILTON, WILLIAM, a merchant, from Port Glasgow to S.C. in 1684. [NAS.E72.19.9]

HAMILTON, WILLIAM, trading between Greenock and Boston, 1744, with Va., 1746. [NAS.E504.15.2]

HAMILTON, WILLIAM, born 1748, a merchant who emigrated via Bristol to Grenada in 1774. [NA.T47.9/11]

HAMILTON, WILLIAM, born 1749, a merchant in N.C. before 1776. [NA.CO5.III]

HAMILTON, and Company, merchants in Va. and N.C.. before 1776. [NA.AO12.47.92]

HAMILTON, GOODISON, and Company, merchants in Glasgow and Va., 1778. [NAS.CS16.1.174]

HAMILTON, WALLACE, and Company, merchants in Greenock trading with N.C. before 1777. [NAS.AC7.56]

HANNAY, WILLIAM, a carpenter and merchant in Spanish Town, Jamaica, later in Wigtown, testament 1760 Wigtown. [NAS]

HANSHALLOT, GEORGE, a merchant, from Scotland to Boston in 1766. [SG#7.4.15][NWI#1/460]

HARDIE, ROBERT, a merchant from Aberdeen who settled in Elizabethtown, East N.J., in 1684. [NLS][Insh#263]

HARDY, THOMAS, a merchant in Norfolk, Va., 1766. [NAS.AC7.51]

HARRIS, WILLIAM, a merchant in Ayr trading with N.Y., 1767. [NAS.E504.4.4]

HARRISON, BENJAMIN, a merchant in James County, Va., trading with Scotland, 1698. [SPAWI.1698.655][NAS.AC.decreets.13.1076/1102]

HART, JOHN, a merchant in Salem, N.J., probate N.J. 1726.

HARVEY, WILLIAM, a merchant skipper in N.Y. from 1756 to 1775, then in Shelbourne, Nova Scotia. [NA.AO13.24.254]

HASTIE, ROBERT, a merchant from Glasgow and by 1781 in N.Y., testament, Edinburgh 1796. [NAS.CC8.8; CS16.1.183]

HASTIE, ROBERT, and Company, Charlotte County. Va., before 1776. [NA.AO13.102.66]

HAY, ALEXANDER, a merchant from Morayshire who settled in Montreal before 1783. [NAS.RD4.239.760]

HAY, FRANCIS, a storekeeper who settled in Dumfries, Va., in 1772. [SFV#60]

HAY, HENRY, a merchant in Edinburgh trading with the American Plantations, 1669. [RPCS.3.113]

HAY, JOHN, a merchant in Glasgow trading with S.C., 1728. [NAS.AC7.34.697]

HAY, JOHN, a merchant in Charleston, 1731, probate S.C. 1733. [SAS]

HAY, JOHN, a merchant from Kilsyth who settled in Va. before 1775. [NAS.RD2.220.10]

HAY, LEWIS, a merchant in Edinburgh trading with Charleston, 1764. [NAS.CS16.1.120]

HAY, PETER, a storekeeper who settled in Surrey and Southampton Counties, Va., before 1776. [NA.AO13.33.297]

HENDERSON, ALEXANDER, born 1737, a merchant from Blantyre, emigrated to Va. in 1756, settled in Colchester, Occoquan, and in Dumfries, Va., died there in 1815. [GA: T-MJ][MAGU#39] [NAS.NRAS.0396.244][Lake Montclair gravestone] [Alexandria Library, Va., letterbook]

HENDERSON, ALEXANDER, a merchant in St Kitts, 1770. [BBR]

HENDERSON, GEORGE, a merchant from Newton Stewart who settled in Kingston, Jamaica, before 1787. [NAS.RS60.177]

HENDERSON, HUGH, a trader, from Glasgow to Boston in 1768. [PAB]

HENDERSON, JAMES, trading between Greenock and Va., 1725. [EUL.Laing.490.65]

HENDERSON, JAMES, a merchant and surgeon who settled in Jamaica, died in Edinburgh during 1755, testament, Edinburgh 1756. [NAS.CC8.8.116]

HENDERSON, JAMES, a merchant, from Glasgow to Boston in 1766. [PAB][SG#7.4.15]

HENDERSON, RICHARD, a factor for John Glassford and Company of Glasgow in Bladenburg, Prince George County, Md., 1766, in Va. 1780, died 1802 in Georgetown. [NAS.GD237.21.51/15; CS16.1.179] [EA.4051/02]

HENDERSON, MCCAUL, and Company, merchants in Glasgow, trading in Va., founded in 1771 by Alexander McCaul, John Glassford, Archibald Henderson, George Kippen, John Kippen, John Shortridge, and Arthur Connell, in Glasgow, plus Neil Jamieson and James Lyle in Va.. [NA.AO12.109.166]

HENDRIE, GEORGE, a merchant, from Leith to East N.J. in 1685. [NAS.E72.15.32]

HENDRIE, JAMES, a merchant in St Kitts, 1782. [NAS.CS17.1.1]

HENDSHAW, JOHN, a merchant in Glasgow then in N.Y., 1755. [NAS.CS16.1.95]

HENRY, HECTOR, trading between Port Glasgow and Antigua, 1748, 1749; between Port Glasgow and Jamaica, 1748. [NAS.E504.28.3/4]

HENSHAW, WILLIAM, born 1643, a merchant in Glasgow who emigrated to the West Indies in 1678. [RPCS.5.474]

HEPBURN, CHARLES, a merchant from Glasgow who settled on Cape Fear, N.C., died there in 1741, testament, Edinburgh 1744. [NAS.CC8.8.107]

HEPBURN, JAMES, a merchant on the Cape Fear River, N.C.., before 1771, partner in Hepburn, Nelson and Company. [NA.AO12.103.21]; James Hepburn and

Joseph Montford merchants at Cape Fear and Halifax, N.C.., 1774. [NAS.CS16.1.161; AC7.55]

HEPBURN, THOMAS, merchant in Va. pre 1784. [NA.AO13.96.458]

HERDMAN, JAMES, trading between Ayr and Antigua, 1774; a merchant in Greenock trading with Antigua, 1782. [NAS.E504.4.6; AC9.3184/3182/184]

HERDMAN, BUCHANAN, and Company, merchants in Greenock trading with Tobago. 1783. [NAS.CS17.1.2]

HERRIES, MICHAEL, a merchant from Glasgow, land grants in Ga., 1750s. [NA.CO5.669][PC.Col.V.591]

HERRIES, COCHRANE, and Company, merchants in Glasgow trading with Va., 1767. [NAS.CS16.1.130]

HEUGH, ANDREW, a merchant and planter from Falkirk who settled in Leek Forest, Montgomery County, Md., and in Va., died 1771, testament, Edinburgh 1791. [NAS.CC8.8.128; RD2.252.1227; CS16.1.143]

HILL, RICHARD, trading between Greenock and Va., 1745. [NAS.E504.15.2]

HODGSON, JOHN, a merchant and bookseller from Glasgow who emigrated to N.E. in 1762, died in 1781. [NAS.SH.20.1.1772][Imm.NE#88]

HODGZART, WILLIAM, a merchant in N.Y., 1783. [NAS.CS17.1.2]

HOG, ROGER, of Newliston, a Scots merchant in London trading with Boston, S.C., and N.Y., 1754-1774. [NAS.CS96.1833/5]

HOGG, JAMES, born around 1730, emigrated to America in 1774, settled as a merchant in Cross Creek, Orange County, N.C.., died there 1805. [UNC; Hogg pp][SM.67]

HOGG, ROBERT, a merchant from East Lothian who settled in Wilmington, N.C.., during 1756, partner of firm of Hogg and Clayton merchants in Charleston, S.C., also in Wilmington, N.C., died in N.Y. 1779. [NA.AO13.120.334][James Hogg, pp, Southern Historical Collection, U.N.C.]

HOGGAN, JAMES, a tobacco factor from Glasgow who settled in Bladensburg, Va., before 1774. [GA: CF1]

HOME, ALEXANDER, a merchant in St Kitts, 1782. [NAS.CS17.1.1/97]

HOME, CHARLES, a merchant in N.Y., 1730s. [NAS.GD1.384.3]

HOME, GEORGE, born 1698, a surveyor and merchant from Berwickshire who emigrated to Va. in 1721, settled in Rappahannock, Culpepper County, Va., died 1760. [VMHB.20.397]

HOME, ROCHEAD, a merchant in Port Royal, Jamaica, 1715. [NAS.RD4.117.295]

HOOD, JOHN, a merchant from Glasgow then in Va. by 1752. [NAS.CS.GMB.50; CS16.1.88/117; AC7.50]

HOOK, JOHN, born 1745, a merchant from Glasgow who emigrated to America in 1758, settled in Blandford and New London, Bedford County, Va., died 1808. [NAS.CS16.1.117/161][VSA.John Hook pp] [VMHB.34.149]

HOPE, JOHN, a merchant from Glasgow who settled in Osburne and in Halifax, Va., before 1776. [GA: T79.25]

HOPKIRK, JAMES, partner of Speirs, French and Company of Glasgow trading to Md. before 1776. [NA.A012.9.49]

HOPKIRK, THOMAS, trading between Port Glasgow and Virginia, 1749; a merchant in Glasgow trading with Boston, 1755. [NAS.E504.28.4; CS16.1.95]

HORN, JAMES, trading between Port Glasgow and St Kitts, 1748. [E504.28/4]

HORSBURGH, ALEXANDER, a merchant from Glasgow who settled in Brunswick and in Petersburg, Va., before 1776, returned to Glasgow in 1777. [GA: T79.1] [SFV.23]

HOUSTOUN, ALEXANDER, trading between Greenock and St Kitts, 1743, 1746, with Jamaica, 1744; trading between Port Glasgow and St Kitts, also Montserrat, 1744, 1745, 1746, 1747; with Jamaica, 1743; between Port Glasgow and Va., 1745; trading between Ayr and N.Y., 1760. [NAS.E504.1/2; E504.28.1/2/3; E504.4.3]

HOUSTOUN, ALEXANDER, a merchant in Glasgow trading with Va., 1769; trading between Port Glasgow and Jamaica, 1744, 1748; trading between Port Glasgow and St Kitts, 1744, 1745, 1747, 1748; between Port Glasgow and Jamaica, 1745. [NAS.CS16.1.134; E504.28.2/3]

HOUSTOUN, ALEXANDER, merchant who settled in Norfolk, Va., before 1776, moved to Nova Scotia. [NA.AO13.24.274]

HOUSTOUN, ALEXANDER, and Company, merchants in Glasgow trading with Grenada, 1777, Va., 1779, Jamaica, 1782. [NAS.CS16.1.171; CS17.1.1;

NRAS.0623/19]; trading with the West Indies 1729-
1781. [NLS.ms8793-800]
HOUSTON, ALEXANDER, late a merchant in Grenada,
1784. [NAS.RS60.66; SH.26.4.1784]
HOUSTOUN, JAMES, a merchant from Glasgow who settled
in Ga. during 1733. [NA.CO5.670.125]
HOUSTOUN, WILLIAM, a merchant from Whithorn who
settled in Newcastle, Delaware, and died there in 1707,
probate Newcastle 1711.[DSA.Misc.1/178]
HUDDLESTON, HUGH, a merchant from Canongate who
settled in Jamaica before 1763, testament Edinburgh
1763. [NAS.CC8.8.119/2]
HULL, RICHARD, a merchant in Philadelphia and burgess of
Edinburgh, 1744. [EBR]
HUNTER, CHARLES, a merchant in St Kitts, 1766.
[GUL][GEU]
HUNTER, DAVID, a merchant from Ayr who settled in Va.
before 1769. [NAS.CS.GMB.53; AC7.53]
HUNTER, JAMES, a merchant from Duns who emigrated to
Va. before 1756, settled in Fredericksburg, King George
County, Va. [NAS.SH.29.7.1756; RS19.17.39;
GD1.384.21]
HUNTER, JAMES, merchant in Ayr, trading between Ayr
and Va., 1743, 1752, 1754, 1757, 1759, 1760, 1765,
1768, 1769, 1770, 1771; between Ayr and St Kitts, 1759;
between Ayr and Boston, 1769, 1770; between Ayr and
Antigua, 1774. [NAS.E504.4.1/3/4/5/6]
HUNTER, JAMES, and Company, trading between
Greenock and Barbados, 1744, with Va., 1744, 1746;
merchants in Ayr trading with Va., 1746, 1761, 1762,
1763, 1766; between Ayr and Falmouth, N.E., 1770.
[NAS.E504.15.1/2; E504.4.1/3/4/5; CS16.1.115]
HUNTER, JAMES, a merchant from Edinburgh who
emigrated to Va. in 1767, merchant at Smithyfield,
James River, and later in Southampton County, partner
of George Blair; 1778 [NAS.RS27.238.226;
RD2.256.112] [NA.AO13.30.616]
HUNTER, JOHN, a merchant trading from Ayr to the West
Indies in 1681/1683. [NAS.E72.3.6/12]
HUNTER, JOHN, trading between Ayr and Va., 1743, 1745,
1749, 1750, 1753, 1754, 1767 ; trading between
Greenock and Va., 1746. [NAS.E504.4.1/2; 15.2]

HUNTER, JOHN, sr., a merchant who settled in Norfolk and in Gosport, Va., died in N.Y. during 1778, probate PCC 1783. [NA.AO13.31.262]

HUNTER, JOHN, jr., a merchant who settled in Gosport, Va., by 1769. [NA.AO13.31.14]

HUNTER, PATRICK, trader in Va. before 1784. [NA.AO13.96.568]

HUNTER, ROBERT, trading between Port Glasgow and Va., 1748; between Port Glasgow and Jamaica, 1749. [NAS.E504.28.4]

HUNTER, WILLIAM, a merchant from Berwickshire, who settled in Fredericksburg, Va., by 1739, died 1754. [WMQ.2.19.118]

HUNTER, ..., a merchant in Antigua, 1779. [NAS.CS16.1.173/175/400]

HUTCHISON, GEORGE, a merchant in Edinburgh trading with Barbados and Jamaica, 1665. [RPCS.2.101/111]

HUTCHESON, GEORGE, a merchant from Glasgow in Boston 1675. [GA: Pollock ms]

HUTCHISON, GEORGE, merchant in Ayr, trading between Ayr and N.Y., 1761, 1762, 1767; between Ayr and Port Hampton, Va., 1763; between Ayr and Falmouth, N.E., 1769; between Ayr and Newfoundland, 1769; between Ayr and Antigua, 1774. [NAS.E504.4.3/5/6]

HUTTON, CHARLES, a merchant from Glasgow who settled in Md. before 1767, later in Nevis, 1779. [NLS.ms8794][NAS.CS16.1.130]

HUTTON, JOHN, trading between Leith and S.C., 1775. [NAS.E504.22]

HYNDMAN, JOHN, trading between Greenock and Va., 1742, 1744, between Greenock and St Kitts, 1744, 1746, 1747; between Greenock and Jamaica, 1744; between Port Glasgow and Antigua, 1744; between Port Glasgow and Jamaica, 1745. between Port Glasgow and Barbados, 1748; between Port Glasgow and Va., 1749 [NAS.E504.15.1/2; E504.28.1/2/3/4]

HYNDMAN, WILLIAM, trading from Greenock to Jamaica, 1744, between Port Glasgow and St Kitts, 1746; a merchant in St Kitts 1765, in Grenada, 1767. [NAS.E504.15.2; 28.2; RS81.7.414; RS81.8.373; SC36.63.13]

IMBRIE, JOHN, a merchant from Falkland, Fife, then in N.Y. 1778. [NAS.CS16.1.174]

INGLIS, ANDREW, a merchant in Savannah, 1770. [NAS.RD4.210.774]

INGLIS, GEORGE, a merchant in Charleston, died 1775. [NA.AO12.99.325]

INGLIS, GEORGE, a merchant in St Vincent, 1787. [NAS.NRAS.0477]

INGLIS, JAMES, jr., a merchant in Edinburgh trading with Grenada, Boston, Philadelphia, Wilmington, and Charleston, 1763-1780. [NAS.CS96.2004-2006, 2249, 2250, and 2258; CS238/J5.69]

INGLIS, JOHN, born 1708, a merchant in Nevis and then in Philadelphia, died there in 1753. [PA#210][PaGaz:23.8.1775]

INGLIS, JOHN, a merchant in Savannah, Ga., before 1776. [NA.AO13.36.11]

INGLIS, JOHN, a sutler and merchant in N.Y. around 1780. [NAS.GD1.46/20]

INGLIS, THOMAS, a merchant trading between Leith and the West Indies during 1611. [NAS.E71.29.6]

INGLIS, THOMAS, a merchant in Charleston, partner in Inglis, Lloyd and Company from 1765 to 1775, then in Kingston, Jamaica, 1784. [NA.AO12.52.249]

INGRAM, ARCHIBALD, a merchant in Glasgow, 1755, 1758, trading between Greenock and Antigua, Va., Barbados, 1743, Va., 1745, 1746; between Greenock and Boston, 1746; between Port Glasgow and Va., 1744. [NAS.E504.1/2; 28.1; CS16.1.100; AC7.47.32]

INGRAM, ARCHIBALD, a merchant from East Kilpatrick, settled in St Kitts before 1769. [GA: CFI]

INGRAM, JAMES, a merchant from East Kilpatrick who settled in Va. before 1769. [GA: CFI]

INGRAM, JOHN, trading between Port Glasgow and Jamaica, 1748; a merchant in Glasgow trading with Va., 1765. [NAS.E504.28.3; CS16.1.122]

IRVINE, ROBERT, a merchant from Dumfries-shire who settled in Antigua before 1729. [NAS.RS22.10.480]

IRVING, THOMAS, a merchant in Charleston, 1773. [SAS]

IRVING, WILLIAM, a merchant and farmer who settled in Va. before 1765. [GA: T-MJ]

IRWIN, WILLIAM, a merchant in Savannah, Ga., probate 1765 Ga..

JACK, JAMES, born 1757, a merchant from Aberdeen who emigrated via Greenock to Jamaica in 1775. [NA.T47.12]

JACK, THOMAS, a merchant in Nansemond County, Va., and N.C.. from 1756 to 1776, returned to Airdrie by 1784. [NA.AO13.30.362]

JACK, WILLIAM, born 1711, a merchant from Elgin who emigrated via Tilbury to Barbados in 1747. [P.2.300][MR#53]

JACKSON, PATRICK, a merchant from Dunbar settled in Va. by 1669. [NAS.RD4.25.629/630; RD4.27.855]

JAFFREY, JOHN, a merchant from Stirling who settled in Salem Town, N.J., probate N.J. 1704.

JAIRDEN, WILLIAM, a merchant from Dumfries in Boston by 1684. [SCS]

JAMIESON, JAMES, a merchant in Charleston, George Town, and Beaufort, S.C., before 1776, died in St Augustine during 1778. [NA.AO13.36.26]

JAMIESON, JAMES, a merchant and surgeon from Greenock, partner in the firm of John Cook and Company merchants in Tobago, died there before 1783, testament, Edinburgh 1783. [NAS.CC8.8.126]

JAMIESON, JOHN, a merchant trading between Port Glasgow and the West Indies in 1683. [NAS.E72.19.8]

JAMIESON, JOHN, a merchant in Glasgow, trading between Greenock and Va., 1742, 1744, 1745, 1746, 1752; between Port Glasgow and the Va. and Md., 1744, 1745, 1747; between Port Glasgow and Jamaica, 1748; between Ayr and Md., 1754. [NAS.E504.15.1/2; 28.1/2/3; 4.2 CS16.1.88]

JAMIESON, JOHN, a partner of the firm George Baillie and Company in Charleston, S.C., and in Savannah, Ga., before 1768, later in Haddington. [NA.AO12.109.178][NAS.CS16.1.146; RD3.279.116]

JAMIESON, JOHN, GEORGE BAILLIE, and ANDREW ROBERTSON, merchants in Charleston, S.C., before 1776. [NA.AO12.109.178]

JAMIESON, NEIL, 1728-1798, merchant from Glasgow who settled in Norfolk, Va., from 1760 to 177-. Partner and manager in Norfolk for Glassford, Gordon Monteith and Company of Glasgow; partner in Henderson, McCaul and Company; in John McDowell and Company of Glasgow; a merchant in N.Y., 1779, later in London.

[NAS.NRAS.0623.T-MJ427/157; B10.15.7174; CS16.1.168] [WMQ.2.22.532][NA.AO13.6.72].
JAMIESON, SAMUEL HEATH, a merchant in Accomack County, Va., before 1776, returned to Glasgow by 1778. [NA.AO13.31.136]
JAMIESON, WILLIAM, trading between Greenock and Va., 1745, 1746; trading between Port Glasgow and Va., 1747. [NAS.E504.15.2; 28.3]
JAMIESON, WILLIAM, a merchant in Jamaica, burgess of Ayr, 1751. [ABR]
JAMIESON, WILLIAM, a merchant from Edinburgh who settled in Va. before 1778. [NAS.CS16.1.173/178; CS17.1.2]
JAMIESON, SEMPLE, & LAWSON, merchants in Glasgow and Md., 1751-1779. [NAS.CS96.1176-1202]
JARVIS, THOMAS, a merchant in Antigua, 1741. [RGG#292]
JEFFREY, ALEXANDER, a merchant from Edinburgh who died in 1768, probate Accomack County, Va., 1769.
JEFFREY, GEORGE, emigrated to Boston in 1676, settled in Portsmouth, New Hampshire, by 1682, a merchant in Piscataque by 1685. [Anc.H.-NE] [SCS][SPAWI.1702]
JERDONE, FRANCIS, born 1720, a factor and merchant from Jedburgh who emigrated to Va. in 1746 and settled in Hampton, Yorktown, and Louisa County, Va., died 1771. [Louisa gravestone][WMQ.2.11.10] [ActsPCCol.1762/475]
JOHNSON, JAMES, trading between Port Glasgow and Va., 1749. [NAS.E504.28.4]
JOHNSON, JAMES, a merchant in Glasgow, land grants in Ga. 1751. [CRG]
JOHNSTON, ANDREW, a merchant from Glasgow who settled in Petersburg, Va., in 1750, died 1785, testament 1787, Edinburgh. [NAS.CS16.1.84; CC8.8.127] [NA.AO13.33.153]
JOHNSTON, ANDREW, a merchant, from Glasgow to Boston in 1769. [PAB]
JOHNSTON, ANDREW, partner in the Thistle Distillery, Norfolk, Va. before 1776. [NA.AO12.34.335]
JOHNSTON, ARCHIBALD, a merchant who settled in Barbados before 1694. [RPCS.25.98]
JOHNSTON, GEORGE, an Indian trader in Augusta, Ga., 1756. [NA.CO5.646/C17]

JOHNSTON, JAMES, a merchant from Glasgow trading in Montserrat, 1691. [NAS.RD2.104.958]

JOHNSTON, JAMES, trading between Port Glasgow and Md., 1745, 1747. [NAS.E504.28.2/3]

JOHNSTON, JAMES, a merchant from Glasgow who emigrated to Va. in 1760. [NAS.CS.GMB.50; AC7.50]

JOHNSTON, JAMES, and Company, merchants in Glasgow, trading with Va. in 1763. [NAS.CS16.1.115]

JOHNSTON, JAMES, a merchant from Orkney who settled in Quebec around 1761, partner of John Purss, died in Quebec 1800. [DCB.IV.399]

JOHNSTON, JOHN, a merchant in Charleston by 1736, probate S.C. 1739. [SAS]

JOHNSTON, JOHN, a merchant from Glasgow who settled in Norfolk, Va., before 1748. [NAS.CS16.1.80/154/161]

JOHNSTON, JOHN, a merchant possibly from Glasgow who settled in Mecklenburg County, Va., before 1776. [GA: 779.1]

JOHNSTON, LEWIS, a merchant from Edinburgh who emigrated to St Kitts before 1756, later in Ga., died there, probate PCC 1798. [NAS.SH.27.4.1756]

JOHNSTON, ROBERT, a merchant in Va., probate 1766 PCC

JOHNSTON, THOMAS, a merchant, trading from Port Glasgow with the Caribee Islands in 1683-1685. [NAS.E72.19.8/9]

JOHNSTON, THOMAS, a merchant in Glasgow trading with Va., 1768. [NAS.CS16.1.133]

JOHNSTON, TIMOTHY, a merchant in Barbados, probate Barbados 1714. [BA: RB37.346]

JOHNSTON, WILLIAM, a merchant in Edinburgh trading with Barbados in 1672, and the American Plantations, 1680. [NAS.E72.15.11][RPCS.6.537]

JOHNSTON, WILLIAM, a merchant in Barbados, probate Barbados 1712. [BA: RB6.7.71]

JOHNSTON, WILLIAM, a merchant from Annandale who settled in Orange County, N.C.., before 1780. [NCSA]

JOHNSTONE, ADAM, a chapman in Boston by 1684. [SCS]

JOSSIE, EDWARD, a merchant trading from Leith to N.Y., 1669. [RPCS.3.46]

JUNES, THOMAS, born 1762, a merchant in St Augustine, East Fla., 1786. [The Spanish Census of St Augustine, 1786]

KEIR, JAMES, a merchant from Stirling who emigrated to Darien in 1699. [RBS#91]
KELLY, JAMES, a merchant, from Scotland to Boston in 1767. [PAB]
KELSALL, ROBERT, a merchant in Ga., 1780. [NAS.RD4.259.758]
KEMP, JOHN, a merchant in Antigua, 1782. [NAS.CS17.1.1]
KENNEDY, ALEXANDER, a merchant in Ayr trading with Va., 1769. [NAS.AC7.53]
KENNEDY, DAVID, born 1733 a merchant and a militiaman of the Va. Regiment, 1756. [VMHB.1.2]
KENNEDY, HUGH, a merchant in Glasgow then in Va. by 1725. [NAS.AC9.925]
KENNON, ROBERT, a merchant from Dumfries who settled in Va. during 1769, died in Petersburg during 1807. [NAS.CS16.1.134][Raleigh Register: 23.7.1807]
KENSINGTON, JOHN, trading between Ayr and Port Hampton, Va., 1763. [NAS.E504.4.3]
KERR, EDWARD, a merchant from Irvine who settled in Va. before 1759. [NAS.CS16.1.103/138]
KERR, GEORGE, a merchant from Irvine who settled in Williamsburg, Va., before 1759. [NAS.CS16.1.103/117/133]
KERR, JAMES, a merchant in Antigua 1765; of Kerr and Burles, merchants in Antigua, 1772. [RGS.108.34; NAS.CS16.1.151/319]
KERR, JOHN, a merchant from Ayrshire who settled in Henrico County, Va., testament, Glasgow 1776. [NAS.CC9.7.70]
KERR, THOMAS, and Company, merchants in Paisley trading with North America, 1778. [NAS.CS16.1.174]
KERR, WILLIAM, a merchant trading between Greenock and Va., 1744. [NAS.E504.15.1]
KIER, WILLIAM, trading between Port Glasgow and Va., 1743. [NAS.E504.28.1]
KINCAID, GEORGE, a merchant in Charleston, S.C., from 1757 to 1774, moved to Jamaica. [NA.AO12.72.17][SAS]
KING, JAMES, trading between Greenock and Antigua, 1743, Greenock and Jamaica, 1743, and St Kitts, 1743, with Va., 1744; between Port Glasgow and Antigua, 1748. [NAS.E504.15.1; 28.3]

KING, JAMES, a merchant in N.Y. who died by 1789.
[NAS.CS17.1.8/24]

KING, JOHN, a merchant in Glasgow trading with Va., 1726.
[NAS.AC9.1056; AC7.34.433-451]

KING, JOHN, a merchant in Glasgow trading to Va., 1734.
[NAS.AC7.40.137]

KING, JOHN, son of John King a merchant in Paisley, a merchant in Kingston, Jamaica, 1779. [NAS.CS16.1.175]

KING, MARGARET, trading between Port Glasgow and Barbados, 1746; between Port Glasgow and Va., 1746.
[NAS.E504.28.3]

KING, MARY, trading between Greenock and Va., 1745.
[NAS.E504.15.2]

KING, ROBERT, trading between Port Glasgow and Jamaica, 1746; between Port Glasgow and St Kitts, 1747.
[NAS.E504.28.3]

KING, WILLIAM, a merchant in Port Glasgow, trading with Jamaica, 1770. [NAS.CS16.1.173]

KINLOCH, ALEXANDER, a merchant who settled at Red Bank, Berkeley County, S.C., by 1723.
[NAS.GD237.10.42/132]

KINLOCH, ALEXANDER, a merchant from Fochabers, Morayshire, to the American colonies in 1748. [OR#10]

KINLOCH, GEORGE, a merchant in Jamaica, 1768. [MBR]

KINLOCH, JAMES, a merchant from Edinburgh who settled in Charleston, S.C., before 1715.[SAS][GBR]
[NAS.GD345; RD2.104.490/1008; RD4.116.1084]

KIPPEN, GEORGE, trading between Greenock and Va., 1745; between Port Glasgow and Va., 1748; trading with N.Y., Md., Va., etc, 1753-1764, [NAS.E504.15.2; 28.4; NRAS.0396.192]; in Goochland Co, Va.

KIRKPATRICK, JAMES, a merchant who settled in Alexandria, Va., before 1779. [NAS.CS16.1.179]

KIRKPATRICK, THOMAS, a merchant in Alexandria, Va., 1779/1782. [NAS.CS16.1.175/177; CS17.1.1/10/411]

KIRKPATRICK, WILLIAM, a merchant in Dumfries trading with Prince Edward Island, 1780. [NAS.CS16.1.181]

KIRKPATRICK and CURRIE, merchants in Dumfries, trading with Nova Scotia and N.Y. in 1776.
[NAS.AC7.60]

KNOX, ALEXANDER, a merchant who settled in Va. before 1781. [NAS.CS16.1.183]

SCOTTISH TRANSATLANTIC MERCHANTS

KNOX, JOHN, trading between Port Glasgow and Jamaica, 1745; between Port Glasgow and Va., 1748; between Port Glasgow and Antigua, 1748. [NAS.E504.28.2/3/4]

KNOX, ROBERT, a merchant from Port Glasgow who settled in Va. and Md., died 1782, probate Fauquier County, Va., 1782, probate Charles County, Md., 1782. [NAS.GD17.1.1.23; CS16.1.183; CS17.1.1; RD5.398.456; SH.8.3.1819]

KNOX, WILLIAM, a merchant who settled in Va. before 1781. [NAS.CS16.1.183]

LAING, JAMES, a merchant in Montreal, 1783. [NAS.CS17.1.2]

LAING, JOHN, a merchant from Cromarty who settled in Md. before 1740. [NAS.AC7.45.666]

LAING, WILLIAM, a book-seller from Glasgow who settled in Boston by 1759, died there before 1765. [SCS] [NAS.CS16.1.122]

LAING, WILLIAM, a merchant in Glasgow trading with N.Y., 1764, and Antigua, 1778. [NAS.CS16.1.117/174]

LAIRD, JOHN, and Company, merchants in Greenock, trading with America, 1783. [NAS.CS17.1.2]

LAIRD, WILLIAM, trading between Port Glasgow and Va., 1749. [NAS.E504.28.4]

LAMB, THOMAS, born in Fife 1729, a merchant in Charleston, S.C., died 1786. [Old Scots Church gravestone, Charleston]

LANG, GABRIEL, trading between Port Glasgow and Jamaica, 1746, 1748, 1749; between Port Glasgow and St Kitts, 1747. [NAS.E504.28.3/4]

LANG, GILBERT, a merchant trading between Greenock and Barbados, 1743. [NAS.E504.15.1]

LANG, JOHN, a merchant in Glasgow then in Jamaica, dead by 1761. [NAS.SH.14.8.1761]

LANG, WILLIAM, trading between Port Glasgow and Jamaica, 1748. [NAS.E504.28.4]

LAUDER, GEORGE, of Pitscandly, formerly a merchant in Jamaica, dead by 1760. [NAS.B18.4.8.16]

LAUGHLAND, THOMAS, a merchant in Boston, 1751. [NAS.CS16.1.85]

LAW, GEORGE, a merchant who settled in Barbados before 1751. [NAS.RD2.170.187]

LAW, ROBERT, a merchant in Barbados, 1718. [St Michael's parish register]

LAWRIE, ANDREW, trading between Ayr and Va., 1758. [NAS.E504.4.3]

LAWRIE, GAVIN, a Scots merchant in London who emigrated to East N.J. in 1684, probate PCC 1696. [NAS.RD2.82.418]

LAWRIE, PETER, a merchant in Guadaloupe then in Swinslee, 1782. [NAS.CS17.1.1]

LAWSON, GAVIN, a storekeeper or merchant from Lanarkshire who settled in Culpepper, Va., before 1776, [NA.AO12.100.311][NAS.RS42.21.92]

LAWSON, HUGH, a merchant in Dumfries trading with Va., 1779/1782. [NAS.CS16.1.175; CS17.1.1]

LAWSON, JAMES, a merchant from Glasgow, trading with Md. in 1765, who settled in Charles County, Md., before 1769. [NAS.CS16.1.122; CS96.3186; GD103.2.442] [MSA.Chancery.46.161] [NA.AO13.33.367]

LAWSON, PETER, a merchant in Bo'ness trading with the West Indies pre 1778. [NAS.AC7.56]

LAWSON, ROBERT, a merchant in Va. before 1776, died in Glasgow 1787, testament, Glasgow 1788. [NAS.CC9.7.73]

LAWSON, WILLIAM, a merchant in Dumfries trading with Va., 1782. [NAS.CS17.1.1]

LEARMONTH, ALEXANDER, trading between Leith and S.C., 1745. [NAS.E504.22]

LEARMONTH, ALEXANDER, a merchant in Charleston, 1764. [SAS]

LEARMONTH, CHARLES, a merchant from Edinburgh who emigrated from the Clyde to Darien in 1699, testament, Edinburgh 1744. [NAS.CC8.8.109]

LEARMONTH, ROBERT, a merchant in Edinburgh trading with Va., 1666. [ETR#107]

LECKIE, JOHN, a merchant in Glasgow trading with the Americans Plantations, 1677. [RPCS.5.227/231]

LECKIE, WILLIAM, a merchant from Glasgow, to the West Indies in 1678. [RPCS.11.136]

LEGG, JOHN, a merchant from Aberdeenshire who settled in Savanna la Mar, Jamaica, and died before 1776, testament Edinburgh 1776. [NAS.CC8.8.123]

LEIPER, THOMAS, born 1745, a merchant from Lanarkshire who emigrated to Md. in 1763, later a merchant in Philadelphia residing in Delaware County, Pa., died in

Philadelphia during 1825. [AP#218][The Aurora: 8.7.1825]

LEITH, ALEXANDER, a merchant who died in Philadelphia before 1750, testament Edinburgh 1750. [NAS.CC8.8.113]

LENNOX, HUGH, a merchant in Dunblane trading with N.Y., 1782. [NAS.CS16.1.184]

LENNOX, JAMES, a merchant who settled in Charleston, S.C., in partnership with David Deas, before 1765. [NAS.RD3.224.627; CS16.1.165/170/117]

LENNOX, ROBERT, born 1759, a merchant from Kirkcudbright who emigrated to America in 1770, settled in N.Y. by 1783 and died there in 1839. [ANY#1.173][NAS.RGS.196/1]

LENNOX, WILLIAM, born 1752, a merchant in Charleston 1776, died 1781. [NAS.CS16.1.165/170][Old Scots Church gravestone, Charleston]

LESLIE, ALEXANDER, a factor in Barbados and St Kitts, 1649. [NAS.GD34.948]

LESLIE, ANDREW, a merchant who died in Barbados during 1765. [SM.27.391]

LESLIE, JOHN, a merchant in Aberdeen trading with Va., 1750, and with Kingston, Jamaica, 1754/1755. [NAS.E504.1.3][AJ#133/337]

LESLIE, JOHN, born 1749, emigrated to America, in Fla. by 1782, a partner of Panton, Leslie and Company, merchants in St Augustine, East Fla., by 1786, died 1803. [AUL.ms#2226/72/15][FHR#18][IT#19/47] [Spanish Census of St Augustine, 1786]

LESLIE, ROBERT, born 1758, emigrated to America, a partner of Panton, Leslie and Company, merchants in Fla.. [IT#19]

LEWIS, ADAM, a pedlar from Dumfries-shire who settled in S.C., probate S.C. 1745.

LEWIS, JOHN, a merchant, from Scotland to Boston in 1764. [PAB]

LEYBURN, PETER, a merchant in Hunger, Dorchester County, Md., from 1771 to 1776. [NA.AO12.8.193]

LIGHTBODY, JOHN, trading between Greenock and Va., 1745; between Port Glasgow and Va., 1745. [NAS.E504.15.2; 28.2]

LIKLY, JOHN, a storekeeper who settled in Fauquier County, Va., before 1771, returned to Glasgow in 1776; a

merchant and shipowner in Wilmington, N.C.., 1786.
[SFV#232][NAS.CE60.11.2/116/79/38/63/65]
LILBURN, WILLIAM, a factor who settled at St Inigo's, St Mary's County, Md., before 1775. [MdHistMag.44.247] [MdArch.11.41][MSA.Prov.Pet.1775]
LIND, GEORGE, a merchant trading between Greenock and Jamaica, 1743. [NAS.E504.15.1]
LINDSAY, ALEXANDER, born 1610, emigrated via Amsterdam to the New Netherlands in 1639, Dutch West India Company trader at Fort Nassau, then at Fort Orange, died 1685. [DP][NWI.I.119]
LINDSAY, ALEXANDER, a factor in Barbados and St Kitts, 1649. [NAS.GD34.948]
LINDSAY, GEORGE, a merchant, from Scotland to Boston in 1764. [PAB]
LINDSAY, JOHN, born 1694, a merchant from Crail, Fife, who emigrated to Philadelphia in 1729, later settled in N.Y., died in Albany during 1751. [NAS.GD203][SP.5.415]
LINDSAY, JOHN, born 1751, a mercer who emigrated via London to Jamaica in 1775. [NA.T47.9/11]
LINDSAY, WILLIAM, a merchant from Kirkcudbrightshire who settled in Charleston, S.C., probate S.C. 1786.
LINKLETTER, ALEXANDER, a trader in Boston before 1776, settled in Halifax, Nova Scotia, by 1783. [NA.AO13.91.35]
LITTLE, GEORGE, born 1756, a merchant from Dumfries who emigrated via Greenock to Jamaica in 1775. [NA.T47.12]
LITTLEJOHN, WILLIAM, born 1740, from Inverness who emigrated to America by 1760, settled as a shipping merchant in Edenton, Chowan County, N.C.., died 1817. [NAS.CS17.1.1/22][NCHGR.I.2]
LIVIE, ALEXANDER, a merchant in Charleston by 1740s, probate S.C. 1756. [SAS]
LIVINGSTON, ROBERT, born 1654, emigrated to America in 1674, a merchant in Albany later a civil servant in N.Y., died 1728. [CTP.36][EBR][CF#6.334] [NAS.GD1.478/880][NYD.3.401]
LOCH, DAVID, a merchant in Leith, trading with S.C., 1755; trading with Madeira and the West Indies, pre 1765; trading with Charleston, 1767. [NAS.E504.22; AC7.51/52]

LOCHHEAD, HENRY, born 1741, a merchant from Glasgow who emigrated to Va. before 1766, settled in Petersburg, then Alexandria, in the West Indies 1781, and by 1784 on the James River. [NAS.B10.12.4; B10.15.7488; CS16.1.125/183; CS17.1.3/354]

LOCKARD, HENRY, a merchant from Glasgow who settled in Alexandria, Va., before 1764. [NAS.CS16.1.117/125/171]

LOCKHART, GEORGE, a merchant trading between Port Glasgow and the West Indies in 1683; settled in N.Y. by 1684; trading from Glasgow to Va., 1690. [NAS.E72.19.8][RPCS.8.377/525/709/711; 15.384/444/590/607]

LOCKHART, JAMES, trading between Ayr and Va., 1763, 1766. [NAS.E504.4.3/4]

LOGAN, GEORGE, a merchant from Glasgow who settled at Kemp's Landing, Princess Anne County, Va., died in Glasgow during 1781, probate PCC 1781. Partner in Logan, Gilmour and Company, also in the Norfolk Distillery [NAS.RD3.211.295; NRAS.0934.488; SH.20.12.1799][NA.AO13.30.71]

LOGAN, HUGH, trading between Greenock and St Kitts, 1743. [NAS.E504.1]

LOGAN, MICHAEL, nephew of above George Logan, emigrated to Va. in 1774, a merchant in Petersburg, Va., in partnership with .... Gordon. [NA.AO13.31.169]

LOGAN, THOMAS, a merchant who settled in Westmoreland County, Va., before 1767. [NAS.CS16.1.130]

LOGAN, WILLIAM, merchant in Ayr, trading between Ayr and Antigua, 1768, 1769, 1770, 1773; between Ayr and N.Y., 1769. [NAS.E504.4.4/5/6]

LOGAN and DUNMORE, store at Cabin Point, Va., before 1776. [NA.AO12.74.335]

LOGIE, FRANCIS, a merchant in Aberdeen trading with Jamaica, 1781. [AJ#1773]

LOMAX, JOHN, a merchant from Glasgow who settled in Md. before 1754, probate PCC 1757.

LOUDON-MACADAM, JOHN, a merchant in N.Y., 1782. [NAS.CS17.1.1/286]

LOVE, ALLAN, a merchant who settled in Va. and N.C. before 1771. [NAS.B10.15.8270]

LOVE, HUGH, a merchant who settled in Va. and N.C. before 1771. [NAS.B10.15.8270]

LOVE, WILLIAM, a merchant who settled in Va. before 1778. [NAS.CS16.1.173][SFV#182]

LOVELL, EBENEZER, a merchant in Boston, 1752. [NAS.RD4.239.1061; RD4.178/1.566]

LOVELL, JOHN, a merchant in Boston, 1755. [NAS.CS16.1.95]

LOW, ALEXANDER, a merchant in Fraserburgh, to Antigua, 1752. [AJ#208]

LOWRY, ARCHIBALD, a factor in Barbados and St Kitts, 1649. [NAS.GD34.948]

LOWTHER, WILLIAM, a merchant in Bertie County, N.C.., before 1776. [NA.AO12.30.378]

LUKE, JOHN, trading between Greenock and Jamaica, 1743; trading between Port Glasgow and Md., 1744, 1745 [NAS.E504.15.1; 28.1/2]

LUKE, ROBERT, trading between Port Glasgow and Jamaica, 1749. [NAS.E504.28.4]

LUKE, WILLIAM, a merchant, trading from Port Glasgow to the West Indies in 1684. [NAS.E72.19.9]

LUMSDEN, DAVID, a merchant from Aberdeen who died in Kingston, Jamaica, before 1763. [NAS.SH.26.2.1763]

LUMSDEN, JOHN, a merchant from Aberdeen who settled in Kingston, Jamaica, and died in 1770. [ACA:APB.4.35]

LUNAN, ALEXANDER, a merchant in Philadelphia, died there in 1770. [AP#228][PaGaz: 2.8.1770]

LUNDIE, ARCHIBALD, born 1750, a merchant from Edinburgh who emigrated via Greenock to N.Y., a merchant in Savannah, Ga., in 1775, later in St Augustine, Fla., 1776, moved to the West Indies. [NA.T47.12; AO13.33.45] [NAS.NRAS.0159.C4; CS16.1.185]

LYLE, JAMES, trading between Port Glasgow and St Kitts, 1744. [NAS.E504.28.1]

LYLE, JAMES, in Va., 1780. [NAS.CS16.1.179]

LYLE, JOHN, a merchant in Montreal, 1781. [NAS.CS16.1.184]

LYLE, LUDOVICK, a merchant tailor in Port Glasgow trading with Va., 1758. [NAS.SC16.1.100]

LYLE & MITCHELL, merchants in Richmond, Va., 1784. [NAS.CS96.1750/1764]

LYMBURNER, ADAM, born 1746, a merchant from Kilmarnock, settled in Quebec, died in London 1836. [MAGU#82]

LYON, GEORGE, a merchant, from Port Glasgow to S.C. in 1684. [NAS.E72.19.9]

LYON, JOHN, a merchant in Glasgow trading with Charleston, 1731. [NAS.AC9.5455]

LYON, JOHN, trading between Greenock and Va., 1745; between Port Glasgow and Jamaica, 1745. [NAS.E504.15.2; 28.2]

MCADAM, JOHN LOUDOUN, a merchant in N.Y., 1781. [NAS.CS16.1.184; CS17.1.1]

MACALESTER, HECTOR, & Company, partners Hector MacAlester merchant in Norfolk, and Robert Donald merchant in Chesterfield County, Va., pre 1774. [NAS.CS16.1.173/174]

MACALLAN, WALTER, a merchant in Grenada, 1777. [NLS#8793]

MACALLISTER, HECTOR, a merchant who settled in Norfolk, Va., in 1760. [UNC.MacAllister pp#3774] [NAS.CS16.1.174][NA.AO13.31.205]

MACALLISTER, HENRY, a merchant who settled in Md. during 1750, died 1768. [MdMag.6.213]

MACALLISTER, WILLIAM, a merchant who settled in Va. before 1769. [NAS.CS16.1.107]

MCALLUM, DANIEL, a merchant in Va., 1784. [NAS.CS17.1.3/375]

MCALPIN, JAMES, born 1761, a merchant from Glasgow who emigrated to Va. before 1776, settled in Philadelphia, died 1847. [AP#236]

MCALPINE, WILLIAM, from Greenock, a bookseller and stationer in Boston from 1754-1776, then in Greenock, died 1788. [NA.AO12.82.1]

MCARTHUR, NEIL, a merchant in Cross Creek, N.C., before 1776. [NA.AO12.34.163]

MCAULAY, ALEXANDER, born 1754, a\merchant from Glasgow who emigrated in 1775 and settled in Yorktown, Va., died there in 1798. [WMQ: 2.22.235; 2.23.509; 11.80]

MCAULAY, GEORGE, born 1744, a merchant in Charleston, S.C., died there 1826. [Old Scots gravestone]

MCAUSLAN, ALEXANDER, a merchant and shipmaster who settled in New Bern, N.C., before 1776, moved to Halifax, Nova Scotia, by 1786. [NA.AO13.80.272]

MCAUSLAND, ROBERT, a merchant from Glasgow then in Newfoundland, 1783. [NAS.CS17.1.2/212]

MCBEAN, ANGUS, probably from Inverness, a merchant in Jamaica, 1778. [NAS.CS16.1.173]

MACBETH, ALEXANDER, a merchant in Elliot Street, Charleston, S.C., 1782. [NA.AO12.92.1b]

MCBRYDE, HUGH, a merchant from Irvine who settled in Dorchester County, Md., before 1775. [NAS.RD2.232.642]

MCBRYDE, WILLIAM, a merchant from Irvine who settled in Dorchester County, Md., before 1775. [NAS.RD2.232.642]

MCCAA, WILLIAM, a merchant who settled in Va. before 1771. [NAS.CS16.1.143/173]

MCCALL, ARCHIBALD, born 1734, merchant from Glasgow who emigrated to Va. in 1752 and settled on the Rappahannock River at Tappahannock, Essex County, died in 1814. [VMHB.73.313][NA.AO13.31.210]

MCCALL, GEORGE, born 1700, a merchant from Glasgow who settled in Philadelphia, died there in 1740. [AP#237]

MCCALL, GEORGE, a merchant in Glasgow trading with Va., 1775, 1781. [NAS.CS16.1.165; AC7.58]

MCCALL, JAMES, a merchant from Glasgow then in Va., testament, 1747 Edinburgh. [NAS.CC8.8]

MCCALL, JAMES, a storekeeper from Glasgow who settled in North Glasgow, Essex County, Va., before 1765. [GA: T79.41]

MCCALL, JOHN, trading between Greenock and Va., 1742, 1744, 1746; trading between Port Glasgow and Va., 1743, 1747; between Port Glasgow and Philadelphia, 1747. [NAS.E504.15.1/2; E504.28.1/3]

MCCALL, JOHN, a merchant in Charleston, 1771. [Charleston Miscellaneous Records, 1771, fo.544]

MCCALL, SAMUEL, trading between Greenock and Va., 1744, 1746; between Port Glasgow and Va., 1747 [NAS.E504.15.2; 28.3]

MCCALL, WILLIAM, trading between Greenock and Va., 1744, 1746; between Port Glasgow and Va., 1747. [NAS.E504.15.2; 28.3]

MCCALL, SMELLIE, and Company, in Glasgow, partners Archibald Smellie, George McCall and Henry Mitchell; trading with Va., property in Fredericksburg, Va. [NAS.NRAS.0623.20]

MCCALLUM, JAMES, a merchant in Granville County, N.C., before 1777. [NA.AO13.91.179]
MCCARTNEY, ROBERT, a factor and merchant in Charleston, S.C., 1727. [NAS]
MCCAUL, ALEXANDER, a merchant from Glasgow, partner in the Thistle Distillery, Norfolk. AM had been a partner from 1760 in the 1749-1771 Glasgow firm George Kippen and Co – other partners being John Glassford, Arch Ingram, George Kippen, John Shortbridge, and Arthur Connell. [NA.AO13.32.116]
MCCAULL, HENRY, a merchant in Glasgow trading with Va., 1728, with Barbados and Antigua, 1734. [NAS.AC7.34.708; AC40.166]
MCCAULL, JAMES, from Whithorn, a merchant from Glasgow who settled in Va. before 1746. [NAS.CS16.1.78]
MCCAULL, JOHN, a merchant in Glasgow trading between Greenock and Va., 1743, 1746. [NAS.E504.15.1/2; CS16.1.78]
MCCAULL, SAMUEL, and Company, merchants in Glasgow trading Guinea, Barbados, Nevis and St Kitts, 1720, and with Va., 1723. [NAS.AC7.33.433-583; AC9.818]
MCCAULL, SAMUEL, trading between Greenock and Va., 1743, 1746, N.E., 1744; trading between Port Glasgow and Va., 1743. [NAS.E504.15.1/2; E504.28.1]
MCCAULL, WILLIAM, a merchant trading between Greenock and Va., 1743. 1746. [NAS.E504.15.1/2]
MCCLEAN, JOHN, a merchant who settled in Norfolk, Va., before 1776. [NA.AO113.31.331]
MCCLELLAN, ROBERT, trading between Ayr and Falmouth, Maine, 1768. [NAS.E504.4.4]
MCCLELLAN, WILLIAM, a merchant from Edinburgh who emigrated to Va. in 1759, settled there until 1766, then a merchant in Tarborough, N.C.., until 1777, moved to London. [NA.AO12.35.118]
MCCLINTOCK, JAMES, a merchant from Glasgow, via Glasgow to S.C. in 1684. [RPCS.9.208]
MCCLURE, ALEXANDER, trading between Ayr and Newfoundland, 1773. [NAS.E504.4.6]
MCCLURE, DAVID, trading between Ayr and Newfoundland, 1765, 1769, 1770, 1771, 1772, 1773,

1774, 1775, 1776; between Ayr and Antigua, 1767. [NAS.E504.4.4/5/6]

MCCLURE, GILBERT, trading between Ayr and Falmouth, Massachusetts Bay, 1766, 1767, 1769; between Ayr and Va., 1768; between Ayr and Antigua, 1769, 1770; between Ayr and Falmouth, N.E., 1769, 1770, 1771, [NAS.E504.4.4/5]; from Ayr, a merchant in Falmouth, Maine, pre 1776. [NA.AO13.95.377-381] [NAS.CS16.1.165]

MCCLURE, THOMAS, merchant in Ayr, trading with Dominica, 1776. [NAS.E504.4.6]

MCCLURE, WILLIAM, born 1747, a merchant from Ayr who emigrated via Greenock to Philadelphia in 1774. [NA.T47.12]

MCCOLL, JOHN, a merchant in Glasgow to N.Y., 1781. [NAS.GD170.1276]

MCCOLL, JOHN, a merchant in Basseterre, St Kitts, 1783. [NAS.RD2.234.787]

MCCOLM, QUINTIN, a merchant from Maybole, Ayrshire, who emigrated to N.E. before 1745, died there in 1746, testament Edinburgh 1752. [NAS.CC8.8.114]

MCCOLME, or MALCOLM, JOHN, a merchant trading between Ayr and Montserrat and the West Indies, 1673. [NAS.E72.3.4]

MCCORMICK, WILLIAM, trading between Ayr and Antigua, 1764; between Ayr and Va., 1766. [NAS.E504.4.3/4]

MCCORMICK, WILLIAM, emigrated to America in 1761, a merchant in Windfield, Pasquotank County, N.C.., before 1776, moved to Edinburgh. [NAS.CS17.1.29/399; CS17.1.39/604] [NA.AO12.34.82][Liverpool Public Library.ms25/271.PA16-31]

MCCRACKEN, JAMES, born 1754, a merchant in Cross Creek, N.C.., died 1812. [Cross Creek gravestone]

MCCRACKEN, WILLIAM, a merchant in Newhaven, Connecticut, before 1776. [NA.AO13.80.278]

MCCRAE, GEORGE, trading between Ayr and Newfoundland, 1763, 1770. [NAS.E504.4.3]

MCCRAE, GILBERT, a merchant in Ayr then in N.Y., 1780, 1783. [NAS.CS16.1.179; CS17.1.2]

MCCREDIE, ANDREW, born 1757, a merchant and shipmaster in Savannah, Ga., died there 1807. [Savannah

Death Register][Colonial Museum and Savannah Advertiser, 24.4.1807][ANY#1/338]

MCCREDIE, DAVID, born 1754, a merchant from Galloway who settled in Charleston by 1774, died 1811. [Old Scots Church gravestone, Charleston]

MCCREE, GEORGE, trading between Ayr and St John's, Newfoundland, 1764, 1769, 1774, 1776; between Ayr and Antigua, 1767; a merchant from Ayr then in America, 1780. [NAS.E504.4.3/4/6; CS16.1.179]

MCCULLOCH, DAVID, born 1718, a merchant from Galloway who settled at Joppa, Baltimore County, Md., before 1756, died 1766, probate Anne Arundel County, Md., 1766. [NGSQ.65.262] [Md.Hist.Soc.: All Hallows Register#145]

MCCULLOCH, EBENEZER, and Company, merchants in Edinburgh, trading with Va. and Carolina, 1771. [NAS.CS16.1.143]

MCCULLOCH, JOHN, trading between Port Glasgow and Boston, 1748. [NAS.E504.28.3]

MCCULLOCH, JOHN, a merchant in Kirkcudbright trading with N.E., 1755. [NAS.CS16.1.95]

MCCULLOCH, THOMAS, a merchant in Gosport, Va., pre 1776 then in Glasgow 1779, died in Lanarkshire 1794, testament, Edinburgh 1795. [NAS.NRAS.0623.T-MJ363; CC8.8.175; CS16.1.175/179][NA.AO13.31.244] [GM.64.1150]

MCCULLOCH & TODD, trading between Leith and S.C., 1755. [NAS.E504.22]

MCCUNN, JAMES, trading between Port Glasgow and Jamaica, 1748. [NAS.E504.28.3]

MCCUNN, JOHN, trading between Port Glasgow and Va., 1744. [NAS.E504.28.2]

MCCUNN, WILLIAM, trading between Greenock and Boston, 1745; between Port Glasgow and Antigua, 1748; between Port Glasgow and St Kitts, 1749. [NAS.E504.15.2/4]

MCDONALD, ALEXANDER, born 1723, a merchant from Ross-shire, to the American colonies in 1747. [P.3.40][MR#82]

MCDONALD, COLIN, an assistant storekeeper from Glasgow who settled in Culpepper County, Va., before 1776. [SFV#229]

MCDONALD, DONALD, a merchant from Edinburgh who died at Cross Creek, N.C., in 1773. [SM.35.223][EA#972]

MCDONALD, JOHN, a merchant in Cross Creek, Cumberland County, N.C.., before 1775. [NA.AO13.91.200]

MCDONALD, JOHN, a merchant in St Vincent, 1780. [NLS.ms#8794

MCDONELL, ALLEN, a merchant in Carleton, N.Y., pre 1776. [NA.AO12.28.286]

MCDOUGAL, DUNCAN, a merchant in St Kitts, 1776 to 1778. [NLS.ms#8793/8794]

MCDOUGALL, Captain GEORGE, a merchant in Detroit, 1768. [ActsPCCol.1768/65]

MCDOUGALL, PETER, a merchant from Inveraray who settled in N.Y. by 1782. [NAS.CS17.1.6/51][ANY#1.175]

MCDOWALL, JOHN, a merchant from Glasgow who settled in Hanover County, Va., during 1750, principal factor and partner of the Glasgow firm Andrew Cochrane, James Donald and Company, later known as Murdoch, Donald and Company. John McDowall was partner in John McDowall and Company in Va. and McDowall Stirling and Company in Glasgow. By 1781 he was resident in Dunbartonshire. In 1784, he was a merchant in Glasgow trading in Bermuda. [NAS.RD4.243] [NA.AO13.31.275] [NAS.NRAS.0631.GDB.4]

MCDOWALL, JOHN, a merchant in St Vincent, 1780. [NLS#8794]

MCDOWALL, PATRICK, a merchant late in Va. 1755, settled in Onancocktown before 1758. [NAS.SH.22.2.1758][NAS.RS23.XVII.337]

MCDOWALL, WILLIAM, a merchant in St Kitts, 1715, 1727. [GBR][MBR]

MCDUFFIE, DUGALD, a merchant in Jamaica, 1765. [Argyll Sheriff Court Book#XVI.20.3.1765]

MCFARLAND, GEORGE, trading between Ayr and Va., 1759; trading between Ayr and Philadelphia, 1760. [NAS.E504.4.3]

MACFARLANE, ALEXANDER, a merchant in Kingston, Jamaica, 1747; burgess of Ayr, 1751. [NAS.AC9.1626] [ABR]

MCFARLANE, ALEXANDER, a factor from Glasgow who settled in Chaptico, Md., before 1761. [GA: CFI]

MCFARLANE, ANDREW, of Blairnairn, Dunbartonshire, a merchant in N.Y. before 1752; in Jamaica by 1780. [NAS.RS10.8.276; RS10.3.501; RD2.171.233/259; NRAS.0623.T-MJ365] [GA: 623.T-MJ386/2]

MCFARLANE, DANIEL, a merchant in St Croix, 1784. [NAS.Greenock Ship Register]

MCFARLANE, GEORGE, trading between Ayr and Boston, 1764; between Ayr and Falmouth, Maine, 1768. [NAS.E504.4.3/5]

MCFARLANE, JOHN, a merchant in Glasgow trading with America and the West Indies, 1717, with Va. and Barbados, 1728, 1729. [NAS.AC7.24.710; AC7.34.708; AC10.138; AC9.1070]

MCFARLANE, WALTER, born 1755, a merchant who emigrated via Greenock to N.C. in 1775. [NA.T47.12]

MCFARLANE, WALTER, a merchant in St Croix, 1776-1778. [NLS#8793-4]

MCFEE, THOMAS, trading between Greenock and Boston, 1743; between Port Glasgow and Va., 1744, 1748; between Greenock and Va., 1745. [NAS.E504.15.1/2; 28.1/3]

MCFIE, JAMES, merchant in Ayr, trading between Ayr and N.C., 1753; between Ayr and Va., 1757, 1770; between Ayr and Antigua, 1758, 1764, 1769; between Ayr and Boston, 1763; between Ayr and West Fla., 1769. [NAS.E504.4.2/3/5]

MCFIE, ROBERT, trading between Ayr and Quebec, 1766. [NAS.E504.4.4]

MCGEORGE, JOHN, a storekeeper in Surrey County and in Southampton County, Va., before 1777. [NA.AO13.33.297]

MCGILCHRIST, LAURENCE, trading between Port Glasgow and Jamaica, 1747, 1748. [NAS.E504.28.3/4]

MCGILL, JAMES, born 1744, emigrated from Glasgow to Canada before 1776, a fur trader, died in Montreal during 1813. [MAGU#55]

MACGILL, ROBERT, a merchant in Nevis, 1770-1780. [NLS#8793-4]

MCGILLIVRAY, ALEXANDER, from Inverness-shire, a merchant in Charleston by 1732. [NAS.CS16.1.70/72/95; RS38.X.88][SAS]

MCGILLIVRAY, JOHN, an Indian Trader in Ga. before 1776. [NA.AO12.109.202]

MCGILLIVRAY, LAUCHLAN, a merchant in Charleston by 1733. [SAS][NAS.CS16.1.95]

MCGLON, ANDREW, a grocer in Philadelphia before 1776. [NA.AO13.71A/155]

MCGOWAN, JOHN, a merchant in Boston by 1695. [SCS][NAS.RD3.92.2]

MCGOWAN, ROBERT, a merchant in Glasgow trading with Va. in 1727. [NAS.AC7.36.328]

MCGOWAN, WILLIAM, trading between Port Glasgow and Jamaica, 1749. [NAS.E504.28.4]

MCGOWAN, WILLIAM, jr., a merchant in Jamaica then in Glasgow, testament, 1770.[NAS]

MCGOWN, ALEXANDER, emigrated to Savannah, Ga., in 1766 as an employee of Cowper and Telfair merchants, from 1773 a partner in William and Edward Telfair and Company in Savannah, then by 1783 a merchant at Montego Bay, Jamaica. [NA.AO13.91.230]

MCHARG, EBENEZER, a merchant from Galloway who settled in Mecklenburg County, Va., before 1763. [NAS.CS16.1.115]

MCILVAIN, JOSEPH, trading between Ayr and Va., 1747. [NAS.E504.4.1]

MCILVAIN, WILLIAM, a merchant in Philadelphia, 1767. [NAS.CS16.1.130]

MCINNES, DANIEL, trading between Ayr and St John's, Newfoundland, 1775, 1776. [NAS.E504.4.6]

MCINTOSH, DUNCAN, a merchant from Edinburgh who settled in Jamaica and died before 1744, testament, Edinburgh 1744. [NAS.CC8.8.108]

MCINTOSH, JAMES, a merchant in Jamaica before 1780, then in Inverness. [NAS.CS16.1.179]

MCINTOSH, JOHN, an Indian trader in Mobile, West Fla., 1764. [NLS#ms119]

MCINTOSH, LACHLAN, born 1725, a merchant tailor from Inverness, from London to Barbados in 1747. [P.3.100]

MACINTOSH, LACHLAN, an Indian trader in Augusta, Ga., 1756. [NA.CO5.646, C17]

MCINTOSH, LACHLAN, a merchant in Charleston, S.C., before 1778 then in Kingston, Jamaica, probate PCC 1789. [NAS.NRAS.0631.GDB.3]

MCINTOSH, MYLES, from Inverness-shire, settled in Charleston, S.C., an Indian trader, died there in 1728, probate Charleston 1729. [NAS.SC29.55.6.215/257]

MCINTOSH, NICHOLAS, a merchant who died in Jamaica before 1770. [NAS.SH.3.1770]

MCIVER, ALEXANDER, born 1753, a merchant in Glasgow who emigrated via Greenock to N.Y. in 1774. [NA.T47.12]

MCIVER, COLIN, a merchant from the Isle of Lewis who settled in Alexandria, Va., probate Fairfax, Va., 1788. [NAS.RD2.254.922; SH.26.6.1789]

MCIVER, JOHN, a merchant from the Isle of Lewis who settled in Alexandria, Va., before 1788. [NAS.RD2.254.922; SH.26.6.1789]

MACKAY, AENEAS, a merchant from Inverness, emigrated before 1745, settled in Boston. [NAS.RD4.178/1.553; RD4.178/2.284; RD4.178.556] [NEHGS/SCS] [NLS.CH3816]

MACKAY, DONALD, a partner in the firm of Donald Mackay and Company, and in Mackay and Spalding, in Ga., before 1768. [GaGaz#247]

MACKAY, EBENEZER, a merchant from Glasgow who emigrated to America before 1763 and settled in Talbot County, Md., and in Va. [MdMag.2.375][NAS.CS16.1.115]

MACKAY, PATRICK, a merchant in Ga. by 1733. [SAS]

MCKAY, ROBERT, a merchant from Glasgow who settled in Va. before 1761. [NAS.B10.15.6729]

MCKAY, WILLIAM, and Company, merchants in Inverness trading with Va., 1729. [NAS.AC10.151]

MACKAY, WILLIAM FREDERICK, a merchant, from Orkney to Boston in 1764. [PAB]

MCKECHNIE, ALEXANDER, of Little Batturich, a merchant in Glasgow who settled in St Kitts and later St Croix before 1769. [NAS.RS10.10.187]

MCKECHNIE, JOHN, a merchant in Glasgow trading with Va., 1769. [NAS.CS16.1.107]

MCKELL, ROBERT, a merchant in Tobago, 1780. [NLS#8793]

MCKENNA, JOHN, a merchant in Edinburgh trading with Carolina, pre 1757. [NAS.AC7.49.1293]

MCKENZIE, ALEXANDER, a merchant who settled in Hampton, Va., before 1748. [NAS.CS16.1.80/99]

MCKENZIE, ALEXANDER, a merchant in Barbados, 1753. [NAS.CS16.1.89/48/92]

MCKENZIE, ANDREW, a merchant in Boston, 1755. [NAS.CS16.1.95]

MCKENZIE, ANDREW, emigrated via Leith to Charleston, S.C., in 1765 as clerk to John Simpson and Company, later a merchant in Charleston before 1776. [NA.AO12.102.189]

MCKENZIE, COLIN, of Strathcathro, a merchant in Jamaica before 1764. [NAS.NRAS.0771/762; RS35.XX.335]

MCKENZIE, COLIN, a merchant from Dingwall who died in Jamaica before 1783. [NAS.RD4.235.344]

MCKENZIE, GEORGE, a merchant from Edinburgh who settled in Elizabethtown, East N.J., in 1684. [Insh#237][N.Y. Deeds 3/614] [SPAWI.1689.352/360]

MCKENZIE, GEORGE, a merchant from Edinburgh who settled in Bridgetown, Barbados, before 1698, died there in 1711, probate Barbados 1711, testament Edinburgh 1733. [NAS.SH.25.10.1704; CC8.8.95]

MCKENZIE, JAMES, a merchant from Glasgow, died in Annapolis, Md., 1748. [MdGaz.178]

MCKENZIE, JOHN, a merchant in Charleston, 1732. [SAS]

MCKENZIE, JOHN, a merchant in Glasgow trading with Philadelphia and Va., 1771-1776. [NAS.CS96.3176]

MCKENZIE, NEIL, trading between Ayr and Va., 1770. [NAS.E504.4.5]

MCKENZIE, PATRICK, merchant in Ayr, trading between Ayr and Antigua, 1766; between Ayr and N.Y., 1767. [NAS.E504.4.4]

MCKENZIE, ROBERT, a merchant in Charleston, S.C., partner of John Tunno, before 1776, moved to Leith. [NA.AO12.51.273][NAS.CS16.17.1/61.123]

MCKENZIE, WILLIAM, a merchant who died in Charleston, S.C., before 1739. [SM.1.44]

MCKENZIE, WILLIAM, trading between Port Glasgow and Jamaica, 1748. [NAS.E504.28.4]

MACKIE, ALEXANDER, a merchant from Glasgow who settled in Va. before 1748. [NAS.B10.12.1, fo.178; B10.5959.6653]

MACKIE, ANDREW, a merchant from Glasgow emigrated to Va. before 1766. [NAS.B10.15.7019]

SCOTTISH TRANSATLANTIC MERCHANTS

MACKIE, RICHARD, a merchant and shipmaster who settled in Nansemond County, Va., before 1776, moved to Nova Scotia. [NA.AO13.31.306]

MCKINLAY, JAMES, born around 1751, a merchant in New Berne, N.C., 'for forty years', died 1819. [Cedar Grove gravestone, Craven County, NC]

MCKINNA, JOHN, a merchant in Edinburgh then in Jamaica, testament, 1766 Edinburgh. [NAS]

MCKINNON, DONALD, settled as a merchant in St Thomas parish, Quebec, from 1763 to 1775. [NA.AO12.109.704]

MCKINNON, JOHN, a merchant at the Bay of Honduras then in London, 1775. [NAS.AC7.55; CS16.1.173/181]

MCKISSOCK, JOHN, trading between Ayr and St Kitts, 1759. [NAS.E504.4.3]

MCKITTRICK, ANTHONY, a merchant who settled in Va. before 1763. [NAS.CS16.1.115]

MCKNIGHT, THOMAS, settled in Norfolk, Va., in 1757, a merchant in Currituck County, and Pasquotank County, N.C.., and in Norfolk, Va., before 1775, moved to Edinburgh. [NA.AO12.34.59][LPL.ns25/271/pa16-1/16/25a] [NLS#5027/216; 5030/215; 5038/209] [NAS.CS17.1.7/344]

MCLACHLAN, ARCHIBALD, trading between Port Glasgow and Va., 1749. [NAS.E504.28.4]

MCLACHLAN, HENRY, a merchant in Georgetown, Md., before 1776. [NA.AO13.31.304]

MCLACHLAN, HUGH, senior, a merchant from Leith then in Kingston, Jamaica, 1755. [NAS.AC7.47.598]

MCLACHLAN, HUGH, a merchant from Dunbartonshire who settled in Kingston, Jamaica, before 1756. [NAS.SH.10.9.1756]

MCLACHLAN, JAMES, a merchant in Md., 1749. [NAS.CS16.1.80]

MCLANE, ARCHIBALD, a factor in Va. 1763. [BM.Add#36218/199]

MCLAREN, DUNCAN, a merchant in Johnstown, N.Y., 1786. [NAS.RD2.241/2.776]

MCLATCHIE, CHARLES, agent for Spalding and Kelsall in the Suwanee River, East Fla., 1774; partner in the firm of Panton, Leslie and Company, Indian traders in Fla., died in St Mark's during 1787. [IT#48][Mowat#25]

MCLAUGHLAN, JAMES, a merchant who settled in Va. in 1753 and in Cecil County, Md., by 1750. [NAS.CS16.1.84/89/115]

MCLAURIN, EUAN, a merchant from Argyll who settled in western S.C. before 1776, died in Charleston in 1782. [NA.AO12.47.266]

MCLEAN, ALLEN, a merchant who died in Kingston, Jamaica, in 1783. [SM.46.111]

MCLEAN, ARCHIBALD, a merchant in Kingston, Jamaica, 1764, trading between Jamaica and Leith. [JHL.30.490]

MCLEAN, DANIEL, a merchant in Glasgow then in America, 1773. [NAS.CS16.1.154]

MCLEAN, DONALD, a merchant from Argyll who died in St Augustine, East Fla., in 1778, testament, Edinburgh 1786. [NAS.CC8.8.127; CS17.1.4/195]

MCLEAN, HUGH, a merchant in Jamaica, 1788. [NAS.CS17.1.7/133]

MCLEAN, JAMES, born 1759, a merchant from Ayr who emigrated via Greenock to Jamaica in 1775. [NA.T47.12]

MCLEAN, JOHN, trading between Port Glasgow and Boston, 1748. [NAS.E504.28.3]

MCLEAN, JOHN, burgess of Ayr, 1751, a merchant in Kingston, Jamaica, trading with Leith, died 1764. [SM.27.55][NAS.AC7.53][ABR][JHL.30.490]

MCLEAN, LAUCHLAN, a merchant in St Mary's County, Md., before 1776. [NA.AO13.91.215]

MCLEAN, MURDOCH, a merchant in Edinburgh then in America, 1776. [NAS.CS16.1.170]

MCLEAN and MOORE, merchants in Jamaica, 1778-1780. [NLS#8793/4]

MCLEAY, CHARLES, a merchant in Newton Stewart then in Jamaica before 1779. [NAS.CS16.1.174]

MCLEHOSE, JOHN, a merchant from Glasgow who died in Jamaica during 1782. [NAS.SH.23.12.1782]

MCLELLAN, JOHN, emigrated to America in 1768 as an apprentice storekeeper, a merchant in Hillsborough, N.C., before 1777, moved to England. [NA.AO12.101.38]

MCLEOD, JOHN, a merchant in Edinburgh trading with Carolina, 1737, and with Md., 1741. [NAS.GD170.3339; RH9.17.308]

MCLEOD, MURDOCH, settled in Montreal as a merchant in 1773. [NA.AO12.101.204]

MCLEOD, NEILL, born 1740, a merchant from Stornaway who emigrated from there to N.Y. in 1774. [NA.T47.12]

MCLEOD, NORMAN, a merchant in Boston from 1761 to 1765, died 1767. [NAS.NRAS.0623.T-MJ.377/C]

MCLIE, KENNETH, a merchant in Charleston, 1745. [NAS.CS16.1.78]

MCLINTOCK, ROBERT, a merchant in Halifax, Nova Scotia, 1780. [ActsPCCol.1780/360]

MCMASTER, JAMES, from Galloway, a merchant in Portsmouth, New Hampshire, and Boston, from 1765-1776, later in Nova Scotia. [NA.AO.12.12.23][PAB][SCS][NAS.CS16.1.173]

MCMASTER, JOHN, from Galloway, emigrated from Leith to Boston in 1765, a merchant in Portsmouth, New Hampshire, and Boston, from 1767-1776. [PAB] [NA.AO.12.12.23]

MCMASTER, PATRICK, from Galloway, emigrated via Glasgow to Boston in 1767; a merchant in Portsmouth, New Hampshire, and Boston, from 1767-1776, later in Nova Scotia. [NA.AO.12.12.23][SCS][PAB]

MCMASTER, ROBERT, born 1750, a merchant from Galloway who emigrated via Stranraer to N.Y. in 1774. [NA.T47.12]

MCMASTER AND INGLIS, merchants in N.Y., in Scotland by 1786. [NAS.CS17.1.5/362]

MCMICKEN, HUGH, a merchant who settled in Portsmouth, Va., before 1774. [NAS.CS16.1.143; CC8.8.123]

MCMILLAN, ALEXANDER, trading between Port Glasgow and Boston, 1748; trading between Port Glasgow and Jamaica, 1748. [NAS.E504.28.3/4]

MCMORRAN, EDWARD, born 1749, a merchant from Dumfries who emigrated from there to N.Y. in 1774. [NA.T47.12]

MCMULLIN, WILLIAM, a trader among the Chickasaw, 1735. [SPAWI.1735.157.XII]

MCMURCHY, JOHN, a merchant in Jamaica, noved to London 1766. [Charleston, SC, Misc. Records, 1766:370]

MCMURDO, GEORGE, from Dumfries-shire, a merchant in Va. 1751. [NAS.CS96/2/2161/20]

MCNAIR, EBENEZER, a merchant in Glasgow then in N.Y. or Long Island, 1781. [NAS.CS16.1.183]

MCNEIL, GILBERT, born 1753, a merchant from Kilmarnock who emigrated via Greenock to N.Y. in 1774. [NA.T47.12]

MCNEIL, HUGH, a merchant from Ayrshire who settled in Antigua and died in Ballantrae before 1762, testament Glasgow 1762. [NAS.CC9.7.64; SC6.60.17]

MCNEIL, JAMES, born 1734, emigrated to Va. in 1762, a merchant in Halifax County, N.C.., before 1776. [NA.AO12.91.32][NAS.CS16.1.173]

MCNEIL, JOHN, a merchant in Tobago, 1771. [NAS.RD2.224/2.646]

MCNEIL, NEIL, a merchant and planter from Knapdale who settled in Hanover, Jamaica, and died in Glasgow during 1749, testament Glasgow 1785. [NAS.CC9.60.73]

MCNEIL, NEIL, from Islay, a merchant in Bristol then in St Kitts, then in St Croix, 1758, 1763, 1764, 1765, 1768, 1774, testament, The Isles 1777. [NAS.CS237.74.1; CS27.907; CC12.2.2; CS16.1.115/120]

MCNEIL, and CLAXTON, merchants in Bristol trading with St Kitts and Glasgow, 1756, merchants in St Kitts, 1758. [NAS.CS16.1.98/100]

MCNEIL, SADDLER, and CLAXTON, merchants in St Kitts, 1756-1781. [NAS.CS237.T41; CS96.4370/30; CS16.1.98]

MCNICOLL, DONALD, a merchant and factor from Glasgow who emigrated to Pittsylvania, Va., before 1760. [GA.CFI]

MACQUEEN, JAMES, born 1716, a merchant in Kingston, Jamaica, died 1765. [Kingston gravestone]

MCQUEY, RICHARD, a merchant late in Va., then in Glasgow. [NAS.NRAS.0623.T-MJ.122]

MCQUHAY, ANTHONY, a merchant in Va., 1778. [NAS.CS16.1.173]

MCRAE, ALLAN, a merchant in Dumfries, Prince William County, Va., 1653. [FKC#134]

MCRAE, ANDREW, a merchant in Va., 1778. [NAS.CS16.1.173]

MCRAE, GEORGE, merchant in Norfolk, Va., before 1776. [NA.AO13.123.129]

MCRAE, WILLIAM, a merchant in Va., 1778. [NAS.CS16.1.173]

SCOTTISH TRANSATLANTIC MERCHANTS

MCTIER, WILLIAM, a merchant in Wilmington, N.C., before 1776, later in the West Indies then in Glasgow. [NA.AO12.37.149]

MCVICAR, DUNCAN, born 1741, a merchant from Glasgow who emigrated to America before 1758 and settled in Charleston, S.C., and in N.Y. [GA.T-MJ427.140]

MCWALTER, DUNCAN, a merchant in Jamaica before 1771. [Argyll Sheriff Court Book XVII.13.6.1771]

MCWHANN, WILLIAM, merchant in Blandford, Va., from 1763, in partnership with John Baird and others in John Baird and Company from 1770. [NA.AO12.109.210]

MAIN, JAMES, trading between Port Glasgow and Va., 1744. [NAS.E504.28.1]

MAITLAND, WILLIAM, merchant in Williamsburg, Va., 1771-1776.[NA.AO13.31.344]

MALCOLM, HUGH, a merchant in Jamaica, dead by 1773. [Argyll Sheriff Court Book, XVII.13.5.1774]

MALCOLM, NEIL, a merchant in Jamaica, 1774. [Argyll Sheriff Court Book XVII.13.5.1774]

MALLOCH, ROBERT, a merchant in Edinburgh trading with Charleston, 1684. [RPCS.8.525-527][EBR]

MAN, JOHN, a merchant in Dundee, trading with the West Indies, 1647. [DA.DSL]

MANSON, WILLIAM, from Orkney, a merchant in Augusta, Ga., 1780. [NAS.NRAS.0627/1015.15]

MAPAS, SINCLAIR, and WARD, merchants in Jamaica, 1783. [NAS.RD2.236/1.651]

MARJORYBANKS, ANDREW, a merchant trading between Leith and Virginia, 1673. [NAS.E72.15.14]

MARJORYBANKS, JOSEPH, a merchant from Edinburgh who emigrated via Leith to Darien in 1698, testament Edinburgh 1707. [NAS.CC8.8.83]

MARR, ANDREW, a merchant in Charleston, S.C., probate 1786 PCC

MARSHALL, JAMES, a merchant and inn-keeper from Aberdeen who settled in St Phillip's parish, Charleston, S.C., died around 1765, probate PCC 1767. [ACA: APB][SAS]

MARSHALL, JAMES, from Glasgow in 1747, a factor, died in Frederick County, Md., 1803. [AJ#2918]

MARSHALL, JOHN, a merchant in Louisa County, Va., 1772/1779. [NAS.CS16.1.151/175]

MARSHALL, PATRICK, a merchant from Dundee who settled in S.C., later in New Providence, probate the Bahamas 1760. [SAS]

MARSHALL, ROBERT, a merchant in Glasgow trading with Va., 1774. [NAS.CS16.1.161]

MARSHALL, SAMUEL, a merchant from Skye who settled in N.C. by 1755, later in Wilmington before 1776, moved to London. [NA.AO12.3.218]

MARSHALL, WILLIAM, a merchant from Glasgow then in Tobago, the West Indies, 1782/1783. [NAS.CS17.1.1/2]

MARTIN, JAMES, merchant in Glasgow then an assistant to Archibald Hamilton and Company in Va. from 1760. [NA.AO12.36.242]

MARTIN, JAMES, emigrated to Charleston, S.C., 1771, a baker and merchant in Savannah, Ga., before 1776, returned to Dundee. [NA.AO13.36.697/705]

MARTIN, JOHN, a merchant in Norfolk, Va., later in Kirkcudbright by 1785. [NAS.CS17.1.4/183]

MARTIN, THOMAS, a merchant in Antigua, 1739. [StABR]

MASON, ROBERT, trading between Port Glasgow and Jamaica, 1746.[NAS.E504.28.3]

MASTERTON, JOHN, a merchant in Edinburgh trading with Barbados and Va. in 1667. [RPCS.2.357]

MATHER, JOHN, a merchant in Kingston, Jamaica, 1779, and in Hamilton by 1780. [NAS.CS16.1.174-177]

MATHIE, GABRIEL, a merchant trading between Greenock and St Kitts, 1742, Md., and Jamaica, 1743, Md., 1744, 1745, S.C., 1745, Boston 1746; between Port Glasgow and Jamaica, 1744, 1745, 1749; between Port Glasgow and Antigua, 1748; between Port Glasgow and Va., 1749. [NAS.E504.15.1/2; E504.28.1/2/4]

MATTHEW, JOHN, trading between Greenock and Va., 1744, 1745; trading between Port Glasgow and Md., 1744; between Port Glasgow and Va., 1744. [NAS.E504.15.1/2; 28.1/2]

MAXWELL, ALEXANDER, trading between Greenock and Va., 1743. [NAS.E504.1]

MAXWELL, DANIEL, a merchant in Beaufort County, N.C., died in 1775. [NA.AO13.95.397]

MAXWELL, Sir GEORGE, of Newark, trading with the Caribbee Islands, 1670. [RPCS.3/3.173]

MAXWELL, JOHN, a merchant trading between Ayr and Montserrat and the West Indies in 1673. [NAS.E72.3.4]

MAXWELL, JOHN, a merchant from Glasgow in Boston, 1686. [RPCS.15.307][DP][SCS]

MAXWELL, JOHN, trading between Port Glasgow and Va., 1749. [NAS.E504.28.4]

MAXWELL, MATTHEW, a merchant in Va. and Md., 1759. [NAS.CS16.1.103]

MAYNE, CHARLES, trading between Leith and S.C., 1745. [NAS.E504.22]

MEIKLE, JOHN, trading between Ayr and Barbados, 1742. [NAS.E504.4.1]

MELVIN, DAVID, a merchant in Boston, 1692, 1717. [SCS][GBR]

MENZIES, NINIAN, a merchant in Richmond, Va., partner in James Todd and Ninian Menzies merchants in Glasgow, in partnership with John Hay, James Baird, Peter Hay and John McGeorge trading as John Hay and Company in Va. and N.C.; died in West Indies 1781. [NAS.CS16.1.165]

MENZIES, WILLIAM, a merchant in Edinburgh trading with the American Plantations, 1691. [RPCS.16.579]

MERCER, CHARLES, a merchant trading between Greenock and Va., 1743. [NAS.E504.15.1]

MERCER, ROBERT, a merchant who settled in N.Y. before 1770. [NAS.GD1.787.36; RD4.261.1068]

MICHIE, ALEXANDER, a merchant in St Michael's, S.C., 1774. [Charleston inventories, Vol.60, ms]

MICHIE, BENJAMIN, a merchant in Charleston, 1740s. [SAS]

MICHIE, HARRY, a merchant in Charleston before 1776. [NA.AO12.50.417]

MICHIE, JOHN, a merchant in Charleston, 1732. [SAS]

MICHIE, KENNETH, a merchant in Charleston by 1738, probate S.C. 1749. [NAS.CS16.1.73][SAS]

MICHIE, WILLIAM, born 1716, a merchant from Montrose who settled in Charleston, died 1771, probate S.C. 1772. [NAS.NRAS#771, bundle 552]

MIDDLETON, ALEXANDER, born 1709, a merchant from Aberdeen who settled in Boston by 1736, died in 1750. [SCS][NAS.AC7.43.493]

MIDDLETON, WILLIAM, a merchant trading between Aberdeen and Virginia, 1750. [NAS.E504.1.3]

MILLER, ANDREW, a merchant in Bermuda, 1780. [ActsPCCol.1780/375]

MILLER, ANDREW, merchant in Halifax, N.C., partner in the firm of Alston and Company and also Alston, Young and Company of Glasgow, later in N.Y., a merchant in N.C. in 1780; died in Charleston 1784. [NA.AO12.37.161][NAS.CS17.1.1/76/179]

MILLER, GEORGE, a merchant possibly from Dumfries who emigrated to Va. in 1758, settled in N.C. in 1763, a merchant in Dobbs County, N.C., before 1776. [NA.AO12.36.174][NAS.CS16.1.168/1]

MILLER, HUGH, a merchant in Mecklenburg, Va., 1779; formerly in Va. 1786. [NAS.CS16.1.175; CS17.1.5/20; CS238/Misc.16/6]

MILLER, JAMES, a merchant from Carshorne who settled in Perth Amboy, N.J., by 1685. [NJSA.EJD.A282; B175]

MILLER, JAMES, trading between Ayr and Va., 1770. [NAS.E504.4.5]

MILLER, JAMES, a merchant in Va., 1774. [NAS.AC7.55]

MILLER, JOHN, a merchant, from Scotland to Boston in 1766. [PAB]

MILLER, WILLIAM, trading between Port Glasgow and Va., 1745, 1747. [NAS.E504.28.2/3]

MILLER, WILLIAM, a merchant in Va. then in Glasgow, 1749. [NAS.CS16.1.81]

MILLIGAN, DAVID, a merchant in N.Y., 1781. [NAS.CS16.1.183]

MILLIGAN, JAMES, a merchant from Kirkcudbrightshire who settled in Philadelphia by 1770. [NAS.RS23.XX.461]

MILLIKEN, HUGH, and Company, merchants in Glasgow, trading with Charleston, 1731, trading between Greenock and Md., also Jamaica, 1743, Va., 1744, 1745, 1746; trading between Port Glasgow and Va., 1744, 1746, 1747, 1749; between Port Glasgow and Md., 1745, 1746, 1747; between Port Glasgow and S.C., 1746. [NAS.AC9.5455; E504.15.1/2; 28/2/3/4]

MILLIKEN, JAMES, trading between Greenock and Va., 1746; between Port Glasgow and Md., 1746, 1747; between Port Glasgow and Virginia, 1747. [NAS.E504.15.2; 28.2/3]

MILLIKEN, THOMAS, a merchant trading between Ayr and the Caribee Islands, 1683. [NAS.E72.3.12]

MILNE, ALEXANDER, jr., merchant in Aberdeen trading with Jamaica, 1767. [AJ#1015]

MILNE, CHARLES, a merchant from Montrose who settled in Georgetown, S.C., probate S.C. 1772.
MILNE, DAVID, a merchant in St Michael's, Barbados, 1699. [St Michael's burial register]
MITCHELL, ALEXANDER, a merchant in Antigua, 1778. [NAS.CS16.1.173/159]
MITCHELL, ALEXANDER, a Scots merchant in London trading with N.Y. and Charleston, 1780-1781. [NAS.CS96.600]
MITCHELL, DAVID, merchant in Ayr, trading between Ayr and Antigua and Montserrat, 1758, 1768, 1769, 1770; between Ayr and Va., 1767, 1768; between Ayr and Falmouth, N.E., 1769, 1770, 1771; between Ayr and N.Y., 1769; between Ayr and Bath, N.C., 1769. [NAS.E504.4.3/4/5]
MITCHELL, DAVID, ALEXANDER OLIPHANT, and Company, merchants in Ayr trading with New Brunswick, 1782. [NAS.CS16.1.120]
MITCHELL, HENRY, settled Va. c1756, factor and partner in Fredericksburg, Va., for McCall, Smellie and Company of Glasgow, then a merchant in N.Y., returned to Glasgow by 1784 [NA.AO13.31.635][GM#IV.264][NAS.CS17.1.2/294]
MITCHELL, JAMES, born 1705, a merchant who emigrated to N.E. in 1730, settled in Weathersfield, Connecticut, died there in 1800. [NAS.RD4.178/2.198]
MITCHELL, JAMES, a merchant trading between Greenock and Va., 1743; between Port Glasgow and the Va. and Md., 1744, 1745. [NAS.E504.15.1/2]
MITCHELL, JOHN, a merchant trading between Ayr and the West Indies, 1673. [NAS.E72.3.4]
MITCHELL, JOHN, a merchant in Glasgow trading with America and the West Indies, 1717. [NAS.AC7.24.710]
MITCHELL, JOHN, a merchant in Aberdeen trading with Va. 1750. [NAS.E504.1.3]
MITCHELL, JOHN, a merchant in St Augustine, Fla., 1776. [NAS.NRAS.0159.C4]
MITCHELL, JOHN, a merchant from Glasgow who settled in Fredericksburg, Va., by 1782, 1783, 1785. [NAS.CS17.1.1/174/282; RD2.241.382]
MITCHELL, JOHN, HUGH LENNOX, and WILLIAM SCOTT, in Fredericksburg, Scott died 1769, Lennox died in 1771.[NA.AO13.102.72]

MITCHELL, PETER, trading between Ayr and Falmouth, N.E., 1769, 1770, 1771, [NAS.E504.4.5]; a merchant in Glasgow trading with Va., 1774, 1775. [NAS.AC7.55]

MITCHELL, WILLIAM, a Scots merchant in London trading with N.Y. and Charleston, 1780-1781. [NAS.CS96.600]

MITCHELLSON, DAVID, a merchant in N.Y., 1785. [NAS.GD5.416]

MOCHLINE, JOHN, merchant in Va., 1749. [NAS.RD2.168.10]

MOFFAT, GEORGE, a merchant who settled in N.Y. during 1699. [DP#143]

MONCRIEFF, GEORGE, a merchant in Antigua, 1757. [EBR]

MONCRIEFF, JOHN, a merchant from Perthshire who settled in Charleston, S.C., in 1772, died there in 1821. [NA.AO13.131.452][Old Scots Church gravestone, Charleston]

MONCREIFF, PHILIP, son of Col. Moncreiff, to Va. 1771, settled as a merchant in Warwick near James River, to Charlotte County in 1773-1775. [NA.AO13.31.640]

MONCREIFF, ROBERT, SCOTT, trading between Leith and S.C., 1765. [NAS.E504.22]

MONRO, ALEXANDER, a merchant in Lisbon, Portugal, testament 13.8.1741, Edinburgh. [NAS]

MONRO, ALEXANDER, partner in a company in Glasgow trading with Va. and N.C. from 1771 to 1776. [NA.AO13.31.642]

MONRO, DAVID, trading between Port Glasgow and Antigua, 1748. [E504.28.4]

MONRO, GEORGE, a merchant in America, 1782. [NAS.CS17.1.1]

MONTEATH, WILLIAM, a merchant on Green Island, Jamaica, 1777. [NAS.RD4.237.607]

MONTEITH, WALTER, a merchant in Glasgow trading with Va., 1765, 1774. [NAS.CS16.1.122/157; AC40.166]

MONTFORD, JOSEPH, a merchant in N.C, 1774, 1775. [NAS.AC7.55; CS16.1.168]

MONTGOMERIE, HUGH, a merchant who died in St Kitts, probate PCC 1700.

MONTGOMERIE, JAMES, the younger, a merchant in Glasgow trading with America, 1694. [EBR]

MONTGOMERIE, JAMES, trading between Port Glasgow and Jamaica, 1744; between Port Glasgow and Antigua,

1748; between Ayr and Va., 1773. [NAS.E504.28.2/4; 4.6]

MONTGOMERIE, PATRICK, trading between Greenock and Boston, 1746; between Port Glasgow and Antigua, 1747; between Port Glasgow and Maryland, 1747; between Ayr and Boston, 1753, 1754. [NAS.E504.15.2; 4.2; 28.3]

MONTGOMERIE, ROBERT WILSON, a merchant from Ayrshire, emigrated to Va. before 1775, returned to Scotland. [HAF.1.290]

MONTGOMERIE, THOMAS, a merchant possibly from Ayr then a partner in the Thistle Distillery, Norfolk, Va., before 1776; possibly naturalised in Charleston, S.C., in 1787, probate S.C. 1796. [NA.AO12.106.47]

MONTGOMERY, HEW, a merchant, from Port Glasgow to Va. in 1685. [NAS.E72.19.8]

MONTGOMERY, JAMES, a merchant trading from Ayr to the Caribee Islands, 1683. [NAS.E72.3.12]

MONTGOMERY, JAMES, jr., a merchant in Glasgow trading with America, 1694, 1696. [EBR]

MONTGOMERY, JAMES, trading between Port Glasgow and Virginia, 1747, 1749; between Port Glasgow and Antigua, 1747. [NAS.E504.28.3/4]

MONTGOMERY, JAMES, JOHN KERR, and Company, merchants in Sussex County, James River, Va., 1765. [NAS.RD2.197.369]

MONTGOMERY, JOHN, a merchant who settled on the James River, Va., before 1776. [NAS.CS161.170]

MONTGOMERY, PETER, a merchant in Glasgow trading with Barbados and Antigua, 1734. [NAS.AC40.166]

MONTGOMERY, THOMAS, a merchant who settled in Norfolk, Va., before 1776, then in Ayr. [NA.AO13.31.643]

MONTIER, JAMES, a merchant in Glasgow trading with Barbados and Antigua, 1734. [NAS.AC40.166]

MOODIE, ROBERT, a merchant in Savannah-la-Mar, Jamaica, then in Leith, 1776. [NAS.CC8.8.123]

MOODIE, THOMAS, a merchant in Carolina, 1772. [NAS.CS16.1.148]

MOODY, ROBERT, trading between Leith and S.C., 1755. [NAS.E504.22]

MOODY, ROBERT, a merchant, from Glasgow to Boston in 1766. [PAB]

MOOR, WILLIAM, a merchant trading between Ayr and the West Indies in 1673. [NAS.E72.3.4]
MOORE, SAMUEL, a merchant trading between Ayr and the West Indies in 1681. [NAS.E72.3.6]
MOORE, WILLIAM, a merchant in Barbados, executor of George McKenzie probate Barbados 1711.
MORGAN, WILLIAM, a merchant in Jamaica, 1700. [NAS.CE60.11.6/22]
MORRICE, JOHN, a merchant in St Croix from 1776 to 1784, then in Irvine. [NAS.NRAS.0396.TD248]
MORRIS, JOHN, trading between Greenock and Va., 1745. [NAS.E504.15.2]
MORRISON, ALEXANDER, a merchant in Penobscot, Maine, before 1776, and by 1786 in St Andrews, New Brunswick. [NA.AO13.22.183]
MORRISON, DONALD, a merchant, from Glasgow to Boston in 1767. [PAB]
MORRISON, JAMES, merchant in Ayr, trading between Ayr and Boston, 1768. [NAS.E504.4.4]
MORRISON, JOHN, trading between Leith and S.C., 1755. [NAS.E504.22]
MORRISON, JOHN, jr., a merchant in Aberdeen, trading with Va. and Md. pre 1747. [NAS.AC8.689]
MORRISON, JOHN, a merchant in Antigua then in Dumfries, testament Dumfries 1770. [NAS]
MORRISON, WILLIAM, JAMES TAYLOR, and Company, merchants in Greenock trading with Philadelphia, Jamaica, and the Bay of Honduras, 1776. [NAS.AC7.55]
MORSON, ALEXANDER, trading between Greenock and Va., 1745; trading between Port Glasgow and Va., 1744, 1747. [NAS.E504.15.2; 28.2/3]
MORSON, ARTHUR, born 1734, a factor from Greenock who emigrated to Va. in 1751, settled in Falmouth,Va., died in Hartwood, Stafford County, Va., 1798. [NAS.B10.15.7174][VG#654]
MOWAT, WILLIAM, a merchant in Aberdeen trading with Antigua, 1751. [AJ#208]
MUDIE, DAVID, a merchant from Montrose, emigrated from there to East N.J. in 1684, settled in New Perth by 1685. [NJSA.EJD.Liber A/196][NLS]

SCOTTISH TRANSATLANTIC MERCHANTS

MUIR, ADAM, a merchant, possibly from Edinburgh, who settled in Md. around 1746, and by 1756 in Va. [MAGU#35][NAS.CS16.1.99]

MUIR, GEORGE, a merchant in Fredericksburg, Va., before 1776, moved to London by 1781. [NA.AO13.31.653]

MUIR, HUGH, a merchant trading between Ayr and the Caribee Islands in 1683. [NAS.E72.3.12]

MUIR, ROBERT, born 1748, a merchant from Dumfries who settled in Alexandria, Va., died 1786. [Christchurch gravestone]

MUIRHEAD, JOHN, a merchant in Philadelphia, 1699. [SPAWI.1699.248]

MUNDELL, ROBERT, trading between Leith and S.C., 1765. [NAS.E504.22]

MUNN, ALEXANDER, emigrated via Greenock to Va. in 1769, settled as a merchant in Wake County, N.C, until 1777, then in N.Y., possibly returned to Wake County. [NA.AO12.35.1][NAS.CS17.1.3/324]

MUNRO, DONALD, a merchant, from Glasgow to Boston in 1768. [PAB]

MUNRO, EBENEZER, a merchant in Glasgow trading with Va., 1756. [NAS.CS16.1.95]

MUNRO, JAMES, a merchant in St George, Grenada, 1779. [NAS.RD3.242.460]

MUNRO, JOHN, a merchant, from Glasgow to Boston in 1768; settled in N.Y. in 1756. [PAB][NA.AO12.12.1]

MURCHIE, ARCHIBALD, trading between Port Glasgow and Va., 1745. [NAS.E504.28.2]

MURDOCH, GEORGE, a merchant trading between Greenock and Va., 1743, with Md. and Va., 1744, 1745, 1747; with S.C., 1745; between Port Glasgow and Va., 1749. [NAS.E504.15.1/2; 28.4]

MURDOCH, JOHN, a merchant trading from Ayr to the Caribee Islands in 1683. [NAS.E72.3.12]

MURDOCH, JOHN, born 1753, a merchant who emigrated via Whitehaven to Va. in 1774. [NA.T47.9/11]

MURDOCH, JOHN, a merchant trading between Greenock and Va., 1743, 1744, 1745; between Port Glasgow and Antigua, 1747; between Port Glasgow and Virginia, 1747, 1749. [NAS.E504.15.1/2; 28.3/4]

MURDOCH, JOHN, merchant in Glasgow, trading to Va. with William Cunninghame and Company died 1776, heir William Miller his grandson. [NAS.SH]

MURDOCH, PETER, and JOHN HAMILTON jr., merchants of Glasgow trading in Va. before 1776. [NA.AO12.109.212]

MURDOCH, SAMUEL, born 1755, a merchant who emigrated via Whitehaven to Va. in 1774. [NA.T47.9/11]

MURDOCH, THOMAS, born 1757, a merchant who emigrated via Whitehaven to Va. in 1774. [NA.T47.9/11]

MURDOCH, WILLIAM, born 1707, a merchant from Callander, emigrated via Liverpool to Va. in 1747. [NA.T1.328][P.3.216]

MURDOCH, DREGHORN, and Company, merchants in Charlotte County, Va., before 1780. [NA.AO13.102.60]

MURRAY, ALEXANDER, a merchant in Charleston by 1737, dead by 1750. [NAS.RD3.210.491][SAS]

MURRAY, ALEXANDER, born 1734, a merchant and shipmaster from Glasgow who settled in Osburne, Va., during 1762, moved to Shelburne, Nova Scotia, by 1783. [NA.AO12.55.61]

MURRAY, ALEXANDER, a merchant in Pittsylvania County, Va., before 1776, later in Shelburne, Nova Scotia, by 1783. [NA.AO12.55.41]

MURRAY, ANDREW, a merchant in Antigua, 1709, [St John's town library, Antigua]; 1717, [GBR]

MURRAY, GEORGE, a merchant in Jamaica, 1771. [NAS.CS16.1.143]

MURRAY, JAMES, born 1713, a merchant from Roxburghshire who settled in Carolina by 1735 then in Boston by 1754, died 1781. [SCS][SAS]

MURRAY, JAMES, a merchant from Leith who settled in Va. before 1744. [NAS.CS16.1.173]

MURRAY, JAMES, a merchant in Fraserburgh trading with Va., 1744. [NAS.CS16.1.73]

MURRAY, JOHN, a merchant, from Scotland to Boston in 1766. [PAB]

MURRAY, JOHN, a tobacco factor from Glasgow who settled in Aquia, Va., before 1770. [GA:T79.21]

MURRAY, JOHN, born 1755, a merchant who emigrated before 1780 and settled in Alexandria, Va., and later N.Y., 1786. [ANY.2.9] [NAS.CS17.1.5/350; CS17.1.6/251; RD3.245.1215]

MURRAY, JOHN, and JAMES MURRAY, merchants in Charleston, 1757. [NAS.GD219.290][SAS]

MURRAY, ROBERT, a merchant in Barbados, 1655, probate Barbados 1716.
MURRAY, ROBERT, a merchant in N.Y., 1786. [NAS.CS17.1.5/350; CS17.1.6; RD3.245.1215]
MURRAY, WILLIAM, a merchant who settled in Va. before 1662. [NAS.RD3.5; RD3.6.606][EMR, 1662]
MURRAY, WILLIAM, a merchant and shipmaster in N.Y., 1764. [NAS.CS16.1.117]
MURRAY, WILLIAM, a merchant in Edinburgh, trading with Charleston, 1767. [NAS.AC7.52]
MUSCHET, ROBERT, of Green, a merchant in St Elizabeth's, Jamaica, 1770s. [NAS.CS16.1.154/170/173/174/175; RD2.218.1162]
NAIRNE, PETER, born 1761, a merchant from Anstruther who settled in Basseterre, St Kitts, died there in 1786, testament, St Andrews 1786. [NAS.CC
NASMITH, JOHN, a merchant from Edinburgh, died in Va. during 1747, testament Edinburgh 1752. [NAS.CC8.8.114]
NEASMITH, ROBERT, trading between Port Glasgow and Boston, 1748. [NAS.E504.28.3]
NEILSON, HUGH, a merchant who settled in Lewisburg, Loudoun County, Va., by 1770, died 1813. [NAS.CS16.1.165]
NEILSON, JAMES, a merchant trading between Greenock and Va., 1743, 1744, 1745, 1746, with Md., 1744; between Port Glasgow and Md., 1745. [NAS.E504.15.1/2; 28.2]
NEILSON, JOHN, trading between Port Glasgow and Va., 1744, 1746, 1748. [NAS.E504.28.2/3]
NEILSON, JOHN, a storekeeper who settled in Dumfries, Va., before 1768, died 1772. [SFV#60]
NEILSON, WILLIAM, a merchant who settled in Lewisburg, Va., before 1775. [NAS.CS16.1.165; CS17.14/231]
NELSON, THOMAS, born 1677, a merchant who emigrated to Va. in 1690 and settled in York, died 1745. [GBR.1716][CAG.1.986/725]
NESBIT, HUGH, a merchant settled in S.C. by 1684. [FS]
NEWAL, ANDREW, a merchant in Westmoreland, Jamaica, 1780. [NAS.CS16.1.179]
NEWAL and CLARK, merchants in Ayr trading with Jamaica, 1780. [NAS.CS16.1.179]

NICHOLSON, WILLIAM, a merchant from Berwickshire who settled in Anne Arundel County, Md., probate Anne Arundel 1731. [MSA.Wills.20.306]

NICOL, JAMES, a merchant in Newport, Rhode Island, later in Leicester, Worcester County, N.E., 1766. [NAS.CS16.1.125]

NICOLL, GEORGE, a merchant in Kingston, Jamaica, 1776. [NLS#8793/4]

NIMMO, JAMES, a merchant from Linlithgow who settled in Princess Anne County, Va., before 1748. [WMQ.5.134]

NISBET, ALEXANDER, a merchant from Edinburgh who settled in Charleston, S.C., by 1715, a merchant in Charleston, died 1753, probate S.C. 1753. [NAS.GD237.10.1.42; GD237.1.153.9; RD4.116.1084; AC9.6455] [GM.24.48][SAS]

NISBET, DAVID, trading between Greenock and Va., 1744. [NAS.E504.15.1]

NISBET, DAVID, a merchant in St Kitts, 1776. [NLS.ms8793/4]

NISBET, PATRICK, a merchant in Glasgow trading with Va., 1757. [NAS.B10.15.7036]

NISBET, ROBERT, an apprentice merchant who emigrated to Charleston, S.C., in 1721, a merchant in Charleston before 1729. [NAS.GD237.10.1.29/ bundle 4/1][SAS]

NISBET, ROBERT, a merchant from Lanarkshire who settled in Nevis and St Kitts, and died in 1740, testament Edinburgh 1743. [NAS.CC8.8.108][NC#2][MWI#98]

NISBET, WALTER, a merchant who settled in Berkeley County, S.C., before 1724. [NAS.GD237.10.1.42]

NISBET, WALTER, a merchant who settled in Nevis before 1743, testament Edinburgh 1743. [NAS.CC8.8.108]

NISBET and KINLOCH, merchants in S.C., 1729. [NAS.GD237.153.19]

NIVEN, DUNCAN, a merchant from Glasgow then in Va. 1786. [NAS.CS17.1.5/351]

NOBLE, THOMAS, born 1704, a merchant from Banffshire who settled in Md. or Va. [GFK#677]

OCHTERLONY, ALEXANDER, born in 1690s, a merchant from Montrose who settled in Philadelphia. [F#5.277]

OGILVIE, ALEXANDER, a merchant in Leith trading with America, 1780. [NAS.CS16.1.181]

OGILVIE, CHARLES, a merchant from Banff who emigrated via London to Charleston in 1751, a merchant there before 1776, moved to Aberdeen, probate PCC 1788. [AUL.ms2740/3][NA.AO12.48.63][SAS]

OGILVIE, JAMES, a merchant from Aberdeen who emigrated to Charleston, S.C., in 1744, and died there in 1745. [ACA:APB.3.135]

OGILVIE, JOHN, a merchant from Dundee then in Charleston, S.C., 1785. [NAS.CS17.1.4/286]

OGILVIE, WILLIAM, trading between Port Glasgow and Jamaica, 1747, 1748. [NAS.E504.28.3/4]

OGILVIE, WILLIAM, a merchant in Banff trading with St Kitts, 1750. [AJ#122]

OLIPHANT, ALEXANDER, trading between Ayr and Antigua, 1763, 1764; between Ayr and Barbados, 1765; between Ayr and N.Y., 1768; between Ayr and Falmouth, N.E., 1769, 1770, 1771; between Ayr and Antigua, 1774, 1775; between Ayr and St John's, Newfoundland, 1776. [NAS.E504.4.3/4/5/6]

ORMISTON, THOMAS, a merchant from Edinburgh who settled in Savannah, Ga., in 1736. [SPAWI.143.148][NA.CO5.670.283/308]

ORR, ADAM, trading between Ayr and Antigua, 1758; between Ayr and Anguilla, 1759. [NAS.E504.4.3]

ORR, HECTOR, trading between Port Glasgow and Jamaica, 1745. [NAS.E504.28.2]

ORR, JAMES, a merchant and writer from Ayr who died in Jamaica during 1750, testament Edinburgh 1758. [NAS.CC8.8.117]

ORR, JOHN, born 1726, a merchant from Berwickshire who settled in Leestown, Loudoun County, Va., before 1786. [NAS.CS17.1.5/45][SOF#151][VG#105][Tylers Qrtly.4.49]

ORR, JOHN, a storekeeper from Lanarkshire who settled in Alexandria, Fairfax County, Va., before 1770. [NAS.CS16.1.141]

ORR, MATTHEW, a merchant from Glasgow who died in Tobago during 1790, probate PCC 1790, testament Edinburgh 1791. [NAS.CC8.8.128]

ORR, ROBERT, trading between Greenock and Boston, 1744. [NAS.E504.15.2]

ORR, WILLIAM, jr., merchant in Ayr, trading between Ayr and Va., 1768. [NAS.E504.4.5]

ORROCH, WALTER, a merchant in Methil trading with Boston, 1754. [NAS.AC7.46.101]

OSBURNE, ADAM, a merchant trading between Ayr and the West Indies in 1681. [NAS.E72.3.7]

OSWALD, ALEXANDER, a merchant in Glasgow trading with the Va. and Md., 1739, [NAS.AC7.44.488; AC9.1443]; trading between Greenock and Jamaica, Va., Antigua, 1743, Va., 1744, 1745; S.C., 1745; between Greenock and St Kitts, 1746; between Greenock and Jamaica, 1746; trading between Port Glasgow and Va., 1736, 1744, 1745, 1747; between Port Glasgow and Jamaica, 1743, 1744, 1745, 1746, 1747, 1748; between Port Glasgow and Barbados, 1746; between Port Glasgow and Antigua, 1747. [NAS.E504.15.1/2; E504.28.1/2/3/4; E512/1455]

OSWALD, GEORGE, of Scotstoun, merchant in Glasgow trading with America, 1763-1767. [NAS.GD1.618.1]

OSWALD, RICHARD, a merchant in Glasgow trading with the Va. and Md., 1739, [NAS.AC7.44.488]; trading between Greenock and Jamaica, 1743, 1746, 1747; Antigua, 1743, Va., 1743, 1744, 1746, 1747; S.C., 1745; between Greenock and St Kitts, 1746; trading between Port Glasgow and Va., also Jamaica, 1743, 1744, 1745, 1746, 1748; between Port Glasgow and Va., 1736, 1745, 1747; between Port Glasgow and Barbados, 1746. [NAS.E504.28.3/4; E504.15.1/2; E504.28.1/2/3; E512/1455]; a Scottish merchant in London who was granted land in Ga., 1751. [NA.CO5/669]; 1779, [NAS.CS16.1.175]

OSWALD, DENNISTOUN, and Company, merchants in Glasgow trading in Fairfax County, Va., before 1776. Partners were Alexander Oswald and James Dennistoun. [NA.AO12.54.173]

PAGAN, JOHN, trading between Greenock and Va., 1746. [NAS.E504.15.2]

PAGAN, ROBERT, emigrated from Scotland to Falmouth, Maine, in 1748, factor for Lee, Tucker and Company of Greenock at Casco Bay, formerly a merchant in Falmouth, 1776. [NAS.SC58.61.13] [NA.AO12.11.71; AO212.81.45]

PAISLEY, JOHN, a merchant in Paisley trading with Boston, 1766. [NAS.CS16.1.126]

PANTON, WILLIAM, born 1742, emigrated to America after 1765, an Indian trader in Savannah, Ga., partner in the firm of Panton, Leslie and Company, later in Pensacola,

West Fla., died 1801, probate PCC 1804.
[IT#18][NA.AO12.109.246]
PARK, ARTHUR, a merchant in Greenock trading with the Va. and Md., pre 1722. [NAS.AC7.26.681; AC9.849]
PARK, JOHN, a merchant in Greenock, trading with Va., 1743, 1744, then in Va., 1752, 1782. [NAS.CS16.1.88; CS17.1.1/97; NAS.E504.15.1/2]
PARK, JOHN, a merchant in Dominica, partner of John Christie and David Currie trading as John Park and Company, 1785. [NAS.RD2.241.103]
PARK, PATRICK, a merchant from Glasgow who emigrated via Leith to Darien in 1698 and died there, testament Edinburgh 1707. [NAS.CC8.8.83]
PARK, RICHARD, a merchant in S.C., 1706. [NAS.RD2.104.490; RD4.99.222][SCA. Register of the Province Conveyances, F.143-6]
PARK, ROBERT, trading between Ayr and Antigua and Montserrat, 1764. [NAS.E504.4.3]
PARKE, WILLIAM, factor in Va. for Dinwiddie and Company of Glasgow, before 1776. [NA.AO13.102.78]
PARKER, HUGH, a merchant in Kilmarnock trading with Jamaica, 1775, 1779. [NAS.CS16.1.165/175]
PARKER, JAMES, a merchant trading between Glasgow and Va. in 1681. [NAS.E72.19.3]
PARKER, JAMES, a merchant from Port Glasgow who settled in Jamaica before 1754. [NAS.SH.24.8.1754]
PARKER, JAMES, born 1729, a merchant from Port Glasgow who settled in Norfolk, Va., from 1746 to 1776. [NA.AO12.54.247][NAS.SH.24.8.1754; CS16.1.95/107][Colonial Williamsburg.M.77.1/3]
PARKER, JOHN, a merchant from Port Glasgow who settled in Va. before 1760. [NAS.CS16.1.107]
PARKER, JOHN, jr., a merchant in Kingston, Jamaica, 1778. [NAS.CS16.1.173/174]
PARKER, JOHN, a merchant in Kilmarnock trading with Jamaica, 1775, 1779. [NAS.CS16.1.165/175]
PARKER, HUNTER, and SMITH, merchants in Kilmarnock trading with Jamaica, 1778, and Va., 1779. [NAS.CS16.1.174/177]
PATERSON, HUGH, trading between Ayr and Charleston, 1756; between Ayr and Bath, N.C., 1769. [NAS.E504.4.3/5]

PATERSON, JOHN, a merchant shipmaster from Glasgow who settled in Boston before 1690. [RPCS.15.307]

PATERSON, JOHN, trading between Port Glasgow and Jamaica, 1749. [NAS.E504.28.4]

PATERSON, PETER, a merchant in Greenock trading with Va., 1779. [NAS.CS16.1.177]

PATERSON, ROBERT, trading between Port Glasgow and Va., 1747. [E504.28.3]

PATERSON, SIMON, from Glasgow to Va. as an assistant storekeeper of William Cunningham and Company of Glasgow, later in partnership with John Pettigrew in Ga. before 1776. [NA.AO12.101.190]

PATTERSON, JAMES, trading between Port Glasgow and St Kitts, 1745. [NAS.E504.28.2]

PATTERSON, JOHN, a shop-keeper in Front Street, Philadelphia, from 1771 to 1777, died in N.Y. [NA.AO12.40.40]

PATTERSON, ROBERT, trading between Greenock and Va., 1745, 1746; trading between Port Glasgow and Va., 1747. [NAS.E504.15.2; 28.3]

PATTERSON, WILLIAM, a merchant in Edinburgh trading between Leith and the West Indies, 1679. [RPCS.6.300/331/335/415]

PATTON, ROBERT, a merchant and factor from Glasgow who settled in Culpepper County, Va., before 1776. [GA.CFI]

PATTULLO, HENRY, born 1726, a merchant and clergyman who emigrated to Va. in 1735, settled in N.C., died 1801. [DAB.14.295]

PEADIE, JAMES, trading between Greenock and S.C., 1745; between Port Glasgow and Va., 1748, 1749. [NAS.E504.15.2; 28/4]

PEARSON, THOMAS, a merchant in Tobago, 1775. [MBR]

PEARSON, ..., and DAVID COCHRANE, merchants in Va., 1783. [NAS.CS17.1.2]

PEDDIE, JOHN, born 1703, a merchant from Arbroath who emigrated via Liverpool to Port North Potomac, Md., in 1747. [NA.T1.328][P.2.250]

PEEBLES, DAVID, a merchant from Edinburgh who settled at Powell's Creek, Va., in 1647. [EBR#129][WMQ#2.13.132]

PENMAN, ARCHIBALD, a merchant from Edinburgh who settled in Fla. by 1785. [NAS.CS17.1.4/193]

PENMAN, EDWARD, a merchant from Edinburgh who settled in Charleston, S.C., by 1784. [NAS.RD3.245.725]

PENMAN, HUGH, a merchant in Charleston, 1783. [NAS.CS17.1.2/343]

PENMAN, JAMES, a merchant from Edinburgh who settled in St Augustine, East Fla., and in Charleston, S.C., before 1772, probate S.C. 1789. [GBR][NAS.AC7.59/1788; NRAS.771.bundle 29/491; NRAS#0181; 11]

PETER, ALEXANDER, a merchant in Va. 1787. [NAS.CS17.1.6/358]

PETER, JOHN, born 1722, a merchant from Glasgow who settled in Surrey County, Va., before 1760, died 1763. [CD#43]

PETER, ROBERT, born 1725, a merchant from Lanarkshire who settled in Georgetown, Frederick County, Md., before 1775. [NAS.CS16.1.165][HM.1.732]

PETER, THOMAS, trading between Port Glasgow and Va., 1749. [NAS.E504.28.4]

PETER, WALTER, a merchant from Glasgow who settled in Surrey County, Va., before 1763, died before 1787. [NAS.GD180.348; CS16.1.174/185; CS17.1.6/358; SH.30.11.1787]

PETER, THOMAS, and WILLIAM BOGLE, merchants in Glasgow trading with Va., 1769. [NAS.CS16.1.134]

PETER, WALTER, and Company, merchants in Va., 1765, 1766. [NAS.CS16.1.122/126]

PETERS, THOMAS, a merchant, from Port Glasgow to N.E. in 1685; 1700. [NAS.E72.19.8][SCS]

PETTIGREW, JAMES, born 1715, a merchant from Glasgow who settled in Va. before 1778. [NAS.CS16.1.173/175/181]

PETTIGREW, JOHN, a merchant from Glasgow who settled in Augusta, Ga., by 1756, a partner of Simon Paterson of Glasgow in Sunbury, Ga., died in Savannah during 1775, probate Ga. 1775. [NA.CO5.646.C10; AO12.101.190]

PITCAIRN, DAVID, a merchant from Dreghorn, died in Jamaica during 1730, testament Edinburgh 1733. [NAS.CC8.8.95]

PITCAIRN, ROBERT, a merchant who settled in St Catherine, Middlesex, Jamaica, before 1780. [NAS.GD1.675.61]

PITTIGREW, JAMES, born 1746, a merchant from Glasgow who emigrated via Greenock to Charleston, S.C., in 1774. [NA.T47.12]

PORTEOUS, EDWARD, a merchant from Newbattle, emigrated via London to Va. in 1675, settled in Petsworth, Gloucester County, Va., in 1685, died there 1700, probate Gloucester 1700, probate 1700 PCC 1700. [NAS.GD297.114][NA.E190.62.5] [VMHB.13.311][Gloucester gravestone]

PORTEOUS, JOHN, a merchant in N.Y., 1786. [NAS.CS17.1.5/310]

PORTER, ABEL, a merchant, trading between Leith to East N.J. in 1685. [NAS.E72.15.32]

PORTERFIELD, ALEXANDER, trading from Greenock to St Kitts, 1742, 1743, Barbados, 1744, with S.C., 1744, 1745, 1746; trading between Port Glasgow and Boston, 1748; between Port Glasgow and St Kitts, 1748. [NAS.E504.15.1/2; 28.3/4]

PORTERFIELD, JOHN, a merchant and a shipmaster who settled in Bristol, N.E., before 1699, later in Trenton, N.J., probate 1738 N.J. [SPAWI.1700.195][SCS][NJSA.Liber 4/136]

POTTER, DAVID, trading between Greenock and Va., 1745. [NAS.E504.15.2]

POTTIE, GEORGE, a merchant in Va., 1781. [NAS.CS16.1.184]

PRATT, WILLIAM, born 1703, a merchant from Peterhead who settled in Gloucester County, Va. [GCE#936]

PRIMROSE, NICOL, a merchant from Musselburgh who settled in Charleston, S.C., during 1780, naturalised there 1783, died there 1796. [EEC#12303][SCSA]

PRINGLE, ROBERT, born 1702, emigrated to Charleston in 1725, a merchant on Tradd Street, died 1776. [see The Letter Book of Robert Pringle, S.C., 1972] [SAS]

PRINGLE, WALTER, a merchant who settled in St Kitts and died there in 1760, testament Edinburgh 1776. [NAS.CC8.8.123]

PYOTT, THOMAS, a flour merchant from Angus who settled in New Berne, N.C., before 1776, later in London. [NA.AO13.123.48]

PYPER, ALEXANDER, a merchant trading with Barbados and Newfoundland, 1698. [NAS.RH15.1013]

PYPER, THOMAS, a merchant, from Leith to N.Y. in 1681. [NAS.E72.15.21]

RAE, ADAM, a merchant in Leith trading with the West Indies, 1611. [NAS.E71.29.6/22]

RAE, GEORGE, a merchant who settled in Va. before 1776. [NA.AO13.32.315]

RAE, GEORGE, and JOHN BROWN, merchants in Norfolk, Va., 1770s. [NA.AO12.99.21]

RAE, JAMES, born 1723, a merchant from Govan who died in Va. during 1764. [SM.26.290][MAGU#17]

RAE, ROBERT, trading between Port Glasgow and Boston, 1748. [NAS.E504.28.3]

RAE, ROBERT, trading between Greenock and Boston, 1745, 1746; trading between Port Glasgow and Va., 1749. [NAS.E504.15.2; 28.4]

RAE, ROBERT, born 1723, a merchant from Little Govan who settled in Falmouth, Va., died 1753. [Bruton gravestone]

RALSTON, DAVID, a merchant from Glasgow who settled at Cabin Point on the James River, Va., before 1762. [GA:CFI]

RALSTON, WILLIAM, a merchant trading between Rhode Island and Darien, 1699. [SPAWI.1699.501]

RAMSAY, ANDREW, a merchant in Glasgow trading with Va., 1724. [NAS.AC9.868]

RAMSAY, ANDREW, trading between Greenock and Va., also Jamaica, 1743; trading between Port Glasgow and Va., 1745, 1747, 1748. [NAS.E504.1; 28.2/3]

RAMSAY, ANDREW, a merchant in the Canongate, Edinburgh, trading with Pa., 1773. [NAS.CS17.1.157/179]

RAMSAY, CHARLES, a merchant in Montrose trading with Jamaica, 1719. [NAS.AC9.647]

RAMSAY, JOHN, a merchant in Glasgow trading with Jamaica, 1726. [NAS.HH11.15]

RAMSAY, JOHN, a shopkeeper in Charleston, probate S.C. 1734. [Caledonian Mercury#2326]

RAMSAY, WILLIAM, born 1716, a merchant from Dumfries-shire, who settled in Alexandria, Va., before 1765, in Va. 1782, died in Alexandria during 1785. [NAS.CS17.1.1/411; SC15.55.2; RS19.376] [VG#88]

RANKINE, JOHN, merchant in Dundee, trading between Dundee and S.C., 1770, 1772, 1773, 1775. [NAS.E504.11]

RAPLAY, JOHN, a merchant in St Kitts, 1727. [MBR]

RATTRAY, JOHN, son of Thomas Rattray a merchant, a merchant from Glasgow who emigrated to Jamaica, 1763. [NAS.B10.15.7056]

REID, GEORGE, factor for the Royal Africa Company in Barbados, before 1684. [SPAWI.1684/2030]

REID, GEORGE, a merchant from Greenock then in Wilmington, N.C.., 1784. [NAS.CS17.1.6/342; RS53.1013]

REID, JOHN, a merchant in Curacao, 1779. [NAS.CS16.1.175]

REID, JOHN, a merchant from Cromarty who settled in Carolina by 1771. [NAS.CS16.1.143]

REID, JOHN, a merchant from Dumfries who settled in Va. during 1740, died in Norfolk during 1791. [SM.53.568]

REID, PATRICK, trading between Ayr and Antigua, 1772. [NAS.E504.4.6]

REID, ROBERT, emigrated to Ga. in 1763, a merchant in partnership with Thomas Reid, and John Storr until 1774, then a planter on Skidaway Island, Ga., before 1776. [NA.AO12.101.352]

REID, THOMAS, son of Thomas Reid a Dundee merchant, a merchant in Jamaica before 1766. [DCA.H1906/1916] [NAS.RS35.16.xxi.439; CS16.1.175]

REID, THOMAS, a merchant who settled in Richmond, Va., before 1776. [NA.AO12.54.161]

REID, WILLIAM, a merchant from Aberdeen who settled at Reidburn on the Chester River, St Mary's County, Md., in 1722. [MSA.MdProvCt.L5/39; Lei/6]

REID, WILLIAM, a merchant and tobacco factor from Glasgow who settled in Fredericksburg, Va., before 1775. [GA:T79.1][NA.AO12.56.292]

REID and STEUART, merchants in London trading with Va., 1749. [NAS.CS16.1.81]

RENNIE, ROBERT, a merchant in Jamaica then in Montrose, 1780. [NAS.CS16.1.181]

RENNY, JAMES, a merchant from Angus who settled in Jamaica before 1783. [NAS.RD3.242.1202/67]

REOCH, ALEXANDER, a merchant in George Town, S.C., dead by 1779. [NA.AO13.80.408]

REYNOLDS, DAVID, a chapman in N.E., 1685. [SCS]
RICHMOND, WALTER, a merchant in Kingston, Jamaica, 1770. [NAS.RD4.211.55]
RIDDELL, ALEXANDER, born 1752, a merchant from Glasgow who settled in Baltimore, Md., died in Glasgow during 1825, probate Baltimore. [MSA.Baltimore Wills.8.406]
RIDDELL, ARCHIBALD, trading between Greenock and Va. and Md., 1745. [NAS.E504.15.2]
RIDDELL, GEORGE, a merchant and physician from West Lothian who settled in Yorktown, Va., in 1751, later moved to Williamsburg, died Va. 1779. [NA.AO13.8.161][NAS.CS16.1.117][SM.41.79/167]
RIDDELL, HENRY, a merchant from Glasgow who settled in Pitscataway, Md., before 1776, moved to Colchester, Fairfax County, Va., by 1779, partner of John Glassford in Md. pre 1776. [NA.AO12.80.17] [NAS.CS16.1.179]
RIDDELL, JAMES, a merchant in Guadaloupe, 1782. [NAS.CS17.1.1/97]
RIDDELL, JOHN, a merchant in Glasgow trading with S.C., 1728. [NAS.AC7.34.697]
RIDDELL, JOHN, a merchant from Glasgow who settled in Dumfries, Prince William County, Va., before 1769. [GA:CFI]
RIDDOCH, ALEXANDER, a merchant trading with the West Indies, 1645. [APS.6.1.457][NAS.GD34.833]
RIDDOCH, ALEXANDER, a merchant, from Leith to East N.J. in 1685. [NAS.E72.15.32]
RIDDOCH, JAMES, trading with the West Indies, before 1645. [APS.VI.i.457][NAS.GD34.833]
RIDDOCH, JOHN, a merchant in Barbados, 1717. [NAS.NRAS#3246, bundle 205]
RINTOUL, JOHN, and Company, merchants in Kirkcaldy, trading with Boston and the West Indies, 1783. [NAS.CS17.1.2]
RIOCH, CHARLES, a merchant in Edinburgh trading with Charleston, 1780. [NAS.CS16.1.181]
RISK, HUGH, a shopkeeper in Charleston before 1776, later in Glasgow. [NA.AO12.122/299]
RITCHIE, ALEXANDER, trading between Port Glasgow and Jamaica, 1745. [NAS.E504.28.2]

RITCHIE, ANDREW, a merchant in Boston by 1769, moved to Annapolis, Nova Scotia, by 1784. [NAS.CS16.1.134/250][NA.AO12.10.157]

RITCHIE, ARCHIBALD, a merchant and factor who settled in Caroline County, Va., in 1740, and in Tappahannock, Essex County, Va., in 1749, died 1784, probate Essex County, Va., 1784. [WMQ.2.18.90; 2.22.345] [DAB.15.328][VMHB.7.2.40]

RITCHIE, HENRY, a merchant who settled at Hobshole, Va., before 1755. [SA#59]

RITCHIE, JAMES, a merchant trading between Greenock and Va., 1744, 1745, 1746; trading between Port Glasgow and Maryland, 1735, [NAS.E512/1455]; trading between Port Glasgow and Va., 1743, 1744, 1745, 1747, 1748, 1749. [NAS.E504.15.1/2/3; E504.28.1/2/3]

RITCHIE, JAMES, a merchant in Glasgow trading with Va., 1769. [NAS.CS16.1.134]

RITCHIE, JAMES, a merchant who settled at Hobshole, Va., before 1775. [SA#59]

RITCHIE, JAMES, and Company, merchants in Glasgow trading to Va. before 1776. [NA.AO12.109.256; NRAS.0623/19]

RITCHIE, JOHN, trading between Greenock and Va., 1742, 1743, 1744, 1745, 1746; trading between Port Glasgow and Va., 1743, 1744, 1745, 1747, 1748, 1749. [NAS.E504.15.1/2/3; E504.28.1/2/3/4]

RITCHIE, JOHN, born around 1745, a merchant in Boston, settled in Annapolis Royal, Nova Scotia, around 1775, died 1790. [DCB.IV.674]

RITCHIE, SAMUEL, trading between Ayr and Philadelphia, 1759. [NAS.E504.4.3]

ROBB, JAMES, a factor from Glasgow who settled in Port Royal, Va. 1753-1756. [GA.T-MJ]

ROBB, WILLIAM, trading between Greenock and Boston, 1744. [NAS.E504.15.2]

ROBERTS, JOHN, born 1745, a merchant who emigrated via London to Ga. in 1775. [NA.T47.9/11]

ROBERTSON, ALEXANDER, a victualler in Charleston, probate S.C. 1724.

ROBERTSON, ANDREW, an assistant storekeeper who settled on the James River, Va., before 1776. [SFV#231]

SCOTTISH TRANSATLANTIC MERCHANTS

ROBERTSON, ANDREW, a merchant who emigrated to America in 1756, partner of John Jamieson and George Baillie in Charleston, S.C., before 1773, then in Savannah, Ga., died in London 1791.
[NA.AO12.51.111][GM.91.190][GaGaz#242]
ROBERTSON, ARCHIBALD, a merchant in New London, N.E., later in Appomatax, James River, Va.,1740s.
[NAS.CS16.1.71/72/75]
ROBERTSON, ARCHIBALD, a merchant in Edinburgh who emigrated before 1743 and settled in Petersburg, Va.
[VMHB.34.77][NAS.SC36.63.2][WMQ.5.185/237]
ROBERTSON, ARCHIBALD, a merchant who settled in Md. before 1750. [NAS.SC26.63.2]
ROBERTSON, ARTHUR, a merchant in Glasgow trading with Va., 1742. [NAS.CS16.1.70]
ROBERTSON, GEORGE, born 1741, a merchant from Aberdeen who emigrated via Greenock to Jamaica in 1775. [NA.T47.12]
ROBERTSON, GEORGE, born 1753, a merchant from Inverness who emigrated via Greenock to Nevis in 1774. [NAS.CE60.1.7]
ROBERTSON, JAMES, a merchant from Morayshire who settled in Jamaica before 1740. [NAS.RS29.6.449]
ROBERTSON, JAMES, a merchant in America, 1773.
[NAS.CS16.1.154]
ROBERTSON, JOHN, trading between Port Glasgow and Va., 1736, 1743, 1745. [NAS.E512/1455; E504.28.1/2]
ROBERTSON, JOHN, a merchant in Glasgow then in Va., 1754. [NAS.CS16.1.95]
ROBERTSON, JOHN BOYD, trading between Ayr and Grenada, 1769. [NAS.E504.4.5]
ROBERTSON, PATRICK, a merchant from Edinburgh who settled in New London, N.E., before 1742.
[NAS.RD4.211.547; CS16.1.70/71/75]
ROBERTSON, PATRICK, trading between Greenock and Va., 1745. [NAS.E504.15.2]
ROBERTSON, PETER, a merchant in Philadelphia, 1740.
[NAS.CS16.1.69/170]
ROBERTSON, ROBERT, a merchant in Glasgow trading with Guinea, Barbados, Nevis and St Kitts, 1720, and Va. and Md., 1725. [NAS.AC7.33.433-583; AC8.310]
ROBERTSON, ROBERT, born 1740, a merchant in N.Y., died in 1805. [ANY.I.218]

ROBERTSON, ROBERT, a merchant from Perth who settled in Philadelphia by 1780. [NAS.CS16.1.170/179]

ROBERTSON, WALTER, a merchant from Glasgow who settled in Petersburg, Va., before 1765. [NAS.CS16.1.173][GA: T-MJ]

ROBERTSON, WILLIAM, a shopkeeper from Aberdeen, to the American colonies in 1769. [AJ#1115]

ROBERTSON, WILLIAM, a merchant in Va., 1771. [NAS.CS16.1.146]

ROBERTSON, WILLIAM, a merchant in Antigua, 1776. [NAS.CS16.1.168]

ROBINSON, GEORGE, a merchant, from Glasgow to Boston in 1767. [PAB]

ROBINSON, JAMES, a merchant from Glasgow who settled in Falmouth, on the Rappahannock River, Va., in 1767. [GA: CFI][NA.AO12.56]

ROBINSON, JOHN, a factor who settled in Falmouth, Va., from 1767 to 1774. [NAS.John C. Brodie pp]

ROBISON, JAMES, a factor from Ayrshire who emigrated via Glasgow to Va. during 1761 and settled on the Rappahannock River. [NAS.NRAS.1892]

ROCHEAD, JAMES, a merchant from Edinburgh who settled in N.Y., probate Monmouth, N.J. 1740. [Monmouth Wills, Liber C, fo.378]

ROCHEAD, JOHN, a merchant in Jamaica, a burgess of Glasgow, 1719. [GBR]

ROLLAND, JAMES, a merchant burgess of Ayr, died in St Kitts 1646. [see testaments, Glasgow, 1648 & 1649, NAS]

ROME, GEORGE, a merchant in Newport, Rhode Island, pre 1776. [NA.AO12.72.93]

ROME, THOMAS, of Clouden, a merchant in Antigua, 1715, 1718. [NAS.RD2.104.657/665/739/991; RD4.117.321; GD78.208; GD135.1615]

RONALD, GEORGE, a merchant from Glasgow who settled on Cape Fear, N.C., during 1738, moved to Bladen County in 1757. [NAS.CC8.8.107][Bladen County Deed Book#23]

ROSE, ALEXANDER, born 1738, a merchant from Inverness who emigrated to America before 1755 and settled in Va. and N.C., died in Person County, N.C., 1807. [RSA#137][NAS.CS16.1.130]

ROSE, CHARLES, a merchant from Tain who settled in Smithfield, Va., before 1776. [NAS.AC7.50/55; CS.GMB.55]

ROSE, DUNCAN, a merchant in Glasgow, settled in Va. before 1764. [NAS.B10.15.6969]

ROSE, DUNCAN, a merchant in Glasgow trading with Va., 1773. [NAS.CS16.1.154]

ROSE, JOHN, a merchant from Forres who died in Va. during 1762. [DRF]

ROSEWELL, ANTHONY, a merchant trading between Leith and Barbados, 1666. [NAS.RD2.16.323; RD4.16.874]

ROSS, ALEXANDER, jr., merchant in Aberdeen trading with Pensacola, West Fla., 1767, with St Augustine 1769, with Grenada, 1783. [AJ#1017/1123/1872]

ROSS, ALEXANDER, a merchant in N.E., dead by 1772. [NAS.SH.10.12.1772]

ROSS, ALEXANDER, a storekeeper in Falmouth, Maine, c1770. [NA.AO12.11.42]

ROSS, ANDREW, a merchant in Musselburgh, trading with S.C., pre 1738. [NAS.AC7.43.213; CS16.1.69]

ROSS, ANDREW, a merchant from Glasgow who settled in Va. and died in 1752. [SM.14.365][MAGU#3]

ROSS, DANIEL, a merchant in Nevis, 1778. [NAS.CS16.1.173/434]

ROSS, DAVID, a physician and merchant who settled in Bladenburg, Md., probate Prince George 1778. [MSA.Chancery.48/390; Prince George County Wills T1/107]

ROSS, DAVID, a merchant in Baton Rouge, West Fla., 1787. [NAS.CS17.1.2/6/15]

ROSS, GEORGE, a merchant in Baton Rouge, West Fla., 1783. [NAS.CS17.1.2]

ROSS, HECTOR, a merchant in Colchester, Va., 1786. [NAS.CS17.1.15/134]

ROSS, HUGH, a shopkeeper in Savannah, Ga., died there 1774, probate Chatham County, 1775. [GaGaz#3/1]

ROSS, JOHN, a merchant from Aberdeen who settled in Norfolk, Va., before 1760. [MSA.Prince George County Record Book, 12.5.1760]

ROSS, JOHN, born 1729, a merchant from Perth who settled in N.Y. in 1762, and in Philadelphia in 1763, died there in 1800. [ANY.I.400][AP#311][NAS.CS16.1.117]

ROSS, JOHN, a merchant in Tain then in Philadelphia, 1764. [NAS.CS16.1.117/141]
ROSS, JOHN, a merchant in Tobago who died in Cork 1781. [GM.IV.78]
ROSS, JOHN, from Aberdeenshire, an Indian trader at Fort Pitt, then a planter and merchant in East Fla., before 1781, then moved to Dominica in 1785. [NAS.GD186]
ROSS, JOHN, a merchant at Loch Broom then in America, 1782, in Edinburgh, 1783. [NAS.CS17.1.1/2; AC7.62]
ROSS, ROBERT, a merchant from Aberdeen who settled at Pensacola, West Fla., in 1764, by 1772 he was a merchant and planter on the Mississippi, moved to Shelburne, Nova Scotia, by 1785. [NA.AO13.26.414] [NAS.CS17.1.2]
ROSS, THOMAS, an Indian trader in Ga., probate Ga. 1766.
ROSS, WILLIAM, a merchant at Port Maria Bay, St Mary's, Jamaica, 1780. [NAS.CS16.1.179; CS17.1.2]
ROSS, WILLIAM, a merchant in Jamaica, son of David Ross in Roslin, 1783. [NAS.CS17.1.22/257]
ROSS, SHORE, and Company, merchants in Petersburg, Va., 1783. [NAS.RD2.237.825]
ROUGHEAD, JAMES, from Berwickshire, a merchant in Port Royal, Jamaica, 1715. [NAS.RD3.144.151; RD4.117.295]
ROWAND, JOHN, a merchant in Glasgow, trading between Greenock and Va., 1742, 1745, 1753, 1756; between Port Glasgow and Va./Md., 1745, 1747. [NAS.E504.15.1/2, 28/2/3; AC7.46.185/212; CS16.1.98]
ROWAND, WILLS, and ROWAND, merchants in Charleston, 1756. [NAS.CS16.1.98/99]
ROXBURGH, WILLIAM, from Kilmarnock, a merchant in Quebec, 1783. [NAS.SH.]
RUGBIE, JOHN, a merchant in Leith and Barbados, 1666. [NAS.RD2.16.323]
RUSSELL, ANDREW, a Scots merchant in Rotterdam trading with Surinam and Boston, 1688. [NAS.MP258.65.308; RH15.106.box 20]
RUSSELL, DAVID, a merchant who settled in Blandford, Va., before 1776, returned to Glasgow. [NA.AO12.109.260]
RUSSELL, FRANCIS, a merchant in Leith trading with S.C. and New Providence, 1750s. [NAS.CS96.1583]

RUSSELL, ROBERT, a merchant trading between Greenock and Va., 1743; between Port Glasgow and Va. and Md., 1744, 1749. [NAS.E504.15.1; 28.1/4]

RUSSELL, SAMUEL, a merchant in Marblehead, Essex County, Massachusetts Bay, 1722. [NAS.GD155.705]

RUTHERFORD, JAMES, a gold and silver merchant from Edinburgh, in Charleston, S.C., 1751. [SCGaz#914]

RUTHERFORD, JOHN, of Bowland, a merchant at Cape Fear, N.C., 1752. [NAS.RD4.178.2]

RUTHERFORD, ROBERT, a merchant who settled in Winchester, Va., by 1765. [NAS.CS16.1.122]

RUTHERFORD, THOMAS, born 1766, a merchant from Glasgow who emigrated to Va. and settled in Richmond during 1783, died there in 1852. [MAGU#123][USNA.M932/982]

RUTHERFORD, WALTER, born 1723, a soldier and merchant who emigrated to America before 1758, settled in Hunterdon County, N.Y., and died in N.Y. during 1804. [NAS.RD2.210.911]

SADDLER, JAMES, a merchant in St Kitts, then in Bristol, 1782. [NAS.CS17.1.1/37/120/183]

SADDLER, WILLIAM, a merchant who settled in St Kitts during 1758 and died there before 1781. [NAS.CS237.14.1; SH.21.2.1781]

SANDELIN, JACOB EVERTSEN, (James Sandeland) to Delaware with Swedish West India Company in 1638, later a merchant skipper on the Delaware River by 1646. [SSD]

SANDS, ALEXANDER, born 1758, a chapman from Edinburgh who emigrated via Leith to Philadelphia in 1775. [NA.T47.12]

SANDS, JAMES, a merchant in Charleston, S.C., by 1763, who died in there during 1769. [SM.31.502][AJ#1133][SAS]

SANGSTER, GEORGE, trading between Greenock and Va., 1745; between Port Glasgow and Va., 1747. [NAS.E504.15.2; 28.3]

SAYERS, JOHN, a merchant in Leith trading with Va. in 1667, 1683. [NAS.E72.15.6/12]

SCHAW, ROBERT, a merchant who settled in N.C. by 1751, partner in the firm of Duncan, Ancrum and Schaw merchants in Wilmington, died 1786. [SCHM] [Wilmington Town Book, 1743-1778, Raleigh, 1973]

SCHEVIZ, ALEXANDER, merchant in Blandford, Prince George County, Va., pre 1776, then in Glasgow. [NA.AO13.4.195]

SCOLLAY, JOHN, a merchant from Orkney who settled in Jamaica before 1788. [NAS.NRAS.0627, box 23, bundle 41]

SCOTLAND, JOHN, a merchant from Edinburgh who settled in Antigua before 1773. [NAS.RD3.232.432]

SCOTT, ALEXANDER, a merchant from Glasgow who settled in Norfolk, Va., before 1755. [GA:CFI]

SCOTT, ALEXANDER, trading between Leith and S.C., 1775. [NAS.E504.22]

SCOTT, ANDREW, a merchant, trading from Ayr to the Caribee Islands in 1683. [NAS.E72.3.12]

SCOTT, ANDREW, a merchant in Md., 1748. [NAS.CS16.1.80]

SCOTT, ARCHIBALD, a merchant in Glasgow, trading between Glasgow, Barbados, and the Caribee Islands, 1670. [RPCS.3.259]

SCOTT, DAVID, a merchant from Edinburgh who settled in Antigua before 1779. [NAS.RD4.226.1004]

SCOTT, DAVID, a book-seller from Montrose who settled in S.C. 1785. [NAS.CS17.1.4/217]

SCOTT, DONALD, & Co. (Robert Scott, James Dennistoun jr., Richard Dennistoun) merchants in Glasgow trading in Hanover,Va., before 1776. [NA.AO12.109.276]

SCOTT, FRANCIS, a Scots merchant in London trading with Va., 1689. [NAS.RH15.14.46]

SCOT, FRANCIS, a merchant in Dumfries then in Va., 1748. [NAS.CS16.1.80]

SCOTT, GEORGE, a merchant in Greenock trading with Jamaica, 1773. [NAS.CS16.1.154]

SCOTT, HUGH, a merchant from Glasgow who settled in N.C., probate Bertie County 1736.

SCOTT, JAMES, trading between Greenock and Va., 1742, 1743, 1744, 1745, 1746, also St Kitts, 1743. [NAS.E504.15.1/2]

SCOTT, JAMES, born 1764, a merchant in N.Y. from 1780, died 1826. [ANY.2.186][F.2.234]

SCOTT, JOHN, a merchant in Duckesburg, Staten Island, N.Y., 1700. [NAS.NRAS.0479/29]

SCOTT, JOHN, trading between Port Glasgow and Jamaica, 1745, between Port Glasgow and St Kitts, 1746. [NAS.E504.28.2]

SCOTT, JOSEPH, a merchant trading between Greenock and Barbados, 1743; between Port Glasgow and S.C., 1745. [NAS.E504.15.1; 28.2]

SCOTT, ROBERT, a merchant in Caroline County, Va., 1764. [NAS.RD2.197.470]

SCOTT, ROBERT, and Company, trading between Greenock and Boston, 1745, 1746. [NAS.E504.15.2]

SCOTT, ROBERT, JAMES WATSON and Company, trading between Greenock and Boston, 1743, 1744. [NAS.E504.1]

SCOTT, ROBERT, ALEXANDER CARLIE, and Company, trading between Greenock and Boston, 1744. [NAS.E504.15.1]

SCOTT, ROBERT, trading between Port Glasgow and Va., 1747. [NAS.E504.28.3]

SCOTT, SAMUEL, a merchant who emigrated via Portsmouth to Barbados in 1776. [NAS.T47.9/11]

SCOTT, THOMAS, assistant storekeeper to John Baird and Company in Blandford, Prince George County, Va., from 1771-1775, then in Glasgow. [see NA.AO12.109.210]

SCOTT, WILLIAM, a merchant from Dumfries who settled in Charleston, probate S.C. 1765.

SCOTT, WILLIAM HENRY, son of Alexander Scott a merchant in Edinburgh, a merchant in St Eustatius, died in Antigua, 1789. [GM.XII.601/212]

SCOURE, WILLIAM, born 1753, a merchant from Stirling who emigrated via Greenock to Antigua in 1775. [NA.T47.12]

SEAMAN, GEORGE, a merchant in Charleston by 1734. [NAS.CS16.1.69; RD3.210.490][SAS]

SEAMAN, GEORGE, born 1735, emigrated in 1749, a merchant from Leith in S.C., 1755, who died in Charleston, S.C., in 1769, probate PCC 1769, probate S.C. 1769. [NAS.CS16.1.120/170; AC7.49.14; AC9.1960]

SEAMAN, JAMES, a merchant in Charleston, 1738. [NAS.AC7.43.213]

SEATON, HENRY, a merchant in St Kitts, 1776; a merchant in the West Indies before 1781. [NLS#8793/21][NA.CO5.Vol.III]

SELKIRK, ROBERT, late a merchant in Boston, 1788.
[ERA]
SELKRIG, ALEXANDER, merchant in Boston, partner in the house of James Selkrig and Company, pre 1773.
[NA.AO12.109.278]
SELKRIG, JAMES, from Lanarkshire, a merchant in Boston, partner in the house of James Selkrig and Company, pre 1773. [NA.AO12.109.278]
SELKRIG, ROBERT, a merchant, from Glasgow to Boston in 1767. [PAB]
SEMPILL, WILLIAM, a merchant from N.Y. trading in Delaware, 1676. [NYHist.msDutch.XX/XXI.102/313]
SEMPLE, JOHN, a merchant from Glasgow who settled in Portobacco, Md., before 1757, later in N.Y.
[NAS.CS230.19/21; B10.15.7082; CS16.1.122]
[PCCol#5.543]
SEMPLE, JOHN, JOHN JAMIESON, and JAMES LAWSON, merchants in Glasgow and Md., 1750s.
[NAS.CS96.1176-1203]
SEMPLE, ROBERT, trading between Port Glasgow and St Kitts, 1748 [NAS.E504.28.3]
SEMPLE ROBERT, a merchant in Boston before 1776.
[NA.AO13.43.69]
SEMPLE, WILLIAM, trading between Port Glasgow and Jamaica, 1744; between Port Glasgow and Montserrat, 1744. [NAS.E504.28.2]
SERVICE, GEORGE, merchant in Boston pre 1778.
[NA.AO13.83.435]
SERVICE, ROBERT, merchant from Saltcoats, settled in Boston by 1765. [SCS][NA.AO13.83.435]
SHANNON, JOHN, trading between Port Glasgow and Va., 1747. [NAS.E504.28.3]
SHARP, ALEXANDER, and Company, trading with America and the West Indies, 1743-1758. [NAS.NRAS.0396.245]
SHARP, ALEXANDER, a merchant in Perth then in America, 1783. [NAS.CS17.1.2]
SHAW, ALEXANDER, a merchant in Va., 1778.
[NAS.CS16.1.173]
SHAW, ALEXANDER, a bookseller, late of Turnbull and Shaw in Va. then in Kingston, Jamaica, 1781.
[NAS.CS17.1.7/90]
SHAW, ALEXANDER, a merchant in Inverness trading with Nova Scotia, 1783. [NAS.CS16.1.2]

SHAW, THOMAS, a merchant in Barbados, probate Barbados 1720. [BA: RB.6.6.137]

SHEDDEN, JOHN, to Va. 1764, merchant in Norfolk, Va., 1783, then in Glasgow by 1785. [NAS.CS17.1.2/248; AC7.60]

SHEDDEN, ROBERT, merchant from Beith, Ayrshire, who settled in Portsmouth and in Norfolk, Va., before 1767. [NAS.SH.17.11.1767; CS16.1.154/161] [NA.AO12.56.104]

SHEDDEN, WILLIAM RALSTON, born 1747, a merchant from Ayrshire who settled in Va., Bermuda, and N.Y., died there in 1798; probate PCC 1852. [NA.AO13.83.389] [NAS.SH.20.12.1771; CS16.1.161; CS17.1.7/265; GD1.67/1] [HAF.1.275][AJ#2661] [ActsPCCol.1780/375]

SHEPHERD, ANDREW, born 1759, a merchant from Aberdeen who settled in Va. [MCA.2.342]

SHEPHERD, WILLIAM, a merchant in Aberdeen trading with Va. 1750. [NAS.E504.1.3]

SHERIFF & GUTHRIE, trading between Leith and S.C., 1765. [NAS.E504.22]

SHERLOCK, ROBERT, a merchant, from Scotland to Boston in 1763. [PAB]

SHIRRAS, ALEXANDER, born 1753, a merchant from Aberdeenshire who settled in Charleston, S.C., in 1781, died 1811. [St Michael's gravestone, Charleston]

SIBBALD, JOHN, from Kirkcaldy, a merchant in Philadelphia, 1772. [NAS.B41.7.8/187]

SIMPSON, ARCHIBALD, a merchant in Islay then in America, 1780. [NAS.CS16.1.179]

SIMPSON, JAMES, trading between Port Glasgow and Va., 1747, 1748. [NAS.E504.28.3]

SIMPSON, JAMES, a merchant in Glasgow then in St Kitts, 1765, settled in Grenada and died before 1779. [NAS.CS16.1.120/177][NLS.Acc.8793/13]

SIMPSON, JOHN, a merchant from Dumfries-shire who settled in Charleston, S.C., before 1764, and in Sunbury, Ga., by 1774, died in Edinburgh, probate PCC 1788. [NAS.SC15.55.2; RD4.212.722; CS16.1.157/165] [GaGaz#291]

SIMPSON, JOHN, born 1728, a merchant from Glasgow who settled in St Vincent before 1750. [NAS.RS42.17.16]

SIMPSON, THOMAS, factor in Hanover Town, York River, Va., for Donald Scott and Company, pre 1776. [NA.AO13.83.404]

SIMPSON, WILLIAM, emigrated to America in 1766, a merchant in S.C. before 1776, returned to Edinburgh by 1784. [NA.AO12.92.2]

SIMSON, JOHN, of Moyret, a merchant from Glasgow who settled in New London, Connecticut, from 1769 to 1772. [NAS.CS16.1.134/151]

SINCLAIR, ALEXANDER, of Auchtergall, a merchant in Kingston, Jamaica, 1781. [NAS.CS16.1.184]

SINCLAIR, ARCHIBALD, a merchant and attorney in Jamaica, 1760. [EUL.Laing.msII]

SINCLAIR, ARCHIBALD, a merchant from Greenock, settled in Kingston, Jamaica, before 1781. [NAS.RD2.235.39; RD2.236.651]

SINCLAIR, GUSTAVUS, a merchant in Edinburgh trading with Boston, 1736. [NAS.AC13.1; AC10.246]

SINCLAIR, KENNEDY, a merchant in Jamaica, 1773. [NAS.CS16.1.154]

SINCLAIR, RICHARD, a merchant in Charleston by 1732, probate S.C. 1733. [SAS]

SINCLAIR, ROBERT, a merchant in Albany, N.Y., 1766, dead by 1777. [NAS.RS18.8.135/227; CS16.1.168/171]

SINCLAIR, BREBNER and Company, merchants in Greenock trading with Newfoundland, Quebec, N.Y., Halifax, Grenada, Jamaica, St Kitts, St Eustatius, St Vincent, and Tobago, 1778-1782. [NAS.CS96.1413-1415]

SINCLAIR and FERRIE and Company, merchants in N.Y., 1780. [NAS.CS236.Misc.6/1, 15/1; RD2.235/1.39]

SKEEN, JAMES, a merchant in Aberdeen trading with the Leeward Islands, 1771. [AJ#1245]

SKENE, ALEXANDER, a merchant in Norfolk, Va., 1730. [NAS.GD237.20.8.32]

SKENE, JOHN, born 1649, a merchant from Aberdeen who settled in West N.J. during 1682. [NYGBR.XXX]

SKINNER, DAVID, trading between Port Glasgow and the Isle of May, 1748. [NAS.E504.28.4]

SLATER, JAMES, a chapman from Glasgow who emigrated via Greenock to N.Y. in 1774. [NA.T47.12]

SCOTTISH TRANSATLANTIC MERCHANTS

SLOWAN, ANDREW, trading between Port Glasgow and Va., 1744; trading between Ayr and Va., 1750, 1754, 1755, 1756. [NAS.E504.4.2; E504.28.1]
SMELLIE, JAMES, trading between Greenock and Va., 1742, 1745. [NAS.E504.1/2]
SMELLIE, JOHN, a merchant from Glasgow who settled in Kingston, Jamaica, before 1729. [NAS.SH.2.5.1729]
SMELLIE AND HOPKIRK, trading between Port Glasgow and Va., 1749. [NAS.E504.28.4]
SMILLIE, JAMES, trading between Port Glasgow and the Va. and Md., 1744; between Greenock and Va., 1746. [NAS.E504.28.1; 15.2]
SMITH, ALEXANDER, merchant in Aberdeen trading with Antigua, 1770, 1772. [AJ#1185/1297]
SMITH, DAVID, a merchant trading between Ayr and Montserrat in 1678. [NAS.E72.3.4]
SMITH, ENGLISH, a merchant in N.Y., 1684. [RPCS.8.377]
SMITH, JAMES, jr. a merchant in Montrose trading with Africa and Antigua, 1754. [NAS.AC7.46.51]
SMITH, JOHN, a merchant in Fredericia, Ga., 1749. [St Helen's marriage register, Beaufort County, S.C.]
SMITH, JOHN, trading between Ayr and Jamaica, 1750. [NAS.E504.4.2]
SMITH, JOHN, trading between Leith and S.C., 1765. [NAS.E504.22]
SMITH, MUNGO, trading between Ayr and Boston, 1764. [NAS.E504.4.3]
SMITH, PATRICK, born 1747, a merchant from Glasgow who emigrated to Jamaica in 1763. [NAS.B10.15.7085]
SMITH, WILLIAM, born 1750, a merchant from Aberdeenshire who settled in Quebec then in Charleston, S.C., from 1784, died 1814. [NAS.CS17.1.8/347][St Michael's gravestone, Charleston]
SMITH, WILLIAM, a merchant in Edinburgh trading with N.Y., 1766. [NAS.CS16.1.126]
SMITH and BAILLIE, merchants in St Kitts, 1766. [NAS.SC29.55.11.331]
SMITH, STRACHAN, & Company, merchants in Dundee, trading between Dundee and S.C., 1756, 1757, 1759, 1760, 1763, [NAS.E504.11]
SNODGRASS, JOHN, a factor or store-manager in Goochland County, Va., before 1776. [NAS.B10.12.4, fo.124-7; AC7.58]

SNODGRASS, NEIL, a merchant from Paisley who emigrated to America by 1758, settled in Norfolk, Va., and in Pasquotank County, N.C., before 1776, died in N.Y. during 1782, testament Edinburgh 1788, probate PCC 1785. [NA.AO12.103.8][NAS.CS16.1.114]

SNODGRASS, WILLIAM, a factor and merchant from Glasgow who settled in Va. during 1766, later in Richmond. [NAS.B10.15.8269; CS.GMB.58; AC7.58]

SOMERVAIL, DAVID, trading between Leith and S.C., 1745. [NAS.E504.22]

SOMERVILLE, GEORGE, a merchant in North America, 1765. [NAS.CS16.1.122]

SOMERVILLE, JAMES, born 1744, a merchant from Midlothian who settled in Baltimore, Md., before 1769, died there in 1806.
[NAS.CS16.1.138][DPCA#213][CD.3.533]

SOMERVILLE, JOHN, trading between Greenock and Va., 1743, Barbados, 1744; between Port Glasgow and Md., 1744; between Port Glasgow and Antigua, 1747.
[NAS.E504.15.1; E504.28.1/3]

SOMERVILLE, JOHN, a merchant who settled in St Mary's County, Md., and Va., before 1763. [NAS.RD4.208.430; CS16.1.122/143]

SOMERVILLE, ROBERT, trading between Port Glasgow and Jamaica, 1748; between Port Glasgow and Antigua, 1748. [NAS.E504.28.3/4]

SOMERVILLE, WILLIAM, trading between Port Glasgow and Jamaica, 1748; between Port Glasgow and Antigua, 1748. [NAS.E504.28.3/4]

SOMERVILLE, GORDON, and Company, merchants in Glasgow trading with Jamaica, 1778. [NAS.AC7.56]

SPALDING, JAMES, a merchant from Edinburgh who settled in East Fla. and Ga. before 1756, partner in the firm of Spalding and Kelsall, in Savannah. [NA.AO13.83.523] [NAS.RS27.201.215; GD174; RD4.259.758; CS16.1.138]

SPARK, ALEXANDER, a merchant from Kincardineshire who settled in Westmoreland County, Va., probate Westmoreland 1767

SPEIRS, ALEXANDER, born 1714, a merchant and planter who emigrated to Va. in 1740 and settled in Elderslie, a merchant in Glasgow by 1781, died there 1782.
[NAS.B10.15.5943; CS16.1.126/183; NRAS.0607.2-7]

SPEIRS, ALEXANDER, & JOHN BOWMAN, merchants in Glasgow trading in Va. pre 1776. [NA.AO12.109.276]

SPEIRS, JAMES, a merchant and planter from Glasgow who settled in Va. before 1754. [NAS.B10.15.6653]

SPEIRS, FRENCH, and Company, of Glasgow trading to Md. before 1776. [NA.AO12.9.49] [NAS.CS16.1.177]

SPENCE, ROBERT, a merchant from Kirkcaldy, emigrated to Va. in 1769, a merchant in Va. before 1776, later in St Augustine, possibly in N.Y., 1781. [NAS.HCR.1.104; CS16.1.184][NA.AO12.102.238]

SPENCE, WALTER, born 1750, a merchant from Edinburgh who emigrated via Greenock to Ga. in 1774. [NA.T47.12]

SPENCE, WALTER, a merchant in N.Y., 1783. [NAS.CS17.1.2]

SPENS, ROBERT, a merchant from Glasgow then in America, 1784. [NAS.CS17.1.3/341]

SPOTTISWOOD, JAMES, of Dunipace, a merchant in Jamaica before 1756. [NAS.GD1.529/255; RGS.103.161][Edinburgh Marriage Register, 25.2.1753]

SPRATT, JOHN, a merchant from Galloway in Boston by 1685, later in N.Y. by 1687. [SCS] [Dutch Reformed Church Register of N.Y.]

SPROAT, DAVID, a merchant in Philadelphia before 1776. [NA.AO12.42.345]

SPROULE, ANDREW, a merchant from Galloway who settled in Gosport, Va., c1733-1775, testament Edinburgh 1779, probate PCC 1782. [NAS.CS16.1.181; CS17.1.1/91; SH.1.2.1777; CC8.8.124] [NA.AO12.54.283]

SPRUILL, JAMES, trading between Port Glasgow and Md., 1745. [NAS.E504.28.2]

STARK, JOHN, merchant in Glasgow trading with Jamaica, 1730; trading between Port Glasgow and Va., 1736. [NAS.AC7.35.1065; E512/1455]

STARK, MARK, a merchant in Dunfermline trading with Pa., 1773. [NAS.CS16.1.154]

STARK, CROSS, and Company, merchants in Glasgow, trading with Va. and Jamaica, 1765. [NAS.CS16.1.125]

STEEL, JOHN, a merchant from Glasgow who settled in Savannah la Mar, Jamaica, before 1782. [NAS.B10.15.8403]

STEUART, CHARLES, a merchant in Va., 1756. [NAS.CS16.1.99]

STEVENSON, ANDREW, trading between Ayr and Newfoundland, 1772. [NAS.E504.4.5]

STEVENSON, JOHN, and Company, trading between Greenock and Boston, also Va., 1743, 1744, 1745, 1746; between Greenock and St Kitts, 1746; between Greenock and Jamaica, 1746; trading between Port Glasgow and Va., 1743, 1744, 1745; between Port Glasgow and Jamaica, 1743, 1744, 1745, 1747; between Port Glasgow and St Kitts, also Va., 1744, 1745, 1748; between Port Glasgow and Antigua, 1744; between Port Glasgow and Jamaica, 1745; between Port Glasgow and Boston, 1746; between Port Glasgow and S.C., 1746; between Port Glasgow and Barbados, 1746, 1748; between Port Glasgow and Va., 1746, 1749; between Port Glasgow and Md., 1747; between Port Glasgow and Boston, 1747; between Port Glasgow and New York, 1747; between Port Glasgow and St Kitts, 1748; between Port Glasgow and the Isle of May, 1748. [NAS.E504.15.1/2; E504.28.1/2/3/4]

STEVENSON, JOHN, a merchant in Glasgow, land grant in Ga., 1751. [NA.CO5.669]

STEVENSON, ROBERT, a merchant, from Glasgow to Boston in 1763. [PAB]

STEWART, ADAM, a merchant from Ayr, partner of Colin Dunlop in Georgetown, Montgomery County, Md., in 1755; a merchant at Rock Creek, Frederick County, Md., before 1776, returned to Ayr. [NA.AO12.8.54]

STEWART, ALEXANDER, born 1725, emigrated to America around 1744, settled in Bath, N.C., as a timber merchant and planter, died 1772. [SFG]

STEWART, ALEXANDER, trading between Ayr and Antigua, 1773. [NAS.E504.4.6]

STEWART, ANTHONY, a merchant from Edinburgh who settled in Annapolis, Md., in 1753. [NAS.CS17.1.2][NA.AO12.6.322]

STEWART, ARCHIBALD, a merchant in Rotterdam later in Tobago, 1778. [NAS.CS16.1.173/313]

STEWART, CHARLES, a merchant who settled in Va. before 1756. [NAS.CS16.1.99]

STEWART, DOUGALL, a merchant who settled in Kingston, Jamaica, and died before 1777. [NAS.RD3.237.36]

SCOTTISH TRANSATLANTIC MERCHANTS

STEWART, HUGH, a merchant in Glasgow, trading with Va. in 1751. [NAS.CS16.1.185]
STEWART, JOHN, a planter and Indian trader in Carolina and Va. from 1689. [FS][SCHGM.32.33]
STEWART, JOHN, a storekeeper who settled in Va. before 1771. [SFV#41]
STEWART, PETER, a merchant in Campbeltown then in St John's Island, 1777/1778. [NAS.CS16.1.171/173]
STEWART, ROBERT, a merchant in Aberdeen trading with Va., 1711. [NAS.AC7.17.352]
STEWART, ROBERT, merchant in Portsmouth, Va., 1780. [NAS.CS16.1.179]
STEWART, ROBERT and ROGER, merchants in Portsmouth, Va., returned to Greenock by 1783. [NA.AO12.54.418]
STEWART, ROGER, a merchant who settled in Portsmouth, Va., before 1776, then in Greenock. [NA.AO13.33.247][NAS.CS16.1.179]
STEWART, THOMAS, born 1666, a merchant from Galloway who settled in Bridgetown, Barbados, died England 1722, probate Barbados 1723.
STEWART, WILLIAM, born 1750, a merchant from Ayr who emigrated via Greenock to Jamaica in 1775; 1779. [NA.T47.12] [NAS.CS16.1.175]
STILL, JOHN, a merchant in Aberdeen trading with Antigua, 1769. [AJ#1105]
STIRLING, ALEXANDER, trading between Greenock and Va., 1743, 1744, 1745; between Greenock and Boston, 1746; trading between Port Glasgow and Va., 1743, 1745, 1749. [NAS.E504.1/2; E504.28.1/2/4]
STIRLING, HUGH, a merchant from Glasgow who settled in Ogychee, Ga., in 1734. [NAS.CO5.670.127]
STIRLING, JAMES, in Kingston, Jamaica, 1765. [NAS.GD201.5.130]
STIRLING, ROBERT, a merchant from Glasgow who 'died abroad' [Darien?], testament Edinburgh 1707. [NAS.CC8.8.83]
STIRLING, ROBERT, son of James Stirling of Keir, a merchant in Kingston, Jamaica, a burgess of Ayr, 1751. [ABR]
STIRLING, WILLIAM, a merchant from Glasgow who settled in Ogychee, Ga., in 1734. [NA.CO5.670.128]

STIRLING, WILLIAM, a merchant in Glasgow trading with N.E., 1772; trading between Ayr and Antigua, 1774. [NAS.CS16.1.151; E504.4.6]

STIVEN, WILLIAM, a merchant from Aberdeen who emigrated to Jamaica in 1715, settled at Gunaboa, died before 1734. [ACA:APB.3.3]

STOBIE, JAMES, a merchant in Charleston around 1773. [ERA]

STOBO, ROBERT, born 1726, a merchant from Glasgow who settled in Williamsburg, Va., 1742, died in Chatham, 1770. [NAS.SC36.63.2][DCB.3.600]

STODDART, WILLIAM, trading between Leith and S.C., 1775. [NAS.E504.22]

STODDART and FAIRBAIRN, merchants in Edinburgh trading with Jamaica and Antigua, 1767-1787. [NAS.CS96.1476, etc]

STRACHAN, CHARLES, an Indian trader in Mobile, West Fla., from 1763 to 1768, returned to Montrose in 1768. [NLS#ms119]

STRACHAN, JAMES, trading between Leith and S.C., 1745. [NAS.E504.22]

STRAITON, THOMAS, a merchant in Jamaica, a burgess of Ayr, 1751. [ABR]

STRAITON, WILLIAM, a merchant in Jamaica, dead by 1743. [NAS.GD170.353]

STRATFORD, DANIEL, a merchant in N.Y., 1750. [NAS.CS16.1.84]

STRUTHERS, A., a merchant in Pensacola, West Fla., 1781. [NAS.NRAS#0174]

STRUTHERS, JAMES, trading between Port Glasgow and Montserrat, 1744. [NAS.E504.28.1]

STRUTHERS, WILLIAM, born 1733, an Indian trader in Augusta, Ga., probate Ga. 1761. [NA.CO5.648.E68]

STRUTHERS, WILLIAM, a merchant in Mobile, West Fla., 1769. [NAS.RD4.205.1]

STUART, CHARLES, a merchant from Leith who settled in S.C. and died there before 1718, testament Edinburgh 1718. [NAS.CC8.8.87]

STUART, FRANCIS, a merchant in Beaufort County, S.C., by 1752. [St Helen's Marriage Register, 28.12.1752][SAS]

STUART, JOHN, a merchant from Edinburgh then in Carolina before 1700, see his wife Henrietta Burnett's testament, [NAS.CC8.8.67]

SUTHERLAND, ..., a merchant from Greenock then in Jamaica, 1757. [AUL.ms1160.5.12]
SUTHERLAND and GRANT, merchants in Montreal, 1783. [NAS.CS17.1.2]
SWAN, JAMES, a merchant in Boston by 1778. [NAS.CS16.1.174; CS17.1.3/140; CS17.1.17/27; CS17.1.16/195][SCS]
SWAN, ROBERT, a merchant in Annapolis, Md., pre 1750, possibly a factor for James Johnston a merchant in Glasgow. [MdGaz#292/293][NAS.CS16.1.89/107/115]
SWINTON, Sir JOHN, a Scots merchant in London trading with Barbados, Md., N.E., and Va., 1670s. [NAS.CS96.3264]
SWINTON, WILLIAM, a merchant from Stirling who emigrated from the Clyde to Darien in 1699. [RSB#91]
SYM, ANDREW, merchant in Glasgow trading between Port Glasgow and Md., 1743, 1745; between Port Glasgow and Virginia, 1747, 1748, [NAS.E504.28.1/2/3]; with Va., 1746, pre 1776, in partnership with William Dunlop. [NA.A013.83.684]
SYM, JOHN, a merchant in Norfolk, Va., partner of John Shedden and Company, before 1776. [NA.AO.13.83.682]
SYME, ANDREW, a merchant in Glasgow trading with Va., 1766. [NAS.CS16.1.126]
SYME, JAMES, a merchant in Massachusetts before 1766. [NAS.CS16.1.125/85]
SYME, JOHN, a merchant in Boston, Massachusetts, then in Westminster, 1766. [NAS.CS16.1.126]
SYMMER, ALEXANDER, a merchant from Edinburgh who settled in Md. before 1756. [SM.18.524]
SYMMER, ANDREW, a merchant from Edinburgh who settled in Md. before 1756. [SM.18.524]
TAGGART, ALEXANDER, a merchant in St Michael's, Barbados, probate Barbados 1696. [BA RB.6.1.30]
TAIT, ROBERT, a merchant in Philadelphia trading with Ayr, 1767. [NAS.E504.4.4]
TARBET, HUGH, a merchant in Boston, 1768. [NAS.CS16.1.133]
TATE, JAMES, trading between Port Glasgow and Va., 1749. [NAS.E504.28.4]
TAYLOR, Dr ALEXANDER, a merchant in Grenada, 1776. [NLS.ms8793]

TAYLOR, JOHN, a merchant in Nevis, 1777. [NLS.ms8793]
TAYLOR, JAMES, and ARCHIBALD LUNDIE, merchants in Savannah, Ga., before 1776. [NA.AO13.34.440]
TAYLOR, SAMUEL, and Company, trading from Greenock to St Kitts, 1742, Boston, 1743, 1746, Barbados, 1743, Va., 1744, 1745; between Port Glasgow and Jamaica, 1745. [NAS.E504.15.1/2; 28.2]
TELFAIR, EDWARD, born 1735, emigrated to Antigua in 1758, moved to America in 1766, settled as a merchant in Va., N.C., and Ga., died 1807. [TSA][Savannah Death Register]
TELFER, ALEXANDER, a merchant from Kirkcudbright who emigrated to America in 1759 and settled in Halifax, N.C.., until 1777, in Va., 1779, died in Liverpool. [NAS.RD2.225.1299][NA.AO12.34.351]
TELFER, DAVID, a merchant from Kirkcudbright who settled in Va. before 1779. [NAS.RD2.225.1299]
TELFER, JOHN, a merchant in Glasgow trading with America, 1778. [NAS.CS16.1.173]
TELFER, PATRICK, a merchant in Glasgow trading with America, Jamaica, and the West Indies, 1778. [NAS.CS16.1.173]
TENNANT, DAVID, trading between Ayr and Antigua, 1774. [NAS.E504.4.6]
TENNANT, JOHN, a merchant in St Kitts, 1765. [NAS.AC7.51]
TENNANT, WILLIAM, from Stirlingshire, an Indian trader in S.C., probate S.C. 1734.
THOMPSON, DAVID, a merchant from Jedburgh who settled in Yorktown, Va., probate N.C. 1749. [WMQ.11.155]
THOMPSON, JOHN, a merchant possible from Dumfries who settled in Halifax, N.C.., before 1777. [NA.AO12.102.125]
THOMSON, ALEXANDER, trading between Port Glasgow and Va., 1747. [NAS.E504.28.3]
THOMSON, ALEXANDER, a merchant who died in N.Y. during 1770. [SM.32.630]
THOMSON, ANDREW, a merchant in Barbados, probate Barbados 1716. [BA: RB.6.4.24]
THOMSON, ANDREW, a merchant in Edinburgh trading with Md., 1745. [NAS.CS16.1.75]
THOMSON, ANDREW, a merchant in Edinburgh then in N.Y., 1769. [NAS.CS16.1.134]

THOMSON, ANDREW, merchant in Glasgow trading with Va. pre 1776, partner of Thomson, Snodgrass and Company. [NA.AO13.33.269; AO13.102.85] [NAS.AC7.58]

THOMSON, ARCHIBALD, a merchant in Nevis, 1778. [NLS.ms8793]

THOMSON, DAVID, a merchant in Kingston, Jamaica, 1761. [NAS.GD180.418]

THOMSON, DUNCAN, a merchant who settled in Va. before 1780. [NAS.CS16.1.179]

THOMSON, GABRIEL, a merchant from Glasgow, from Leith to the West Indies in 1678. [RPCS.6.76]

THOMSON, JOHN, a merchant in Jamaica, 1779. [NAS.CS16.1.175]

THOMSON, JOHN, a merchant in N.Y., 1782. [NAS.CS17.1.1]

THOMSON, JOHN, from Edinburgh, a merchant in Charleston, probate S.C. 1763.

THOMSON, PATRICK, from Aberdeen, a merchant in Barbados, testament 1719 Edinburgh. [NAS]

THOMSON, PATRICK, a merchant from Edinburgh in N.Y., 1768, 1769. [NAS.CS16.1.134; CS17.1.133]

THOMSON, PATRICK, a merchant in Hartford, North America, 1772. [NAS.CS16.1.148]

THOMSON, WILLIAM, a merchant from Glasgow who settled in Kingston, Jamaica, and died there before 1783, testament Edinburgh 1783. [NAS.CC8.8.126]

THORNSON, ANDREW, born 1754, a merchant from Glasgow who emigrated via Greenock to Charleston, S.C., in 1774. [NA.T47.12]

TOD, ALEXANDER, a merchant in Philadelphia, 1777. [NAS.RS27.232/276; RD4.718.858; RD4.247.269]

TOD, CHARLES, a merchant in Jamaica, 1762. [NAS.AC7.50]

TOD, JOHN, a merchant in Jamaica, 1762. [NAS.AC7.50]

TOD, OLIVER, a merchant in Edinburgh trading with Jamaica, dead by 1762. [NAS.AC7.50]

TOD, ROBERT, merchant in Va., 1744, 1748. [NAS.AC10.335; AC11.231; AC9.1658]

TODD, DAVID, a merchant in Suffield, Hartford County, Connecticut, 1785. [NAS.CS17.1.4/325]

TODD, GEORGE, a merchant in Philadelphia, 1782. [NAS.CS17.1.1/318]

TODD, JAMES, & NINIAN MENZIES, merchants in Glasgow trading with Va. pre 1776. [NA.AO12.109.192]

TOLMIE, NORMAND, born in Skye, emigrated to America in 1756, a ship chandler in N.Y. pre 1776. [NA.AO12.22.389][ANY.1.70]

TORRANCE, ..., an assistant storekeeper who settled in Falmouth, Va., before 1776, returned to Scotland. [SFV#209/213]

TOWER, JOHN, a merchant in Aberdeen trading with Boston, 1753. [NAS.CS16.1.92]

TOWER, JOHN, a merchant in St Croix, 1784. [NAS.RD3.244.530]

TRAILL, JOHN, a merchant from Kirkwall who died in Boston before 1750. [Imm.NE#200]

TRAILL, ROBERT, a merchant from Orkney who settled in Boston by 1731. [SCS][Imm.NE#200]

TRAN, ARTHUR, a merchant in Glasgow trading with Antigua, 1716, with Guinea, Barbados, Nevis and St Kitts, 1720, with the Va. and Md., 1725. [NAS.AC9.584; AC7.33.433-583; AC8.310]

TRAN, HUGH, born 1730 son of Arthur Tran, a merchant from Glasgow who settled in St Kitts from 1767 to 1782, then in Dominica 1782. [NAS.CS17.1.1/2/282; B10.15.7141; CS16.1.174; B64.1.9.134/9; SH.12.2.1768; RD2.224/2.650]

TRENT, LAWRENCE, a merchant from Newbattle, trading with the Plantations by 1671, who settled in Barbados before 1689; probate Barbados 1693.[RPCS.2.407] [NAS.SH.28.7.1703][BA: RB.6.2.60]

TRENT, MORRIS, a merchant in Leith trading with Barbados, during the 1660s and later with West N.J. [ECA#186.13.4][SPAWI.1695.2304][NAS.E72.1.2/7]

TRENT, ..., a merchant in Pa., 1757. [NAS.CS16.1.100]

TROTTER, JOHN, in Kingston, Jamaica, 1755. [NAS.AC7.47.598]

TROUP, GEORGE, a merchant in Savannah, Ga., died in Liberty County 1789. [GaGaz#3/1]

TUILL, JOHN, a merchant, from Scotland to Boston in 1766. [PAB]

TUNNO, JOHN, a merchant in Charleston, S.C., by 1768. [NA.AO12.52.279][SAS]

TURNBULL, CHARLES, a merchant from Glasgow and agent in Va. for Buchanan, Murdoch and Company,

1747, settled in Dinwiddie County, Va., pre 1775.
[NAS.B10.15.5943; CS16.1.165/170][WMQ.2.16.99]
TURNBULL, GEORGE, a merchant in Glasgow then in
Dinwiddie County, Va., dead by 1777.
[NAS.CS16.1.170]
TURNBULL, ROBERT, a merchant from Glasgow who
settled in Dinwiddie County, Va., before 1775.
[NAS.CS16.1.165]
TURNBULL and SHAW, merchants in Va., 1778.
[NAS.CS16.1.173]
TURNER, ANDREW, a merchant, from Glasgow to Boston in
1763. [SCS][PAB]
TURNER, JAMES, a merchant in Va. 1782.
[NAS.CS17.1.197]
TURNER, JOHN, a storekeeper in Fauquier, Rocky Ridge,
Va., 1768. [SFV#135]
TWEED, ALEXANDER, a merchant in Charleston, 1764.
[SAS]
URQUHART, WILLIAM, a merchant from Tain then in
N.Y., 1782. [NAS.CS17.1.1]
VANS, HEW, a merchant in Boston, 1722, 1730s, 1750.
[SCS][NAS.AC7.36.506; AC7.40.86; AC9.1196;
RD2.168.313]
VAUSS, HUGH, a merchant from Ayr who settled in Boston
by 1731. [NAS.AC7.36.506; AC7.40.86; AC9.1196;
AC9.1297; AC9.1425; CS16.1.72]
VEITCH, ALEXANDER, trading between Port Glasgow and
Va., 1749. [NAS.E504.28.4]
VEITCH, GEORGE, a merchant in Edinburgh trading with
Va., 1768. [NAS.CS16.1.134]
VEITCH, SAMUEL, born 1668, emigrated to Darien in 1698,
moved to Boston by 1700, an Indian trader in Albany,
N.Y., 1700, died 1732 in London. [NEHGS: SCS]
VERNOR, JOHN, a merchant, from Port Glasgow to Va. in
1684. [NAS.E72.19.9]
VILANT, DAVID, a lawyer from Edinburgh who emigrated
via Leith to East N.J. in 1684, a merchant in Amboy,
N.J., and in Pa., 1699. [NAS.RD3.91.605; RD4.55]
WACHOPE, JOHN, a merchant in Charleston, probate S.C.
1739.
WALKER, ALEXANDER, a merchant from Port Glasgow
who settled in Va. before 1749. [NAS.CS16.1.81/84/85]

WALKER, ALEXANDER, a merchant in Glasgow, land grant in Ga., 1751. [NA.CO5.669]

WALKER, DAVID, a merchant who settled in Va. during 1766 and in Portobacco, Md., by 1770. [NAS.CS16.1.125][SFV#18]

WALKER, GEORGE, a surveyor and merchant from Clackmannan who settled in Georgetown, Md., in 1787. [ANY.1.260]

WALKER, JAMES, trading between Greenock and Va., 1744. [NAS.E504.15.2]

WALKER, JAMES, a merchant in Glasgow, land grant in Ga., 1751. [NA.CO5.669]

WALKER, JOHN, emigrated to Charleston, S.C., in 1760, a merchant there until 1775, moved to Dundee then returned to Charleston. [NA.AO13.132.262] [NAS.CS17.1.2/317; 5/269; 4/250; GD1.128.43]

WALKER, JOHN, a merchant who settled in Norfolk, Va., before 1776, moved to Barbados. [NA.AO13.32.643]

WALKER, JOHN, a merchant from Glasgow who settled in Norfolk, Va., before 1776, later Nassau, the Bahamas, died 1784, probate Williamsburg, Va.[NA.AO13.32.643]

WALKER, WILLIAM, emigrated in 1770, a merchant in Portsmouth, Va., then in Glasgow, testament 1786 Glasgow. [NAS.CC9] [NA.AO13.32.648]

WALKINSHAW, WILLIAM, a merchant, from Port Glasgow to Va. in 1682. [NAS.E72.19.8]

WALKINSHAW, WILLIAM, trading between Port Glasgow and Va., 1745, 1749. [NAS.E504.28.2/4]

WALLACE, ALEXANDER, a merchant in N.Y. City, settled there in 1752, partner of brother Hugh Wallace. [NA.AO12.20.61]

WALLACE, HUGH, trading between Port Glasgow and Va., 1746. [NAS.E504.28.2]

WALLACE, HUGH, a merchant in N.Y. City, settled there in 1748, partner of his brother Alexander Wallace. [NA.AO12.20.240]

WALLACE, JAMES, a merchant in Greenock trading with the Va. and Md., pre 1722. [NAS.AC7.26.681; AC9.849]

WALLACE, JOHN, born 1712, son of Thomas Wallace in Kilmarnock, a West Indian merchant, died 1805. [GA]

WALLACE, MICHAEL, born 1744, a merchant from Lanarkshire in Nansemond County, Va., partner of brother John Wallace, John Laurie, Hugh Wyllie, and

SCOTTISH TRANSATLANTIC MERCHANTS

George Brown, in Norfolk, Va., 1771; resident partner of John Wallace and Company in Va. 1771-1775, moved to Halifax, Nova Scotia, died 1831. [NAS.B10.13.4, FO.8][NA.AO12.55.106][DCB.10.798]

WALLACE, THOMAS, a merchant in Glasgow in Jamaica pre 1730. [NAS.AC7.35.485]

WALLACE, THOMAS, sr., trading between Port Glasgow and Va., 1744; between Port Glasgow and Md., 1745, 1748; between Port Glasgow and Jamaica, 1748. [NAS.E504.28.2/3]

WALLACE, THOMAS, jr. and Company, trading between Greenock and Va., 1743, 1744. [NAS.E504.15.1]

WALLACE, WILLIAM, trading between Greenock and Va., 1744; between Port Glasgow and Va., 1749. [NAS.E504.15.1/2; 28.4]

WALLACE, WILLIAM, a merchant in Jamaica, a burgess of Edinburgh, 1752. [EBR]

WALLACE, WILLIAM, a merchant in Charleston, S.C., by 1735, probate the Bahamas 1765. [SAS]

WALLACE, WILLIAM, trading between Port Glasgow and Md., 1745, 1748; between Port Glasgow and New York 1747. [NAS.E504.28.2/3]

WALLIS, JOHN, born 1717, a merchant in Kingston, Jamaica, died in 1746. [Kingston gravestone]

WALTON, JOHN, a merchant in Barbados, 1786. [NAS.CE60.11.1/90]

WARDEN, HUGH, a merchant from Perth, who settled in Va. from 1763 to 1770, and briefly in N.Y. [NA.AO12.54.52][NAS.CS16.1.157]

WARDEN, JAMES, trading between Greenock and Va., 1742, 1743, 1744, 1745, 1746. [NAS.E504.1/2]

WARDEN, JAMES, from Greenock, a merchant in Boston, 1774. [NAS.RS81/9]

WARDEN, JAMES, a merchant in St Kitts and St Croix, 1778. [NAS.CS16.1.173/322]

WARDROP, DANIEL, a merchant 1765-1791, died in Va. [NAS.B10.13.4. fo.8]

WARDROP, JAMES, a merchant, trading from Port Glasgow to the West Indies in 1684. [NAS.E72.19.9]

WARDROP, JAMES, a merchant who settled in Md. before 1761. [NAS.CS16.1.110]

WARDROP, JOHN, trading between Port Glasgow and Md., 1745, 1748. [NAS.E504.28.2/3]

WARDROP, JOHN, a merchant in Md., probate PCC 1767.
WARDROP, WILLIAM, a merchant in St Kitts, 1774. [NAS.CS16.1.157]
WARDROPE, JOHN, trading between Greenock and Va., 1745; between Greenock and St Kitts, 1746. [NAS.E504.15.2]
WARDROPE, JOHN, a merchant from Glasgow who settled in Brunswick County, Va., died 1789, testament Edinburgh 1791. [NAS.CC8.8.128][SM.51.309]
WARRAND, JOHN, a merchant in Glasgow trading with S.C., 1772. [NAS.CS16.1.151]
WARWICK, ANTHONY, a merchant in Nansemond County, Va., partner of Cumming, Warwick and Company in Glasgow, a merchant in Va. during 1760s and early 1770s. [NA.AO12.56.225]
WATSON, ALEXANDER, a merchant burgess of Glasgow, to Jamaica in 1668, died on Nevis. [NAS.Unextracted Processes, 1671]
WATSON, ANDREW, a merchant in Greenock trading with Tortula, 1784. [NAS.AC7.61]
WATSON, JAMES, a merchant in Edinburgh trading with Boston, pre 1739. [NAS.AC7.44.185]
WATSON, JAMES, and Company, trading from Greenock to Barbados, 1742, 1746, with Va., 1744; between Port Glasgow and Jamaica, 1745 [NAS.E504.15.1/2; 28.2; CS96.1919/22]
WATSON, JAMES, a merchant who settled in Kingston, Jamaica, before 1749. [NAS.RD2.170.264; RD2.167.216]
WATSON, JAMES, a merchant from Berwickshire who settled in Jamaica before 1749. [NAS.RS18.15.353]
WATSON, JOHN, a merchant, trading from Ayr to the Caribee Islands in 1683. [NAS.E72.3.12]
WATSON, JOHN, a merchant from Edinburgh then in Va., trading with Va., Md., Pa., Barbados, Jamaica, and the West Indies, from 1696 to 1713. [NAS.CS29.1752.3309]
WATSON, JOHN, a merchant in Greenock trading with Madeira, Barbados, Antigua, and Va., 1738-1750; Va., trading between Greenock and Va., 1743. [NAS.CS96.1919-1922; E504.1]
WATSON, JOHN, jr., a merchant from Edinburgh who settled in Charleston, S.C., by 1743, and died there in 1756,

testament Edinburgh 1756. [SAS][NAS.CS16.1.69]
[NAS.CS16.1.72/73/78; CC8.8.116/1; GD219.290.53]

WATSON, THOMAS, a merchant from Arbroath, emigrated to the American colonies in 1746. [P.3.392][MR#92]

WATSON, WILLIAM, a merchant from Aberdeen who settled in Port Royal, Jamaica, by 1689, executor to John McFarlane probate Jamaica 1690.

WATSON, WILLIAM, trading between Port Glasgow and Va., 1748, 1749. [NAS.E504.28.3/4]

WATT, JAMES, a merchant trading between Greenock and N.C.., 1743, 1744, Va., 1745; trading between Port Glasgow and Va., 1747. [NAS.E504.15.1/2; 28/3]

WATT, JAMES, born 1740, a merchant from Angus who settled in Caroline County, Va., before 1764. [NAS.RD2.197.470; SH.22.11.1775]

WATT, ROBERT, a merchant from Edinburgh who settled in N.Y. before 1717. [REB#213]

WAUCHOPE, HENRY, a merchant formerly in Va. and Md., pre 1754. [NAS.AC7.46.185]

WAUGH, THOMAS, a factor and surgeon from Jedburgh who settled in N.Y. before 1782. [NAS.GD5]

WEBSTER, JAMES, a merchant from Dundee who settled in Richmond Vale, Cornwall County, Jamaica, before 1780. [DA.TC.CC15.91]

WEIR, GEORGE, a factor who settled in Va. before 1775. [NA.T79/73]

WEIR, HUGH, trading between Port Glasgow and Va., 1747. [NAS.E504.28.3]

WEIR, JAMES, a merchant from Lanarkshire who settled in Fredericksburg, Va., in 1785. [NAS.CS17.1.6/268; RD2.240.479]

WEIR, JOHN, merchant in Glasgow trading with Md., 1720. [NAS.AC9.712]

WEIR, THOMAS, a merchant in Glasgow trading with the American Plantations, 1692. [NAS.RD3.78.32]

WEIR, THOMAS, a merchant who settled in Jamaica then in London, died 1736, testament Edinburgh 1740. {NAS.CC8.8.103]

WEIR, THOMAS, emigrated to America 1773, a factor and storekeeper in Wilmington, N.C.., before 1776, died in London, 1784. [NA.AO12.100.247]

WEIR, WILLIAM, a merchant from Aberdeenshire, who settled in St James County, Jamaica, and died before 1753. [ACA: APB.3.182]

WELCH, WILLIAM, a merchant from Edinburgh, probate Delaware 1687

WELSH, JOHN, a merchant in Leith then in Jamaica, 1769. [NAS.AC7.53]

WELSH, JOHN, a merchant who settled in Norfolk, Va., before 1773. [NA.AO13.32.691]

WELSH, SAMUEL, a merchant in Edinburgh trading with Boston, 1736. [NAS.AC13.1; AC10.246]

WESTON, SAMUEL, in Edinburgh, trading with Jamaica, pre 1734. [NAS.AC10.94]

WHITE, ANDREW, a merchant in Norfolk, Va., then in Greenock, testament 1766, 1776 Glasgow. [NAS.CC9]

WHITE, ARCHIBALD, from Greenock, a merchant in Norfolk, Va., then in Greenock, dead by 1763, probate Norfolk 1765; testament Glasgow 1772. [NAS.RS81.7.496; CC9]

WHITE, HUGH, a merchant from Glasgow then in Boston, 1766. [NAS.CS16.1.126/130/171]

WHITE, HUGH, a merchant from Glasgow then in Crown Point, N.Y., 1778. [NAS.CS16.1.174]

WHITE, JOHN, a merchant in Philadelphia, 1768. [NAS.CS16.1.133]

WHITE, PATRICK, a merchant from Fraserburgh who emigrated before 1749 and died in the Leeward Islands during 1754. [ACA: APB.3.177]

WHITE, WILLIAM, born 1734, a merchant who emigrated via London to Jamaica in 1774. [NA.T47.9/11]

WHITELAW, THOMAS, a merchant in Jamaica then in Glasgow, 1779, 1782. [NAS.CS16.1.175; CS17.1.2]

WHYTE, HENRY, a merchant in Boston, 1763. [NAS.CS16.1.117/59]

WIGHT, ALEXANDER, a merchant in Jamaica, testament 1786 Edinburgh. [NAS]

WIGHTMAN, CHARLES, son of Charles Wightman a merchant in Anstruther, a merchant in Tobago by 1778. [NAS.CS16.1.174]

WIGHTMAN, CHARLES, and ARCHIBALD SMITH, merchants in Tobago, 1780. [NAS.AC7.57]

WILKIE, JOHN, a merchant in Gloucester County, Va., before 1776 and later in Shelburne, Nova Scotia. [NA.AO12.102.203]

WILLIAMS and TOD, merchants in Philadelphia, 1778. [NAS.CS16.1.173]

WILLIAMSON, JOSEPH, a merchant who settled in Rappahannock, Va., from 1764 to 1776. [NA.AO13.32.700]

WILLOX, GEORGE, a merchant in East N.J., 1684. [NJSA.EJD.A266][NAS.RD4.67.97]

WILLS, ROBERT, a merchant in Charleston, 1758. [NAS.CS16.1.100]

WILSON, ARCHIBALD, a merchant from Renfrewshire, from Scotland to Boston in 1768. [PAB][SCS]

WILSON, CUMBERLAND, a merchant from Kilmarnock emigrated to Va. in 1760, partner in Colin Dunlop and Company before 1775. [NA.AO12.109.306]

WILSON, GEORGE, merchant in Aberdeen trading with the West Indies, 1769. [AJ#1096/1141]

WILSON, JAMES, trading between Port Glasgow and Va., 1749. [NAS.E504.28.4]

WILSON, JAMES, a merchant, from Scotland to Boston in 1766. [PAB]

WILSON, JAMES, & SONS, merchants in Kilmarnock [partners – James Wilson and his sons James, Cumberland, and William], trading in Va. and Md. from 1757 to 1776; trading between Ayr and Quebec, 1766; between Ayr and Va., 1767; between Ayr and Antigua, 1774; between Ayr and Halifax, Nova Scotia, 1776. [NAS.E504.4.4/6] [NA.AO12.109.306] [NAS.CS16.1.95/168/170/171]

WILSON, JOHN, trading between Greenock and Va., 1742, 1743, 1744, 1745, 1765; between Port Glasgow and Va., 1746, 1748. [NAS.E504.15.1/2; 28.2/3; CS16.1.120]

WILSON, JOHN, a shipmaster and merchant from Ayr who settled in Nansemond County, Va., dead by 1771. [NAS.CS16.1.168; SH.2.1771]

WILSON, PATRICK, trading between Port Glasgow and St Kitts, 1748. [E504.28.4]

WILSON, PHILIP, a merchant in St Kitts, 1783. [NAS.CS17.1.2]

WILSON, ROBERT, trading between Greenock and Va., 1743, and Barbados, 1744, with Va., 1744. [NAS.E504.1]

WILSON, WILLIAM, a merchant in Boston, burgess of Ayr, 1716. [AyrBR]

WILSON, WILLIAM, a merchant in Charleston from 1769 to 1779, died there in 1779. [NA.AO12.48.363][SAS]

WILSON, WILLIAM, a merchant from Kilmarnock who settled in Alexandria, Va., and in Md., from 1768 to 1776. [NAS.AO13.33.367]

WILSON, WILLIAM, jr., a merchant in Glasgow then in Va. from 1768 to 1776, then 1786. [NAS.CS17.1.5/351][NA.AO12.109.312]

WINCHESTER, JAMES, a merchant in Fraserburgh trading with Antigua, 1749. [AJ#103]

WINTER, THOMAS, a merchant in Spanish Town, Jamaica, 1782. [NAS.CS17.1.1]

WITHERSPOON, JAMES, a merchant who emigrated from Glasgow to Md. in 1734 and settled in Charles County. [MdGaz: 25.1.1749]

WODDROP, WILLIAM, a merchant from Edinburgh who emigrated before 1772 and settled in Tappahannock, Va. [NAS.SH.22.1.1772][GA.CFI]

WODDROW, ALEXANDER, a merchant who settled in Va. before 1778. [NAS.CS16.1.173][HAF.2.509]

WOOD, JOHN, a merchant from Glasgow then in Va., before 1760. [NAS.AC7.50]

WOOD, JOHN, a merchant from Glasgow who settled in Flower de Hundred, Va., before 1783. [NAS.CS17.1.2.170]

WOOD, WILLIAM, jr., merchant in Ayr, trading with Dominica, 1776. [NAS.E504.4.6]

WOODROP, WILLIAM, a merchant in Charleston, 1745. [Charleston Miscellaneous Records, 1769-1742] [NAS.CS16.1.73/78][SAS]

WOODROP, WILLIAM, a factor from Glasgow who settled in Essex County, Va., before 1770. [GA:CFI]

WOODROW, ANDREW, a merchant in Va., 1778. [NAS.CS16.1.173]

WOODROW, WILLIAM, trading between Greenock and the Va. and Md., 1744. [NAS.E504.15.2]

WOODRUP, WILLIAM, a merchant in Nevis, 1675; merchant from Glasgow who settled in St Kitts, died there in 1687. ['Isle of Wight County, Va., Will and Deed Book', 1/573][MWI#54]

WOODS, JAMES, a merchant in America then in Ayr, 1787. [NAS.CS17.1.6/334]

WOTHERSPOON, JAMES, from Rutherglen, settled in Charles County, Md., then a merchant on the James River, Va., from 1733 to 1738. [NAS.B64.1.6.5.7][VaGaz#112][MdGaz#198]

WRIGHT, CHARLES, a merchant in Charleston, 1755. [NAS.CS16.1.95]

WRIGHT, DANIEL, trading between Port Glasgow and Va., 1747. [NAS.E504.28.3]

WRIGHT, JERMYN, a merchant in Charleston, 1755. [NAS.CS16.1.95]

WRIGHT, JOHN, a merchant in Jamaica, a burgess of Ayr, 1751. [ABR]

WRIGHT, WILLIAM, a merchant in Stirling, trading with Grenada, 1779. [NAS.CS16.1.175]

WRIGHT, ..., an Indian trader in Mobile, West Fla., 1764. [NLS#ms119]

WYLLIE, HUGH, merchant in Glasgow and Va., trading with Barbados, 1765, died 1782 Glasgow. [NAS.CS16.1.122]

WYLLIE, HUGH, a merchant from Glasgow who settled in Williamsburgh, Granville County, N.C., 1787. [NAS.RD2.242/1.757]

WYLLIE, ROBERT, from Ayrshire, a merchant in Queen's Creek, Gloucester County, Va., before 1776. [NA.AO13.87.295]

WYLLIE, ..., a merchant in Mobile, West Fla., 1764. [NLS#ms119]

WYLLY, ANTONY, an Indian trader, died 1742. [ESG#102]

YOOL, JOHN, a merchant from Paisley then in Boston, 1778. [NAS.CS16.1.174]

YOUNG, ALEXANDER, merchant in Aberdeen trading with the West Indies, 1769. [AJ#1096]

YOUNG, JAMES, born 1718, a merchant from Glasgow who settled in Albemarle County,Va., before 1745. [GA.CFI][VMHB.1/2]

YOUNG, JAMES, of Netherfield, formerly a merchant in N.C., 1780. [NAS.CS17.1.1/76/179/183]

YOUNG, JOHN, a merchant in Tobago then in Glasgow, 1771. [NAS.RD2.224/2.646]

YOUNGER, GEORGE, & Company, in Petersburg, Va., before 1776. [NA.AO13.102.88]

YUILL, ALEXANDER, a merchant in Boston, 1781. [NAS.CS16.1.183; CS17.1.1.307]

YUILL, ARCHIBALD, and JAMES HAMILTON, merchants in Port Glasgow trading with Boston, 1734. [NAS.AC7.40.86]

YUILL, JAMES, a merchant from Lanarkshire who settled in Boston by 1753, possibly settled in Truro, Nova Scotia, in 1761. [NAS.RS42.15.96; CS16.1.115]

YUILL, THOMAS, a merchant trading between Greenock and Va., 1743, 1744, 1745; between Port Glasgow and Antigua, 1746. [NAS.E504.15.1/2]

YUILLE, GEORGE, a factor who settled in Va. before 1755. [Colonial Williamsburg ms]

YUILLE, JOHN, born 1719, a merchant from Dunbartonshire who died in Williamsburg, Va., in 1746. [GA.CFI] [Bruton, Va., gravestone][Va.Hist.Colln.11/67] [NAS.B10.15.5959]

YUILLE, THOMAS, a merchant in Glasgow trading with Va., 1728. [NAS.AC7.34.708]